Violent
JUSTICE

Violent JUSTICE

How Three Assassins Fought to Free Europe's Jews

FELIX & MIYOKO IMONTI

Prometheus Books

59 John Glenn Drive
Amherst, New York 14228-2197

Photograph of Samuel (Shalom) Schwartzbard courtesy of Yivo Institute of Jewish Research, New York, NY. Photographs of Simon Petliura, David Frankfurter, Wilhelm Gustloff, Herschel Feibel Grynszpan, and Ernst Vom Rath courtesy of Keystone Press AG, Zurich, Switzerland.

Published 1994 by Prometheus Books

98 97 96 95 94   5 4 3 2 1

Library of Congress Cataloging-in-Publication Data

Imonti, Felix.
   Violent justice / Felix and Miyoko Imonti.
      p.   cm.
   Includes bibliographical references and index.
   ISBN 0-87975-925-9
   1. Jews—Biography. 2. Assassins—Biography. 3. Shvartsbard, Shalom, 1886–1938. 4. Petliura, Symon Vasyl'ovych, 1879–1926—Assassination. 5. Frankfurter, David, 1909-   . 6. Gustloff, Wilhelm, 1895–1936—Assassination. 7. Grynszpan, Herschel Feibel, 1921–ca. 1943. I. Imonti, Miyoko. II. Title.
DS115.I48   1994
940'.004924—dc20   94-35322
                                                         CIP

Printed in the United States of America on acid-free paper.

Contents

Introduction   7

PART ONE: THE FEVER OF REVOLUTION

1. Starting with Murder   13
2. An Education in Barbarism   21
3. Hate and Revolution   29
4. A Taste of Revolution   35
5. Wars within Wars   43
6. A Crude War   49
7. Playing with Power   59
8. The Third Enemy   69
9. An Eye for a Thousand Eyes   75
10. The Hunter and the Hunted   81
11. You, the Jury   89
12. A Thousand Eyes for an Eye   105

PART TWO: THE ENEMY WITHIN

13. The Nest of the Hawk   111
14. Hitler's Missionaries   119
15. Heal Thyself   125

16. The Fifth Column   131
17. A Cure for Society   141
18. Because I Am a Jew   149
19. An Inconvenient Martyr   165
20. The Politics of Justice   173
21. The Davos Cure   183

PART THREE: A TASTE OF JEWS

22. The Eastern Jewish Question   193
23. Perpetual Strangers   197
24. The Paper Prison   205
25. The Voice of the Gun   217
26. Men of Honor   225
27. A German Hero   233
28. A Festival for Wolves   237
29. Reaping the Harvest   247
30. The Price and the Cost of Justice   255
31. In the Vise   263
32. Wolves and Sheep   271
33. The Problem Child   283

Epilogue   293

Endnotes   297

Bibliography   303

Index   311

Introduction

It was 1096. From every part of Christendom, men took up the cross and arms, to go forth to liberate the holy places from the "heathen Mohammedans." The Crusades were beginning.

On the banks of the Rhine near the city of Cologne, an armed horde gathered to begin its march across Europe on its way to the Holy Land. Before it reached Hungary, where an indigenous army was forced to end its trail of pillage and murder, the Crusaders had sacked the Jewish communities at Cologne, Worms, Mainz, Prague, and elsewhere. Five thousand Jews had been slaughtered. The Holocaust was beginning.

As news spread ahead of the horde of marching Crusaders, Jewish leaders petitioned local bishops and lords for protection from the attackers. Even when it was offered, the pledges were frequently hollow in the face of armed marauders who had on their minds vengeance for the crucifixion and a desire for loot. To appease the rabble force, Jewish leaders offered them silver coin and appealed for their mercy. Usually, the Crusaders took the Jewish money. Then, they took Jewish lives. Rarely did the Jewish victims resist. They died meekly, going as martyrs to their mass graves.

Their meekness fostered a tradition. Whenever local rulers

needed an easy source for cash, the Jewish community was threatened with destruction or expulsion, unless compensation for some contrived crime was made. In response to the threat, Jewish elders gathered the extortion money to give to their oppressor, petitioned that same oppressor for mercy, and petitioned others to intervene on their behalf, after which the community waited passively to learn its fate. If the Jews were fortunate, the demagogue would be satisfied for a time; but sooner or later, another demand would be made, or the mobs would erupt to plunder and murder.

Like the snows of winter and the heat of summer, pogroms followed the seasons of history. At the time of the expulsions of the Moors from Spain and of Columbus's voyages, it was the season of intolerance and of hatred. Jews were expelled from the kingdom of the "Most Catholic" rulers of newly united Spain. During the time of the Thirty Years War, Jews were driven westward from Eastern Europe. After the assassination of Czar Alexander II in 1881, the most recent and the most violent of the pogroms began and spread over much of Europe, to end in the rubble of Berlin. Across the continent and over the sixty-four years of violence, it was unusual for Jews to oppose their oppressors. "After surveying the damage, the survivors had always proclaimed in affirmation of their strategy the triumphant slogan, 'The Jewish people lives [Am Yisrael Chaij].' This experience was so ingrained in the Jewish consciousness as to achieve the force of law."[1]

National Socialism fashioned an ideology that cloaked the traditional hatred in a philosophy giving to pure human madness the facade of an intellectual and scientific foundation. As demonstrated repeatedly for a millennium and throughout the European continent by the conduct of the Christian population, Hitler voiced what others already believed and practiced. "One must not have mercy with people who are determined by fate to perish."[2]

Although passivity was the rule, there were exceptions that by their unusualness make them conspicuous within the European tradition of Jewish society. Between the two world wars, there were three such exceptions: Jews who turned to violence to deal with violence.

These three Jewish assassins, Samuel Schwartzbard, David Frankfurter, and Herschel Grynszpan, were strangers who came from different backgrounds; their common bond was their Jewishness. Nonetheless, they followed remarkably similar paths. All worked without the support of an organization; each confronted his victim face to face; after committing the assassinations, all surrendered voluntarily, admitted guilt, and prepared to defend their actions in the courts before the whole of society. Using the criteria of the Jewish philosopher and author Emil Ludwig, these features of the three assassins gave their deeds a moral foundation of righteousness.

During the first third of this century, Ludwig established a reputation among scholars and philosophers. He wrote numerous biographies and essays, which were less concerned with factual accuracy than with presenting his view of history and the condition of humanity. Among his subjects was David Frankfurter, who in the end had fallen just short of the role of hero, because of his legal defense strategy.

All three viewed their actions as moral statements that the circumstances of their time had compelled them to make. As each in one form or another revealed, his deed was committed for the benefit of all Jews. If that required them to sacrifice themselves for the greater good, then all stood ready to do so in the tradition of the Jewish martyrs who died willingly rather than to forsake their faith.

While these three assassins followed similar courses, the reactions of the general Jewish community between 1926, when Samuel Schwartzbard committed the first killing, and 1938, when Herschel Grynszpan perpetrated the third, remained consistent and unyielding. The violence was condemned, and the killers were denounced. Only a minority of Jews agreed to support violent opposition against their own oppression. Historical conditions had no impact upon the unyielding moral code of the Jewish community. It had little tolerance for deviants.

Samuel Schwartzbard killed as an act of retribution for past crimes against the Jews of the Ukraine by a former Ukrainian leader, Simon Petliura, who would surely have escaped punishment for the crimes attributed to him by the vast portion of the Eastern European Jewish population. David Frankfurter killed Wilhelm Gustloff, to remove what he and a large portion of the Swiss population believed to be a clear and present danger to the survival of the small mountainous nation. Herschel Grynszpan shot Third Secretary Ernst vom Rath as an act of revenge for the brutal expulsion of twelve thousand Polish Jews and a response to the growing menace of Hitlerism.

Underlying the actions of the three assassins was the prevailing sense of their own impotence. They were alienated from the general European society and were a part of a minority committed to nonviolent action. They came from a tradition of debate with God and with other human beings. When dealing with a reasonable person, debate makes sense. When dealing with violence, it is the road to destruction. However the assassins and a minority of Jews viewed the realities of the moment, the law of passivity, the moral superiority of nonviolence, was upheld, no matter what the circumstances of the time. The assassins were orphaned by the very society they believed would be preserved by their individual sacrifices.

Unlike the Jewish community, the views of Gentiles in Europe varied with the seasons. Samuel Schwartzbard was proclaimed a hero following his assassination of Simon Petliura, and the French National Assembly amended its citizenship laws to welcome Jewish refugees from the pogroms of Eastern Europe. Just twelve years later, those same supporters were declaring Jews a threat to the survival of France and were condemning the liberalized citizenship laws.

The lives of these three men, three exceptions of their times, reveal the essence of the Jewish place within a European context. The stories of their lives were lost in the horrors of the Holocaust, but they disclose much of the nature of human folly.

Part One

The Fever of Revolution

1

Starting with Murder

The killing of Czar Alexander II by Narodnaya Volya, a Russian revolutionary movement, was intended to be a statement against the oppression of the masses. Assassination of the ruler of All the Russias had been decreed by the need to nourish the movement with the blood of the symbol of autocracy. There was nothing personal in the plans of the revolutionaries to relieve the czar of his life, because a revolutionary who has killed to forward the cause has not murdered a human being. He has made a political statement. Six times the agents of Narodnaya Volya had attempted by Alexander's death to proclaim the coming of the liberation of the people. The men and women of the movement gambled their lives to achieve the destruction of that one symbol.

The imperial train had been a repeated target. On several occasions, the railway line had been mined, but each effort had been thwarted by the security agents in the escort train that preceded the czar. Finally, the revolutionaries managed to explode a mine under what was believed to be the imperial train, but their efforts managed only to destroy a shipment of dried fruit from the imperial orchards on the Black Sea coast. For that one time, the order of the trains had been reversed.

On another occasion, one terrorist somehow managed to slip through the security barrier around the Winter Palace in St.

Petersburg. In the garden the revolutionary came face to face with the unguarded symbol of oppression. At close range, the assassin emptied his revolver and missed.

The most daring and ingenious scheme was attempted in 1880, when Narodnaya Volya was able to penetrate the Winter Palace itself and place a hundred pounds of high explosives beneath the floor of the family dining room. The bomb exploded during the supper hour, causing the room to collapse into the basement. Guards and servants died in the rubble, but no one from the imperial family was injured. On that night, Czar Alexander had delayed his meal and postponed his exit from life.

So often had the czar faced sudden violent death and escaped uninjured that he had begun to see his life as being protected by the divine hand of Providence. His safety came from a source far more powerful than the imperial secret police, Ochrana, that had to preserve the czar's life from terrorists. In March 1881, Ochrana agents had caught the scent of a fresh conspiracy.

People on the street Malaya Sadovya in St. Petersburg directed the attention of the police to a cheese shop that showed little interest in selling cheese. There was plenty of merchandise on display. Regardless, the couple behind the counter made no effort to attract customers.

No one in the neighborhood knew them, and the strangers had not followed the custom of visiting the other shopkeepers and residents. That, though, was only half of the story. The real mystery occurred at night, when silent shadows came and went into and out of the shop. Then, there were the strange sounds emanating nightly from the darkened business.

It was all of serious interest to the secret police. Malaya Sadovya was the road that Czar Alexander traveled every Sunday morning and afternoon. Such a predictable schedule was perfect for the preparation by terrorists of a plan to ambush his sleigh.

Ochrana was on special alert for trouble after arresting on February 28 the leader of the Narodnaya Volya, Zheliabov the Terrible. Where the leader was, his followers were certain to be. Where a group of terrorists from Narodnaya Volya was, the plotting of violence was sure to be as well.

Police agents dropped into the cheese shop on Saturday, March 12, 1881, to investigate the rumors. Upstairs, the proprietor seemed to be a legitimate businessman without a known police record. Downstairs in the cellar, the agents found several barrels that had moisture seeping from them.

"Spoiled cheese," the proprietor told them.

The explanation seemed plausible, so the police did not raise the lids of the barrels or move them aside to examine the wall of the cellar. But had they been more thorough in their investigation, the Ochrana agents would have found a tunnel the revolutionaries had dug under the street. Contained in the moist barrels was some of the earth that had been excavated. It was all there for the police to see, but they saw nothing and left the cheese shop to pursue their investigation elsewhere.

Members of Narodnaya Volya had discovered the czar's weekly routine and had plotted a new method of destroying the symbol of autocracy. On Sunday March 13, 1881, they intended to detonate a massive bomb in the tunnel beneath his passing sleigh. The blast would have leveled most of the surrounding buildings and killed many of the residents as it blew the ruler of All the Russias to bits.

Suddenly, everything had changed. Zheliabov had been arrested, and the secret police were showing too much curiosity about the shop. How much they might know, what they might be planning made urgent the need to act quickly. Sofya Perovskaya, Zheliabov's mistress and the second in command, summoned the other Narodnaya Volya members to the cellar to hear her new, desperate plan. The scheme was simple and built upon pure chance. Next afternoon, she would position herself at a point advantageous for watching the passage of the sleighs containing the czar and his police escort. Four members of the movement, with bombs, were to be stationed at strategic points along the two possible routes. Perovskaya's role in the scheme was to signal them onto which road the czar had turned.

All present in the cellar voted to support the impromptu strategy. Then, they abandoned the cheese shop and gathered in an apartment. Throughout the night, the conspirators rehearsed their plan and prepared their bombs. Each of four kerosene containers was filled with five pounds of nitroglycerine and pyroxylin. By early dawn, they were ready. They left the secret apartment and disappeared into the city to wait for the afternoon, when they were to take up their positions.

Ochrana knew that somewhere in St. Petersburg there were terrorists determined to kill the czar. Aided by the czarina, the police urged the ruler to remain within the walls of the palace, where he could be protected; he would have none of it. For years, he had attended the Sunday ceremony of the trooping of the colors, to which diplomats of military rank and important personages were invited. He, the ruler of All the Russias, would not permit a gang of terrorists to imprison him within his own palace. Besides, the capture of Zheliabov the Terrible convinced the czar that the threat to his life had been reduced.

On his way to the Manege, where the imperial cavalry performed the ceremony, he passed the spot where the conspirators would be waiting for his return. Surrounded by friends and diplomats, while the troops performed the ceremony, the czar was feeling buoyant, as though a great burden had been taken from him. That morning, before he had left the palace, he had affixed his signature to a document that would, on the next day, March 14, 1881, introduce constitutional government to Russia, to bring the autocratic, isolated empire into the mainstream of European political thought.

Opposition in the imperial government had been strong. The czar's own son, Czarevitch Alexander III, disapproved of the weakening of central rule.

Even the members of Narodnaya Volya objected to the constitutional reforms. Narodnaya Volya had declared violence to be the only language understood by a tyrant. If the czar reformed the despotic regime without violent revolution, then the whole basis of the movement would be lost. Killing him before the constitution became the law of the land was necessary to preserve the cause of revolution.

As a conclusion to his afternoon outing, Alexander stopped for tea at the nearby palace of his cousin, Grand Duchess Katerina Mikhailovna. At 2:15, he started for home, for a scheduled stroll with the czarina in the snow-covered palace gardens.

The czar traveled in a convoy of four sleighs with an escort of six mounted Cossacks. His sleigh was at the front of the entourage with his bodyguards following close behind. Scattered along the route, police agents kept a watch for anything out of the ordinary. Afternoon traffic was light, and the driver of the sleigh was able to keep a good pace on Engineer Street. Then, he turned off to take the shorter road, Katerina Quay, which ran next to the Katerina Canal. His driver whipped the horses into a full gallop. As they turned onto the Quay, Sofya Perovskaya waved her handkerchief. Down the quay, two bombers took their places. There were to have been four bombers with two to cover each road, but one of the bombers, Yemelyanov, failed to keep the appointment. That had left only one man to ambush the czar on the unused route. Once the alternate road had been selected, that lone bomber was free to flee before the assassins on Katerina Quay struck.

Further along the quay, the speeding sleigh passed an off-duty army officer and a delivery boy with a tray of pastries for an afternoon gathering. On the edge of the canal, a young man with a package tucked under his arm stood daydreaming, seemingly unaware of the passage of the emperor.

Among the pedestrians on the side of the road, there was a second young man with a bundle wrapped in newspaper. He paused as the first sleigh reached him. A moment later, the bundle arced through the air and landed beneath the feet of the horses.

A sphere of flame erupted beneath the tramping feet of the animals. The thunder of the explosion was followed immediately by the screams of the torn, dying horses. Caught directly by the blast, the driver of the sleigh was killed instantly. The delivery boy carrying his pastries lay in a pool of his own blood.

After the smoke cleared, a hand emerged from the splintered wreckage of the sleigh. Again, as it had on ten previous occasions, Providence had protected the czar from certain death.

The czar's would-be assassin was less fortunate. After he had hurled his bomb, Rysakov had tried to flee, but he had slipped on a patch of ice and fallen. Before he could get to his feet, two policemen had captured him.

Immediately, a crowd formed at the scene. Police urged the czar to leave in one of the other sleighs, before a second attempt could be made. Among the curiosity seekers, there might be another assassin waiting his chance to strike. Death had been turned away from his door so frequently, that Czar Alexander II had no fear of it. Instead, he insisted upon seeing the injured Cossacks and the man who had tried to blast him into eternity.

"Are you sure that you are not injured?" a policeman asked.

"I am not injured. Thank God," Czar Alexander replied. Rysakov laughed aloud. "Don't be too quick to thank God," he told the czar.

When it was obvious that the first bomb had failed to finish the job, the daydreamer, Grinevitsky, had moved away from his position on the edge of the canal and mixed into the thickening crowd. He still carried his deadly bundle under his arm, and no one challenged him even as he pressed nearer to the czar. He threw his five pounds of nitroglycerine and pyroxylin at the feet of the ruler of All the Russias. A second blast mushroomed from the frozen earth. Suddenly, the curiosity seekers were mangled and dead. Grinevitsky himself was lying among the corpses.

His legs mangled and his body torn beyond medical help, Alexander II was carried to his palace. At 3:45, his reign ended; the brief life of the constitution was over. Both the extreme right and the extreme left celebrated the preservation of despotism.

The celebration by the conspirators of Narodnaya Volya was to be brief, abbreviated by Ochrana, which had Rysakov to interrogate. To save himself, the revolutionary sold his friends. Before long, the police had arrested all of the conspirators from the cheese shop. Five of them, including Rysakov, were executed, while the others went to prison.

Hessia Helfmann was one of those to be sentenced to death for her involvement in the assassination, although she had not participated in the attempt. Because of her pregnancy, her execution was delayed, until she gave birth. Shortly after that, she died in the Peter and Paul Fortress. Although Hessia Helfmann was an insignificant member of the movement, Ochrana considered her to be the most important of the conspirators. She was the only Jew, and that was to be the source of a broad Jewish conspiracy.

She had been born in 1855 into a wealthy Jewish family in Mazir near Minsk. At the age of sixteen, she ran away from home and joined the revolutionary movements. In 1875, she was imprisoned for two years, after which she was banished. Helfmann escaped from banishment and joined Narodnaya Volya in St. Petersburg, where she distributed revolutionary literature to university students.

All of the conditions existed to ignite the latent hatreds that Czar Alexander II had kept under control. His heir had no thoughts of liberalizing the society. On the contrary. On Easter Sunday, 1881, the results of Czar Alexander III's policies erupted into pogroms in the Ukraine. The Jewish district of Balta was ravaged. Even Narodnaya Volya saluted the attacks. A pamphlet of August 30, 1881, placed the left and the right in common hatred of the Jewish minority.

> Good people, honest Ukrainian people! Life has become hard in the Ukraine, and it keeps getting harder. The damned police beat you, the landowners devour you, the kikes, the dirty Judases, rob you. People in the Ukraine suffer most of all from the kikes. Who has seized the land, the woodlands, the taverns? The kikes. Whom does the peasant beg with tears in his eyes to let him near his own land? The kikes. Wherever you look, whatever you touch, everywhere the kikes. The kike curses the peasant, cheats him, drinks his blood. The kikes make life unbearable.[3]

By the time of her death in 1882, Hessia Helfmann had seen herself transformed from a revolutionary opposed to the autocratic regime of the emperor to a standard-bearer for an insidious Jewish conspiracy. The first of the pogroms in Balta was to be just one in a continuous reign of terror promoted by the extremist supporters of the czar, the Black Hundred, and by Narodnaya Volya and its successor, the Bolsheviki.

Anti-Semitism became a popular fashion and a political tool. The containers of nitroglycerine and pyroxylin had ignited it on March 13, 1881, on Katerina Quay in St. Petersburg, and it continued across Europe to end in Berlin on May 7, 1945. Before the end, in the ruin of Berlin, it had touched, each in its own way, most nations of Europe.

2

An Education in Barbarism

Balta was just a forerunner of what was to come. Fourteen months after Czar Alexander II was assassinated, the full impact struck Jews across the Russian Empire, when on May 15, 1882, the May Laws were imposed. The brief taste of imperial liberalism under the late Czar Alexander II was over. Under the new codified oppression, vast regions of the empire were forbidden for Jewish habitation; the ownership of land was restricted severely; numerous occupations and professions were prohibited to Jews. Eventually, the oppression would drive two million Jews beyond the reach of imperial retribution. Waves of immigrants sought their safety and their prosperity in North America.

Only a handful of the refugees formed the vanguard of the Zionist pioneers who were to repopulate the ancient homeland in Palestine. Leo Pinsker of Odessa was among the early founders of the Zionist movement, which sought, mostly unsuccessfully, to recruit immigrants for the rebirth of Israel. Even as the pogroms ravaged numerous Jewish communities, there was little interest in building a Jewish state. Between 1882 and 1914, a mere forty-five thousand settlers traveled to Palestine, and only a portion of these came from the land of the pogroms. The majority of the others preferred to gamble that the horrors would pass, or sought their futures in Western Europe.

Trapped in the Ukraine, Yitzhak Schwartzbard could only dream of escape to the new promised lands of North America or even to the lesser hope of Western Europe. He was one of the prisoners of poverty forced to survive within the tumult that seethed throughout the empire. To this Yitzhak Schwartzbard added the peril of defiance—he resided beyond the "Pale of Settlement," the area of permitted Jewish habitation. If caught, he faced the mercy of a regime that offered little.

Out in the forbidden lands, Schwartzbard had started his family. His first born, Shalom, was only seven days old in 1888 and about to be given his name when news came that a sweep to catch illegal residents was beginning.[4] The Schwartzbard family took to the roads to escape, running for the Jewish territory of Balta, where the pogroms had begun seven years earlier.

Balta, with a 47 percent Jewish population, was as far as an empty pocket could take Yitzhak and his family. It was there, in the cradle of the pogroms, where he decided to set his roots and establish a grocery shop in the Christian sector of the city.

Hope and peace were short-lived in their refuge. Less than three years after their arrival, another pogrom ravaged the Jewish quarter. Homes and shops were looted and burned. Jews were beaten, raped, and murdered. At the Schwartzbard home, while the three-year-old Samuel watched, their Christian neighbors broke through the door, carried away what few possessions they had, and beat his pregnant mother. Soon afterwards, Chaia Schwartzbard gave birth to her second child, Meir, and died.

Before he could walk or comprehend the world into which he had been born, Samuel had an education in barbarism. There was no escape from fear or poverty in that world. Hope was as distant as the shores of that unreachable land in North America and as near as the Psalms in the Bible.

Over the next years, the young boy turned inward to armor himself in his traditions and religion. Elders in the temple marveled at his knowledge of the Psalms and the depth of his piety. If Samuel doubted the sincerity of human beings and the purpose of life, he never doubted his Judaism. God was his inner confidant; his family was his society. Nothing more was needed.

That world, too, was destined to change when his father remarried. To Samuel, the new woman was an invader he could not repel from what had been a closed world. Worse, his unwelcome stepmother in rapid succession added four more brothers and sisters to the family and deepened hardship into misery. By the age of twelve, Samuel was scrounging for every kopeck, to add a few more crumbs to the table.

In order to feed the expanding family, every luxury had to be eliminated. Counted among the unnecessaries were his lessons at the yeshiva. When those vital lessons ended, Samuel's link with the traditions for which he was forced to suffer was broken. From then on, whatever he would understand about his faith had to be deduced through self-study. Samuel was a brilliant and eager student, but the teacher lacked the knowledge to broaden his scope of understanding.

Instead of studying the Torah, Samuel was expected to learn a trade that would put food on the table. His teacher was to be a watchmaker, Israel Deck, to whom he was apprenticed for five years. Later, Samuel recalled with bitterness the years of drudgery and exploitation at the hands of Deck and his sense of abandonment by his father and his stepmother.

Deck had no intention of fulfilling the agreement to teach his apprentice the trade. As far as the watchmaker was concerned, the boy was there to do his and Mrs. Deck's bidding. If Samuel were not cleaning the shop or serving customers, he was running errands for Mrs. Deck or cleaning the house. Only at the end of the five-year contract, did Deck teach Samuel a little of the trade.

During those years in the Decks' house, Samuel strengthened the wall he had begun to build around himself. His companionship came from his library of religious books, into which he immersed himself to escape the misery of the real world. Inside his separate universe he fashioned his own doctrine, which drew little from others, who had always deceived him. So, their philosophies had nothing to offer.

Samuel's real training was outside of the shop. On a Saturday, while going to the temple, another boy urged Samuel to follow. The mysterious guide led him out of town to a ravine, where a group of men and women had gathered secretly. Among them were shop workers and office clerks, students and laborers.

They were the heirs of Narodnaya Volya, the precursors of the Bolsheviki, the followers of Lenin. Marxism was their map to the future, and it led them along a road of violent revolution. Their movement, "The Spark," would ignite the way into the new age.

Samuel Schwartzbard became a convert, but there was a conflict between his and their views. He could not abandon God, while they believed that God had abandoned them.

Their prophet, Karl Marx, had said, "Religion is the opiate of the people." To the others, Samuel was addicted to his Judaism, in which he claimed to have found the foundations of socialism. Separated by that unbridgeable gap, Samuel formed a party of one who subscribed to the principles of revolution but was rejected by his fellow revolutionaries, who had no tolerance for a Jewish heretic.

Just as the long-anticipated popular revolution seemed imminent in 1905, Samuel Schwartzbard was freed from the hold of Israel Deck. The seventeen-year-old revolutionary joined two other missionaries of Marxism, Grisha and Yussel, to spread news about the coming class struggle. Unable to read the pamphlets given to them, the peasants used them for their toilets, until frightened landlords put a price upon the pieces of paper.

When Schwartzbard and his two companions nailed one pamphlet to the front door of a landlord's house, the police were alerted that revolutionaries were at large in the vicinity; the hunt began. The threat of arrest frightened Grisha and Yussel, who fled to the United States. Schwartzbard remained to serve the revolution.

In the village of Kruchi the young Marxist warrior faced his first real battle. A squad of Russian troops had decided to amuse themselves by attacking Jews. Schwartzbard, as he described the events, seized a cane and attacked the soldiers. Several good blows were struck before he was knocked unconscious.

"How did you dare fight so many Gentiles?" the Jewish residents of the community asked. During the rampage of the soldiers, they had hidden from the danger. Once the soldiers had left, the frightened citizens emerged and cared for the injured teenager.

"How do so many dare not fight so few?" he admonished.

Kruchi was no longer a safe place for Schwartzbard. Already, the police had connected him with the pamphlets and would certainly charge him for an attack against imperial soldiers. If trouble came, he did not expect the Jews of Kruchi to shelter him. Already in his career as a revolutionary, Schwartzbard learned not to rely on the Jews for whom he had chosen to fight. What little safety he expected to find was in Balta, where his defiant and rebellious father was organizing a self-defense committee. Joined in their common cause, Schwartzbard rebuilt the family bonds that had been severed five years earlier.

Although a very small minority among the Jews of the Ukraine, there were a number of people there who shard Schwartzbard's view of the use of violence to halt violence. Across the Ukraine, teams of Jews were traveling to the Jewish communities to give instructions about organizing defense units. Booklets explained how to acquire weapons and how to use them. In Balta a mere forty men had joined the sparse ranks of volunteers. Vladimir Jabotinsky, who led the movement, raged against the Jewish indifference to their own survival.

Apathy was the common fatal ailment that Yitzhak and Samuel Schwartzbard confronted, but there was an even worse disease. A number of Jews had joined the radical socialist movement, which interpreted the pogroms as a sign of the approaching class revolution. According to their radical theory, Jews were a necessary sacrifice for the cause. To assure the success of the revolution, the radicals opposed self-defense and labeled it counterrevolutionary. These radical socialist Jews provided fuel for government fostered anti-Semitism.

Upheavals throughout the Russian Empire threatened the

survival of imperial rule. Under such dangerous conditions, Ochrana and the Black Hundred redirected the anger of the mobs away from the aristocracy and the autocracy and toward the Jews. Their program was aided by the priests of the Russian Orthodox Church who fueled the anti-Semitism.

In 1905 Ochrana wrote one of the most long-lived propaganda tools for arousing public hatred against the Jews, "The Protocols of the Elders of Zion." Using as its basis an 1897 conference of Zionists in Basel, Switzerland, the secret police fashioned a program of a Jewish global conspiracy to rule the world.

The document was a propaganda instrument employed by the extreme left as well as the extreme right. Later, it was adopted by German National Socialists to prove the need to destroy all Jews. It continues to be cited throughout the world.

On October 17, 1905, the danger to the Jewish population appeared to pass. Czar Nicholas II, twenty-four years after the assassination of Alexander II, introduced long-postponed reforms. There was dancing in the streets of Balta. Freedom and brotherhood had come to the blood-stained lands of Russia, or at least so the celebrants imagined.

The next day, the Black Hundred rode. A hundred miles away from Balta, the worst pogrom in recent times swept Odessa. Floods of Jewish blood drowned the moment of hope. The forty defenders of Balta awaited their day of battle. It came, led by the mayor of the city.

So thoroughly was the pogrom institutionalized that it followed an established course. First, the Jews were charged with a collective crime. Then, the authorities imposed a punitive tax to compensate for the fictional crime. Inevitably, the elders collected the tax and paid. Once the money had been collected, the general public from the Christian community were given the opportunity to share the booty. Led by religious and civil authorities, the mobs were granted license to pillage.

During October 1905 in Balta, the well-established routine was repeating itself. As the attackers assembled outside the Jewish quarter, elders from the Jewish community went to appeal to and reason with the mayor and his followers. The petitioners were the first to die. Following the usual pattern, the attackers waited for sunset on Friday, when the majority of the Jews would be at prayer for Sabbath services. Inside the synagogues, they were trapped sheep ready for the slaughter.

At sunset the forty volunteers barricaded the streets with flaming barriers. The pogromists were met at the barricade. For a while, the defenders held, beating back the attackers; but soon they were overwhelmed, and the quarter was sacked by the pogromists' wives and children, who carried away the booty. It was during the pogroms that the meaning of the Russian proverb, "Man is a wolf to man," could best be understood.

The courage of the defenders did not inspire the community to support them. When the police arrested Samuel Schwartzbard for inciting the Jews to violence, the public did not rally to him. Once again, he felt betrayed. Betrayal had become a common feature of his life and reason for him to lock himself more firmly in the fortress of his own, privately created philosophy. Schwartzbard's protection of the Jewish community earned him a prison sentence of three months.

By the time of his release, he had given up his hope for the Jews of the Ukraine and joined the generations of "wandering Jews." With him Schwartzbard carried the hope that somewhere there would be a corner of the world where a Jew could find his place. He passed through Bukovina, Lemberg, Vienna, Budapest, and Italy. There, his brother Meir joined him, and the two wandering Jews made their way to Paris, the capital of revolution. For a time, until the call of revolution in the Ukraine summoned him to return, Paris was to be their home.

3

Hate and Revolution

The Russian masters of the Ukraine built into their colony a pool of hatreds. In the cities, whence they controlled the institutions of the state and the instruments of commerce, they were separated from the subject people. The cities were Russian islands in a sea of Ukrainian discontent.

Russia used an imported Polish aristocracy to control the mass of peasants. Ninety percent of the land was given to the Polish lords and divided into large estates. If the peasants rose against their masters, it would be Poles who would be lynched.

The tradesmen and the merchants in the villages were imported Jews from Poland. When a peasant needed a cooking pot or salt, he was forced to buy from a Jew. When he could not afford the prices that were in good part fixed from the cities, it was a Jew he blamed.

Yet, it was the remote, isolated Russians in the cities who were the masters of the colony. But it was a colony they denied existed. The fiction of the imperial Russian government was that the Ukrainian people were extensions of the Greater Russian nation, the little Russians. To force the fiction to become fact, Ukrainian language books could not be printed, and all education was in Russian. Whenever a Ukrainian sought to escape the crushing poverty of the peasant class, he had to cease to be a

Ukrainian. The system maintained a cultural gulf between the educated elite and the common people on the land.

Beneath the blanket of oppression, the seeds of the culture managed to survive. During the first half of the nineteenth century, the Ukrainian poet Taras Shevchenko put into writing the nationalist passion that continued to flame.

> Oh bury me, then rise ye up
> And break your heavy chains
> And water with the tyrants' blood
> The freedom you have gained.
> And in the great new family,
> The family of the free,
> With softly spoken kindly word,
> Pray, men, remember me.[5]

Nationalism in the second half of the nineteenth century was made more virulent by the marriage of radical socialism with the drive for a cultural identity. Among the nationalists radical socialism had a strong appeal because it was an attack against Poles and Jews who were the visible masters of the economy. No matter how many generations the minorities had lived in the Ukraine, they remained distinct ethnic groups that controlled the lives of the vast majority.

The arrival of the railway in the latter half of the century added an explosive element to an inherently unstable social order. Previously remote regions were opened to the global economy, and the landlords turned to the production of cash crops— sunflower seeds for cooking oil, potatoes for alcohol, or sugar beets for sugar.

Each estate became an agricultural factory that required a small number of permanent employees and large numbers of seasonal workers. As had happened in England with the enclosure movement,* tenant farmers were evicted from the land and forced into the cities, where they provided the kindling for revolution. Between 1907 and 1914, 1.6 million people left for North America or for Siberia, but enough remained to give the Russian masters reason to tremble. In order to divert the hatred of the restive displaced peasants, the Black Hundred and the Orthodox priests fed their anger with the loot and the blood of the pogroms.

A small circle of Ukrainian intellectuals did emerge. They were educated in the language of the conqueror, but many remained Ukrainian. To study in their own language, young men had to cross into West Galicia, the Austria-controlled sector of the Ukraine. The use of the language was legal there, and Dr. Mikchail Hrushevsky used the freedom to develop a core of literature and philosophy. Illegal books and journals were smuggled back into the Russian area, where young men carried the ideas and materials to the secret circles of intellectuals that had been organized in most Ukrainian cities.

Among the young men in the secret circles was Simon Vassilievich Petliura. He hailed from Podolia. His father, Vassili Petliura, a cab driver, was the transition between the poverty of the land and the achievement of an educated Russified Ukrainian. Simon was the beneficiary of his father's ambition and attended a seminary school that would raise him to a new plateau in society.

Simon was born on May 12, 1879, when Ukrainian nationalism was being kindled. Young men like him were to be the fuel of the coming surge in cultural nationalism. The youthful scholar should have graduated from school and entered a position with a lucrative salary and a respectable future. That had been the intent of Petliura's hard working father. Instead, he was caught

---

*During the latter half of the fifteenth century, large acres of southern England were cleared of tenant farmers and converted to grazing pastures for sheep and cattle. The converted lands were enclosed within fences and hedgerows, from which the movement derived its title, "the enclosure movement."

up in the cultural renaissance which had been infected by the socialist movement in Russia itself.

For seven or eight years Petliura was adrift, wandering from city to city throughout the southern regions of the Russian Empire. In each city he joined the illegal circles of intellectuals and participated in the writing of underground pamphlets and the performance of defiant plays. Eventually Ochrana took note of him, as it did every potentially rebellious element.

The young rebel arrived in Kiev in 1905, at the time when the imperial reforms were coming into effect under Czar Nicholas II, and when the Ukrainian Socialist Democratic Labor Party was being created out of parts of the Ukrainian Revolutionary Party. The URP had been established in 1900. Among the founding members was Volodymyr Vynnychenko. During its brief existence, the party had contained a broad spectrum of philosophies, too diverse to survive within a single association. In 1905, Vynnychenko helped to make from the socialists within the URP a Ukrainian version of Lenin's Russian Social Democratic Labor Party. Petliura joined the new party and the staff of the radical newspaper *Slovo,* "The Word."

For Ukrainian intellectuals, unconcerned about the plight of the Jewish minority, the constitutional reforms that had brought misery and death to Jews offered a sign of hope to their nationalist cause. After a century and a quarter, their language was recognized and it became legal to publish newspapers. Around Kiev newspapers sprouted from the previously barren land. A bookshop to sell the flood of Ukrainian language books and periodicals opened to fill a hitherto hidden demand.

Most of the newspapers were directed to the agrarian population, to which 75 percent of Ukrainians belonged. The broad majority of the peasants were landless, illiterate, and scattered. The constitutional reforms and the unreadable newspapers were irrelevant to their lives. They wanted land. *Slovo* spoke about land for the landless and social reform. These were dangerous ideas, too dangerous for the censors to ignore.

By 1912, the spread of political opposition and the multiplicity of newspapers prompted Czar Nicholas II to end the few years of relaxation. Repression returned. *Slovo* and other newspapers had to cease publication. Once again, illegal publications from Austrian Ukraine and the secret circles provided the foundation of the nationalist movement.

Simon Petliura was thirty-four years of age and had just married Olga Bilska when oppression returned to the land. Gone were the days of the wandering nationalist. Instead of remaining in the radical movement, he went to St. Petersburg, to work as an accountant and insurance inspector, until he joined the staff of the conservative, Russian-language paper *Ukrainian Life*. The rebel had mellowed, but the Ukraine had just begun to boil.

Return to autocracy in 1912 in the Russian Empire was as remote to Samuel Schwartzbard in Paris as was the sinking of the *Titanic* in the same year. Schwartzbard had rejected the Ukraine as a hopeless cause and turned his attention to his new life in the far more liberal atmosphere of the French Third Republic.

He had taken employment in a factory, where he became an active union organizer and protested worker exploitation by the capitalist employers. Schwartzbard earned his living with his hands, but the self-educated refugee saw himself as a poet and philosopher. He had begun to lay the foundation of his future career.

4

A Taste of Revolution

When on March 15, 1917, Czar Nicholas II was driven off his throne, the masses felt the burdens of corruption, starvation, and oppression lifted from their backs. Long-suppressed hopes emerged in a storm of impatient expectation, as the news of their liberation spread with the fury of flaming oil on a turbulent sea.

Dr. Hrushevsky, who after the constitutional reforms of 1905 had returned to the Ukraine from Austrian Galicia and become leader of the Ukrainian Progressive Organization in Kiev, sent a telegram of congratulations to Prince Lvov, the prime minister of the provisional government in St. Petersburg. Soon after, a delegation of Ukrainians was dispatched to make known to the new government the desires of the Ukraine. Besides the general reforms wanted throughout the empire, the Ukrainians sought an autonomous national government and separate military units for the Ukrainian troops in the Russian Army.

In St. Petersburg the delegates were received coolly. The question of autonomy was postponed until at some time in the uncertain future a constituent congress could be called to deal with many problems. As for the formation of separate Ukrainian units in the armed forces, that had been achieved by the troops themselves. Ukrainian soldiers had rebelled against their Russian officers and withdrawn from their former units to form their own.

Simon Petliura was elected by soldier committees to take command of the emerging Ukrainian army. Thus, the reluctant rebel was dragged into the midst of the seething revolution and thrust into a position of leadership. Nothing in his training or experience qualified Petliura for the office to which the soldiers elected him. At the outbreak of the war, he had left his position in St. Petersburg and worked as an administrator in the Red Cross. Nonetheless, the soldiers chose him. Among the peasant soldiers he was the rare figure of a literate Ukrainian who had not grown apart from the uneducated peasant masses. Infected by the fever of revolution, they needed no other justification for their actions beyond the one fact that they had made the decision.

Two and a half years earlier, on August 4, 1914, Dr. Hrushevsky and Petliura had traveled to Lemberg in Austrian Galicia to attend the founding session of the Union for the Liberation of the Ukraine. The conference had been sponsored by Galician Ukrainians, but the ULU was composed of exiled Ukrainians who had left the Ukraine to escape from Ochrana or to enjoy the chance of being Ukrainian.

The central program of the ULU was the independence of the Ukraine from the Russian Empire. Behind them in the shadows was the Austrian government, which employed Ukrainian nationalism to destabilize the imperial Russian government and thereby keep the czar from intruding into the Balkans, where the Russian promotion of pan-Slavism threatened the Austrian position. Both imperial Austria and imperial Russia were attempting to secure their control over the region. Ukrainian nationalism and pan-Slavism served as instruments of the different imperialisms.

Hrushevsky and Petliura, who were the official delegates from the Social Democratic movement in the Ukraine, opposed a program of independence. Among the small circle of socialist intellectuals, reform within the context of the Russian Empire was the extent of their nationalism. After 146 years of forced Russification, many of them had come to think as Russians and were as remote from the masses of Ukrainian peasants as were the Russian rulers. In a letter dated December 18, 1914, to Dr.

Osyp Nazaruk, a Ukrainian politician and journalist, Petliura repeated his support of Russian rule: "Every step, word, or deed which tends toward creating in the Russian Ukraine conditions subversive to the unity of the Russian state, or toward a weakening of that state at the present time [of war], is severely condemned in the Ukraine [by public opinion], because it is considered harmful also to Ukrainian interests."[6]

Three years of the horrors of World War I brought a major change in the drift of Ukrainian thought. On June 10, 1917, the first Ukrainian Central Rada* met in Kiev. Hrushevsky was president. Simon Petliura, who had returned with the support of the soldiers, was named minister of the army. The Central Rada issued the "First Universal Proclamation." It advocated the formation of an autonomous Ukrainian state within a federal system.

> Let the Ukraine be free! Without separating from all of Russia, without breaking with the Russian state, let the Ukrainian people have the right to manage its own life on its own soil. Let a National Ukrainian assembly [Soim], elected by universal equal, direct, and secret balloting, establish order and harmony in the Ukraine. Only our Ukrainian Assembly has the right to establish all laws which can provide that order among us here in the Ukraine.[7]

In St. Petersburg the provisional government continued to ignore the moderate demands of the Ukraine. Despite the general discontent, the first concern of the failing government was to continue the war against Germany. That unwillingness of the provisional government to meet the demands of the general public fed the fury of revolution.

Revolutionary fever spread far beyond the Russian frontiers. Among the infected was Samuel Schwartzbard, who believed that he had discovered within the principles of Marxism the

---

*Rada is the Ukranian word for parliament.

solution to the many miseries being suffered by humankind. The ink of his philosophy had come from the mud and blood of the trenches along the front.

On August 25, 1914, Schwartzbard and his brother enlisted in the French Foreign Legion. A Teutonic avalanche had swept over Belgium and was rolling toward Paris. The brothers volunteered to add their lives to the crumbling French wall of defense. During the Battle of Carency on March 1, 1916, the brothers suffered multiple shrapnel wounds, and both received the Croix de Guerre for valor. After undergoing surgery, Samuel was sent to a Catholic monastery to recuperate.

Those were to be some of the happiest days of Schwartzbard's life. Over long hours, he enjoyed philosophical conversations with the monks for whom he developed a deep affection. In the monks he found the simple sincerity that other men always seemed to lack. Here were men without the ambition for power or the lust for material wealth. They, too, lived in a separate world.

For Schwartzbard the war had ended. Once he completed his recuperation, he was granted a medical discharge and was free to resume his life.

Behind those tranquil walls the world of violence had been abandoned for a time, but it hadn't disappeared; it refused to be ignored. Some men were charging into machine gun fire; others were slashing at each other with bayonets. The barbarism seemed to have no end or limit, but Schwartzbard believed that it was for a purpose; it was only part of a natural historical progression. Along with the rotting corpses were the decaying remnants of capitalism. According to the tenets of his ideology, when the war ended, the old world would be replaced by the new world order as humanity advanced from one Marxist stage to the next higher state. What Schwartzbard saw in the Bolshevik Revolution in Russia was the birth of the new order. There, humankind would find peace, equality, and brotherhood.

On August 5, 1917, Schwartzbard and his wife, Anna, sailed for Archangel, a port town on the White Sea in northern Russia. On board his ship were hundreds of returning Russian soldiers.

Before the ship reached Russia, the men were infected by the revolutionary fever. Disorders erupted, and Schwartzbard was blamed for inciting the men.

From the moment he set foot in the new Russia, Schwartzbard saw men and women intoxicated by the spirit of the revolution. Shackles of fear had been cut from their ankles and wrists. For some, their new freedom was an opportunity to exploit. On his way from Archangel to the Ukraine, another face of the revolution showed itself. This was a grotesque face of pillage and death. Without order, there would be violence and murder. The gun was law; the gang was power. Frequently, the victims were the Jews, the people whom the new order was supposed to rescue from their history of suffering.

Schwartzbard began to experience his first doubts along the road of misery to the Ukraine. Revolution was a medicine that ravaged many of the sickest members of the suffering society. The weak would not live long enough to enjoy the liberty that the "new world order" was expected to bring. Wherever government existed, it was powerless to direct the affairs of the society. Bands of soldiers—Russians, Ukrainians, and others— who were sworn to uphold the state and the governing regime, left their trenches to join the chaos and contribute to the anarchy. As they wandered, they pillaged and murdered. Minister of the Army Simon Petliura issued orders, but no one heard them. He was minister of a nonexistent army. In Kiev the Central Rada issued "Universal Proclamations," sent delegates to St. Petersburg, and debated. It was all meaningless. The peasant masses were rising and destroying the old order.

The "First Universal Proclamation" called for the confiscation of the land, but the peasants did not wait for the decision from Kiev or St. Petersburg. They had the weapons from the returning soldiers and no government with the means to stop them. From the Poles they took the land. From the two million Jews, scattered through six hundred communities, they took money, goods, and lives. If Russian law had not prohibited Jews from owning land, the peasants would have seized that, too.

Since Russian rule had been imposed over the Ukraine, the Russian, Polish, and Jewish minorities had enjoyed advantages over the Ukrainian peasants. To the surprise of no one, the Central Rada did not receive support from the minorities, from whom the property was being confiscated by the laws of the new government and by the deeds of the vengeful peasants.

Automatically, the change in the regime guaranteed unrest within the Ukraine as the Russian, Polish, and Jewish minorities sought to recover their former positions and to survive the sweep of madness. The minorities, however, did not unite in common cause against the Ukrainian revolutionaries. Instead, they fought each other as eagerly as they opposed the nationalists.

Into this sea of blood and hatred, Samuel Schwartzbard plunged. Where was the brotherhood that he had expected to find? Schwartzbard's dreams succumbed to the claws and fangs of reality. If the Jews were to survive to enjoy the new order, then they would have to defend themselves, but the former soldier of the French Republic had seen how unwillingly Jews took up arms in their own defense.

Between 1903 and 1905, while still in his youth, Schwartzbard had witnessed the pogroms. In some of the communities defense committees had been organized. Men armed themselves, learned how to fight, and formed combat units. In some cases, they repelled their attackers and inflicted casualties. There were too many other occasions, however, when the committees were too weak to stop the attackers, because the elders wanted to appeal for mercy from murderers and to debate against bayonets and bullets, while the wealthy wanted to buy peace from vandals. In the end, the communities were defeated from within.

Where the defense units were formed, their transformation into a united, alert community did not last long. As soon as the wave of violence passed, the few who had organized disbanded, shed their arms, and forgot their experience.

Back in his town of Balta, Schwartzbard organized a Jewish defense force. Later, a unit of Russian troops passed through the town. The Russians saw an armed Jewish sentry at every street corner. No insults were hurled; no shots were fired. Balta had demonstrated its strength and courage, but those virtues in Jews did not make them better men. Instead, their strength gave them the courage to be cruel. Schwartzbard caught several of his soldiers beating a Ukrainian child.

Once again Schwartzbard left his home, leaving it to its own fate, while he turned his attention to the immediate matter of earning a living. As much as he was caught up by the desire to save the Jews of the Ukraine and to promote the revolution, he had not arrived with a full purse. To live, Schwartzbard would have to work at the only trade he knew. So, he looked to Odessa, where he opened a small watch repair shop. With its large Russian population and centers of education, Odessa had been one of the communities in which Jews had joined to defend themselves and were aided by sympathetic, enlightened Russians. In that Russified city, Schwartzbard was in the midst of the ferment of the revolution, where the fire would not be drenched by Jewish or Ukrainian ethnic hostility toward something Russian. Schwartzbard had found the Bolshevik Revolution, the real revolution, the one he anticipated would bring the solution to all of the misery of humanity and especially to Jews. Among Schwartzbard's enemies was Simon Petliura and the Ukrainian nationalists, who had been moving steadily away from their demands for cultural identity and regional autonomy toward pure independence.

In the midst of the historical ferment, Samuel soon abandoned his trade to respond to the Siren's call of the Revolution. On November 7, 1917, Lenin had declared in St. Petersburg the birth of the first Soviet socialist society. The peoples of all the Russias were expected to follow the Red banner and accept the orders of the Central Committee of Lenin's party.

"Who will follow me?" Schwartzbard asked of a group of young Jews in Odessa. A hundred responded. From them, he organized an army unit of Jewish volunteers, the Rasala Battalion, and marched them across the Ukraine to defend the Revolution.

His small army fought in the name of the Marxist cause,

while remaining independent from the Bolsheviki or any of the other numerous armies on the march. They were fighting for a society of brotherhood, a society in which Jews could stand with their heads raised with other men. Schwartzbard had not yet found where it existed, however, so while they were fighting for that ideal society, he kept his forces independent as a means to secure it.

5

Wars within Wars

Responding to Lenin, the Central Rada in Kiev announced on November 20 the "Third Universal Proclamation," declaring the creation of a socialist Ukraine a political entity with national autonomy in association with Russia. Before he claimed power, Lenin had agreed to the principle of national autonomy. Once in office, however, he redefined his interpretation of national autonomy as the local administration of policies formulated in Russia.

The dispute over autonomy was the second rift between the Ukrainian socialists and the Bolsheviki. Their first important area of disagreement had arisen in 1907, when the Ukrainian delegates to the Second International rejected the principle of the "dictatorship of the proletariat." When the disagreement had surfaced at the conference in Stuttgart, Lenin drummed the Ukrainians out. That wound to his leadership had never quite healed, and the Ukrainians had never felt comfortable in a movement with their dominant Russian brethren. Suddenly, the old hostility emerged over the question of autonomy.

Whatever government ruled in Russia under whatever philosophy, their attitude toward the Ukraine was consistent. Russia was the unquestionable ruler. The Ukrainians were the prisoners of geography and economic necessity. Through the Ukraine Russia gained access to the Black Sea and therefore the Mediterranean and beyond. Ukrainian wheat fed the empire, and Ukrainian coal and steel provided 75 percent of Russia's vital resources.

The "Third Universal Proclamation" was a rejection of central control. On December 18, Lenin created the Ukrainian Soviet Socialist Republic, with its capital in Karkov, and declared war on the chaotic Ukraine. The social reformers of August 1914 had been branded the rebellious counterrevolutionaries of December 1917.

A committee of intellectuals had evolved reluctantly into a government without experienced governors or a stable, cooperative society to govern. Whether Russian or Ukrainian, whether socialist or capitalist, the nature of the government was of little importance to the majority of illiterate peasants, who had no sense of nationality or statehood. Land and crops were their only interests.

Simon Petliura had the practical task of restoring order over thirty million Ukrainians and waging war against the Red Army and numerous other forces, including the small unit of Jewish volunteers led by Schwartzbard. Petliura assumed the responsibility of an office for which he was wholly ill-prepared. His sole military experience had been as a member of the Red Cross. Weapons and strategies were foreign concepts. Under his command was a rag-tag army of untrained, poorly equipped peasant soldiers whom the bankrupt state could not pay. They were as unprepared for their assignment as was their commander.

On December 15, a ceasefire between the Bolsheviks and the Central Powers enabled Lenin to turn all of his attention upon the rebellious Ukraine. The ceasefire preceded negotiations to conclude a peace treaty between the Soviet government and the Central Powers, which were to begin on December 22 at Brest-Litovsk. On the following day, an Anglo-French conference in Paris decided upon a policy of disrupting the German effort to end the war on the Eastern Front. The Paris conference gave to France responsibility for the region north of the Black Sea, where France had vital economic interests in the oil fields of East Galicia.

French General Berthelot in Jassy, Romania, sent two secret missions to keep the war active in the east. One mission was sent to Kaledin, the leader of the Don Cossacks. The agents had available to them $60 million to purchase Cossack support and finance the formation of a White Russian army from the imperial Russian officers who had fled to Cossack territory. The second secret mission operated in Kiev. The principal Allied agents here were General Tabouis, who was based in Kiev to oversee French interests, and British Consul John Picton Bagge. They had $36 million and a briefcase full of promises to offer to the Ukrainian Central Rada.

The sole objective was to keep the Ukraine fighting, to stall for time. British and French leaders feared that they could not hold the line against the Germans on their own. The United States had entered the war earlier in 1917, but the new ally was not ready to take its place in the trenches. If the Germans transferred troops to the Western Front before fresh American troops were on the line, there was a good chance that the Allied Powers could be defeated.

The Central Rada was in no condition to continue the war against the Central Powers, expel the invading Bolsheviks, and restore order inside the country. The government lacked the weapons to equip an army, the food to feed the troops, or the money to pay the men and the officers. France made many promises of support, but between French promises and Odessa, where food and arms were to be delivered, were Turkish guns at the choke point of the Dardanelles.

The Ukrainians wanted one small gesture of faith from the Allied Powers, one act of sincerity in the form of a declaration of diplomatic recognition. That, though, was far too much, far too dangerous. The Allied Powers could not reveal that they were talking to the Ukrainians, while at the same time pledging to the White Russians to support a united Russia under the rule of St. Petersburg.

By January, a third secret mission arrived in St. Petersburg, to talk to Lenin. If Lenin would keep fighting, then a French military assistance group would organize and train the Red Army. As a down payment for Red Army support, $1 billion of British and American supplies in Vladivostok would be released.

Leon Trotsky directed the negotiations with the Central and Allied Powers. In the tea leaves of his philosophy, he had foreseen the future. Coming quickly was the world revolution that would destroy the rotting structure of capitalism. At any moment, the workers were going to break their chains, unite under the Red banner, and dedicate their lives to the dictatorship of the proletariat, which, of course, would be led by Lenin and himself. Trotsky's ally was time. By keeping the pressure on the warring nations, the ferment of the discontented workers would have the opportunity to explode. Time was what Trotsky needed. His tactic was to delay everywhere.

Time was what the Ukrainians did not have. When the three Ukrainian delegates arrived in Brest-Litovsk on January 12, 1918, to join the negotiations, Trotsky's tactic of delay was jeopardized. The German delegates had tired of the Bolshevik game. To force Trotsky to negotiate seriously, the members of the Central Powers offered the Ukraine diplomatic recognition in exchange for a rapid settlement. It was the best offer the Ukrainians would get from anyone. Out of desperation, they signed.

On January 22, the Central Rada issued the "Fourth Universal Proclamation," which declared the birth of a socialist Ukrainian People's Republic.

> From this day forth, the Ukrainian People's* Republic becomes independent, subject to no one, a free, sovereign state of the Ukrainian people. . . .
>
> The Council of People's Ministers will use all means to ensure that the transfer of land from the land committees to the working people takes place without fail before the beginning of spring tilling.

---

*The name of the Ukranian Republic changed twice. "Ukrainian People's Republic" was the name at the time of this quoted excerpt. Later the name changed to the "Ukrainian National Republic."

Forests, waters, and all mineral resources—the wealth of
the Ukrainian working people—are transferred to the jurisdiction of the Ukrainian People's Republic. . . .[8]

On February 9, the peace needed desperately by the Central
Powers and the Central Rada was concluded. The Ukrainian
National Republic (UNR) was granted the diplomatic recognition
that announced to the world the birth of another state. The Germans trained and equipped a unit of fifteen thousand Ukrainian
prisoners, the Sich Rifles, as a gift to the UNR to give Simon
Petliura a real army to fight the Bolsheviks and establish order.
To assure Petliura's success, on February 18, the Germans entered
the Ukraine to drive Bolshevik forces out of Kiev, which had
been taken by Bolshevik troops while the negotiations were
underway in Brest-Litovsk. Then the Sich Rifles arrived, as both
a reward to the new Ukrainian state for its neutrality and to
assure that the Ukrainians fulfilled their portion of the agreement.

The Ukrainians were not being given a free lunch. For the
Central Powers to affix their signatures to the peace treaty, the
UNR agreed to provide one million tons of grain and access to
vital resources. It was called by the starving Germans the
Brotfrieden (the "bread peace").

In their desperation to get an agreement, the Central Rada
had made promises that could not be kept, because the harvest
of 1917 had not been a good one. Much of the land had just
been seized from the dispossessed Polish aristocracy by peasants
who had not had time to organize a new agricultural structure.
German troops had to be used to force the peasants to surrender
their grain, and the peasants resisted. As far as the newly liberated
peasants in the countryside could see, the Central Rada was no
better than the foreign soldiers, no better than the Polish landlords, no better than the wandering bands of looting marauders.
Any hope for the Central Rada to win public support was killed
by German bayonets.

The Germans had expected the Central Rada to collect and
deliver the grain for the starving populations in Germany and

in Austria. Instead, the Germans received endless arguments and continuous debate. By April 28, the impatient Germans took control of the Central Rada and installed their own government.

The Ukrainian Hetmanate,* abolished in 1768, was reestablished. Pavlo Skoropadsky, a descendent of one of the former Hetmans, was placed on the throne. To meet the demands of the Germans who had put him into power and kept him in office by force of arms, he allowed the Polish aristocracy to repossess their estates, if they delivered 20 percent of the grain.

The new government did what all of the old governments had done. It demanded grain from the peasants who, as they had before, fought against the government, something they would do again when Stalin repeated the practice. More than 300,000 German and Austrian soldiers, with the aid of men from the army of Skoropadsky, emptied granaries and filled graves, their own and those of the peasants.

On July 12, the Hetman arrested Simon Petliura and other members of the deposed government. Soon after, he released them in return for a pledge not to seek to overthrow his government. They could afford to promise anything. In a few months, the winds would shift, and new circumstances would dictate new tactics. Nothing in Ukraine was permanent.

While the Germans struggled under the weight of their ally, Allied Powers viewed the treaty of Brest-Litovsk to be an act of treachery. In Jassy, General Berthelot received reports from White Russian officers that the leaders of the UNR, especially Volodymyr Vynnychenko and Simon Petliura, were socialists of the caliber of the Bolsheviks. After losing $36 million to the Central Rada and seeing the Germans freed to increase pressure in the West, the French needed no more reasons to seek revenge.

---

*Kingdom or monarchy.

6

A Crude War

The betrayal at Brest-Litovsk, the swindle of $36 million, these were for the French sufficient cause to seek revenge. The threat to vital petroleum supplies, the danger to a strategy for national security, these were sufficient hazards to justify severe action. If avenging old injuries and preventing future harm could be accomplished with a single blow, then General Barthelemy would have been a blessed man. The general was the French chairman of the Armistice Commission, to end the fighting between the Ukrainian-Galician forces, the army of Simon Petliura, and the besieged Polish army in Lemberg. If he had allowed the Poles to be defeated, then French policy would have been the first casualty.

Among the many problems that the diplomats had to settle in the aftermath of the war, the Ukrainian situation did not rank high on the agenda. The Allied Powers Peace Conference in Paris had not had time to draw the eastern frontiers of Poland or to settle the questions of the Ukraine, when the Polish troops in Galicia were facing certain defeat. On March 14, 1919, the Allied Powers ruled to impose an armistice upon the combatants and to follow the French urging to move the fifty thousand troops of Haller's army from France, where there was no longer an enemy to fight, to Poland, where there was the red menace of the

Bolsheviki. While accepting the French position, the other members of the Allied Powers cautioned the French not to permit Haller's army to become embroiled in the conflict. It was to be a neutral peace-keeping force with the assignment of establishing stability in order to give the Allied Powers time to decide upon the status of the region.

Colonel Jozef Haller had commanded Polish troops in the Imperial German Army, until he and his troops defected to the Russians. Before he could escape, the Germans chased him down and battered his force. After losing most of his army and much of his honor, he fled to France, where the French heaped praise upon him and raised him to the rank of general. Then they gave him an army of Polish exiles.

His army was ready in March 1919. It was too late to be employed against the Germans but was just in time to promote French policy in Poland, where the French postwar interest was concerned with vital scarce oil, which in turn required French diplomats to contemplate the destruction of the Ukrainian nationalist movement.

On February 22, three weeks before the Allied Powers in Paris had ruled on the conditions in Galicia, General Barthelemy led the four-power Allied Commission into Lemberg to negotiate a ceasefire. The city was the last position held by the surrounded Poles, who were on the verge of defeat at the hands of Simon Petliura and his Galician ally in command of the combined armies of Galicia and the Ukrainian National Republic. After their experience with the Central Rada in Kiev, the prospect of a victory by Petliura was not easy for the French to accept. At stake were bruised French honor and major petroleum investments.

On October 18, Galicia had declared her independence from the dying Austro-Hungarian Empire. Independence was to be the first step toward unification with the Ukrainians in both the Ukraine and Hungary, to form a Greater Ukraine to house all of the Ukrainian nation. In Galicia the policy had grown over twenty years into a determination, declared final on January 22, 1919.

On October 31, 1918, Poland declared her independence. The Poles celebrated their new statehood by invading West Galicia to incorporate into Greater Poland a region with a population that was 74 percent Ukrainian. In the Polish pocket there was a license to act.

The Poles had formed in 1915 the Polish National Committee, to persuade the Allied Powers of the need for an independent Polish state. A part of the Polish argument in support of their independence was the granting of portions of the Ukraine to Poland to enable Poland to serve the interests of France and Britain by functioning as a counterweight to Germany. The Poles, therefore, advocated the need for their independence as a means of abandoning that independence in favor of French and British interests as if those interests would always be the same. The policy was described in great detail in a Polish document released by the Polish National Committee in July 1918.

> The safety of the lands of the Lithuanians and Ruthenians, extending in the east, from being overrun by the direct or indirect expansion of the German domination could be secured while the Lithuanian and Ruthenian territories, since it is really impossible to establish the independent states of the Lithuanians and Ruthenians, should be put partially under the Polish and partially the Russian domination in order not to allow the German influence there to grow.[9]

The French and the British endorsed the policy. In 1917, U.S. Secretary of State Robert Lansing echoed their endorsement of a strong Poland. He told Roman Dmowski of the Polish National Committee, "Galicia is not part of historic Austria, and might and ought to go to the Poland of the future. But what is the Poland of the future? That, I think is now, as it has been ever since the great crime of partition was accomplished, the greatest crux of European diplomacy."[10]

On January 4, 1918, President Wilson presented in his Fourteen Points the prescription for the creation of a "New World Order."

Article 13 formalized the statement of Secretary of State Lansing to Roman Dmowski about the formation of an independent Polish state. Wilson, however, added the caution that the incorporation of other territories must be with the consent of the people.

> XIII. An independent Polish state should be erected which should include the territories inhabited by indisputably Polish populations, which should be assured a free and secure access to the sea, and whose political and economic independence and territorial integrity should be guaranteed by international covenant.[11]

French Prime Minister Georges Clemenceau remarked, "God gave us the Ten Commandments and we broke them. Wilson gave us the Fourteen Points. We shall see."[12]

General Barthelemy was not distracted by the admonition of President Wilson or interested in the wishes of the Ukrainian majority in Galicia. If Simon Petliura refused to sign the armistice, then he would face the wrath of the Allied Powers. Otherwise, he could accept quietly, and allow the Peace Conference in Paris to play out the fiction of considering what had long before been decided by the French and accepted by the others. As the French general presented the agreement to the Ukrainians to sign, he delivered a speech that reflected the French carrot and the club:

> We, the representatives of the Entente Powers, that is, England, France, United States, and Italy, conscientiously and thoroughly have investigated the matter which we have to decide. We demand sacrifices from both sides. These sacrifices will be temporary, until the decision of the Peace Conference. It is true that your position is good today but it can change tomorrow to your disadvantage. . . . If you will not accept our proposition then you will have a war with the Poles, who will have in support the brave and well-organized army of General Haller, consisting of six divisions. We, in France, are convinced of the courage of this army. On the other hand, the Bolsheviks are advancing and they already have Kyyiv [i.e., Kiev] and a major

part of your territory, and they are found before your gates. If you will accept our proposition, we will make efforts to have your sovereignty recognized. The fact that we talk to you and turn to you with this proposition is, to a certain extent, a recognition of your statehood because one does not talk with someone who does not exist. Then with our help you will be victorious over the Bolsheviks, you will regain the occupied areas, and you will not appear at the Peace Conference empty handed. Our decision will influence the outcome of the talks of the Directorate with Entente representatives in Odessa because our authority is more extensive than that of represen- tatives in Odessa. We will make efforts that your delegates be allowed at the Peace Conference. We will send a mission to you which will remain with you and will notify our countries of your needs. We will establish relations between your gov- ernment and the Entente Powers. Remember the proverb: Help yourself and Heaven will help you. This heaven is the Allied Powers. Your decision will be the beginning of new life for you and for your national happiness. You will never again have a better opportunity as today. This moment is great and festive. The fate of your nation is in your hands.[13]

Despite the presence of four representatives on the commis- sion, France set the policy. Even after the defeat of the Central Powers, the understanding of the Anglo-French Agreement of December 23, 1917, remained in force. Galicia was a French sphere of activity, and the French were concerned with a Polish counter- weight to a resurrected Germany and particularly to the free flow of oil. As was revealed in the proposal, the foremost interest of the armistice agreement was to protect the oil properties developed with French capital.

Article 9. On the same territories during this armistice no concessions will be given for the right to exploit the petroleum fields outside the realm of private property.

Article 10. With the reservation that the petroleum installations and all of the rail road lines were not subjected to any serious damage, the Polish military authorities during the duration of armistice will be obliged to supply the Ukrainian authorities monthly for a payment by rail and the rail road station in Stryy a certain tonnage of raw petroleum and its products. . . .

Article 11. The Ukrainian army will have the duty to protect during the evacuation the evacuated strip, and especially the exploitations and petroleum installations against any attempts, any destruction and any kind of damage; after its withdrawal it will turn over the maintenance of order to the local civil authorities.[14]

Galicia ranked eighth on the list of world oil producers. Although she was a small player, the region had become an important weapon in the French arsenal for the new industrial war that came on the heels of the bloodletting. Simon Petliura and the army of the Ukrainian National Republic that advocated the nationalization of industry in much the same fashion as did the Bolsheviki. This threatened the French grand strategy. During the war, the absolute need for such a strategy had made itself too clear to be ignored.

Ten days after the war ended, British Secretary of State for Foreign Affairs Lord George Nathaniel Curzon told a gathering, "We floated to victory on a sea of oil."[15] How true that was! The frightening unspoken truth, however, was that it had been an American sea. A foreign power had controlled the destinies of France and Britain. Ninety percent of the fuel burned in naval vessels, aerocraft, or tanks had come from across the Atlantic Ocean. The United States and Mexico produced 80 percent of the oil in the world, and the industry was dominated by one corporation, Standard Oil.

The Federal Trade Commission in Washington charged the industry with profiteering. Profits had risen from 15 to 21 percent as prices, despite government controls, increased from $1.80 to $4.00 per barrel.

Peace gave the industrial nations time to think about their vulnerability. In the last year of the war worldwide oil production rose by twenty-five thousand barrels per day, an increase of 1 percent. A healthy industrial economy could not be constructed upon such a meager growth in supply. America was consuming petroleum at a rate twenty times more per capita than Europe. For the health of the American economy, the supplies to the rest of the world might be cut off, or the world could be held hostage to American demands. In the opinion of the French, Galicia was too important to be left to a group of radical socialist Ukrainians.

The Germans and the Austrians knew how important the Austrian province was. Before the war, Galician wells produced 450,000 tons of oil per annum, which was exactly how much the war machines of the Central Powers burned. If they had had the oil, then there would have been a likelihood that the Central Powers would have won the war. Instead, the fields had been taken by the Russians during the first month of fighting. By that one triumph, the Russians had inflicted a fatal injury to the Austrians and Germans. The last great German offensive with troops transferred from the Eastern Front to the Western Front floundered in the muck of France in great part because of the lack of fuel to launch aircraft and to move trucks and tanks.

Petroleum had been the weakness of Germany's strategy to be a major power. In 1913, 91 percent of world oil came from Standard Oil. Germans, like the British and French, were dependent upon a foreign supplier.

A desperate effort had been made to escape the grip of John D. Rockefeller, but the Germans moved too late. The Deutsche Bank had been investing in Galicia and Romania, while the real hope was in Turkish-controlled Iraq. A railway was planned. "Baghdad to Berlin," the slogan of the optimists announced. Iraq was to make Germany independent, except that the Germans were too slow to make the move into the region, and they never achieved their energy independence.

French investors had seen the necessity to go abroad long

before their own or the German government had. At the beginning of the century, the French investor had caught black gold fever. Spies Petroleum, North Caucasian Oil, Lianosoff, and Grosny were the toys of speculators. Traders on the Paris Bourse could speak familiarly about the Bukovina, Jaslo, Boryslaw, and Kolomea fields. The Rothschild Banks of France had formed oil companies in Galicia and Romania and sold the shares to private investors.

The prices of crude oil and shares in petroleum companies soared with the ever-growing demand for energy. From 1880 to 1910, world oil production expanded from 35 million tons to 328 million tons. Every drop had a customer.

The Rothschild financial interest in the petroleum industry of the region and other Jewish investments in the Boryslaw field added to the struggle for control of a vital resource the still more explosive force of anti-Semitism. As the struggle for control of Galicia raged, Ukrainians had little difficulty fashioning from the situation a vision of a virulent Jewish conspiracy. For Ukrainians, who had come from an environment in which the local Jewish merchants had dominated commerce, expanding that deep-rooted distrust and hatred was a natural process. Who was more the symbol of Jewish economic control of the world than Rothschild?

Lemberg, the capital of Galicia, became the capital of the petroleum industry, the Houston of Austria. On February 28, 1919, Lemberg was the cage in which Polish hopes had been trapped. Closing in for the kill were the combined Ukrainian armies. If French policy were to succeed, the city had to be secured for the Poles. General Barthelemy believed that he held the key to Polish acquisition of the rich territory, which would give to France indirect control, but the Galician representatives defied the wrath of the Allies, challenged Polish claims, and refused to sign. Defeated and humiliated, General Barthelemy resigned.

His successor, General Botha, presented new proposals. The Poles, however, had begun to modify their policy toward the French manipulation of the situation. During the negotiations, the Poles believed that the advantage had swung in their favor.

Polish authorities decided that they did not have to accept whatever crumbs were being offered by the French, when they could have the entire cake—territories of West and East Galicia with a rich icing of petroleum.

Supporting Polish confidence was Haller's army, which had arrived in Poland and was advancing toward Galicia. At the same time, the Poles had struck a secret agreement with the Romanians to provide assistance. The Poles were confident that the French could be persuaded to support the Polish plan and that the other members of the Allied Powers were indifferent to the rights and interests of the Ukrainian-Galicians.

Simon Petliura's army had to face the formidable power of the fresh, well-equipped troops of Haller's army and the Romanians. He had an ally, however, in the Rasala Battalion, Schwartzbard's Jewish volunteers. They engaged the Romanians. Those two military commanders had been united by the global struggle for the control of oil.

Henri Berenger, wartime oil commissioner of France and post-war ambassador to the United States, noted in a memorandum,

> He who owns the oil will own the world, for he will rule the sea by means of the heavy oils, the air by means of the ultra refined oils, and the land by means of petrol and the illuminating oils. And in addition to these he will rule his fellow men in an economic sense, by reason of the fantastic wealth he will derive from oil—the wonderful substance which is more sought after and more precious today than gold itself.[16]

7

Playing with Power

Out in their fields the peasants caught the scent of the blood of the wounded beast. The Ukrainian Skoropadsky government, their oppressor, could no longer rely upon German and Austrian bayonets to preserve it. For six months, Skoropadsky had done the bidding of the foreign occupiers. Collection teams went into the countryside to take the food off the tables of those who had produced it in order to put bread into the stomachs of Germans and Austrians. Every loaf of that stolen bread had been leavened by the blood of the occupiers. Nineteen thousand Germans and Austrians had died for the "bread peace." They had been killed by angry peasants and by the advancing Bolsheviks. When World War I ended on November 11, 1918, they had gathered little bread and had found no peace.

For the surviving occupiers, finally, the war was over. Their only thought was to go home quickly and safely. As the defeated army without authority, their former puppet, Skoropadsky, was no longer their concern. On November 15, Volodymyr Vynnychenko, the chairman of the Ukrainian National Union, summoned the peasants to rise against the undefended Skoropadsky Hetmanate. Here was to be a classical Marxian demonstration of a popular uprising to sweep away an oppressor. Waves of peasants came to settle long-festering scores. As the mobs ravaged the suburbs of Kiev, Vynnychenko saw in the ruins the foundation of his ideology. The blood of the revolution was to wash away the old order and fertilize the land for the new peasant society. Blood would be the essence of justice.

> Our offensive has started. . . . There is no hope for victory at Kyyiv [Kiev], but either a retreat or a consent to the conditions of the German command . . . would mean a much worse solution. . . . If we were defeated this time physically, then spiritually, nationally, and socially we are now united and at a proper time, later on, our cause shall have full support of all people.[17]

Outside of Kiev, at the headquarters of the Sich Rifles, Simon Petliura sent his own call for the peasants to rise and follow him. The peasants knew Petliura better than they did Vynnychenko. In a few weeks, Petliura's army grew from the professional fifteen thousand men of the Sich Rifles to a horde of one hundred thousand. Among the masses of peasants, men arose, called themselves leaders, and claimed to control a band of peasant soldiers. Those who pledged their allegiance to the supreme commander, Generalissimo Simon Petliura, were given the title of "ataman." The generalissimo gave out handfuls of money to the instant commanders, issued his instructions, and imagined that he was the leader of a grand movement. Of the Petliura horde Vynnychenko wrote, "There was neither punishment, nor justice, nor trials, nor control over these criminals and enemies of the revolution and the national movement. The whole system of military authority was constructed and consciously based, by the chief and by the lesser atamany, on the principle that there would be no control."[18]

It was a good time for the peasants to harvest booty. The harvest from the land was over. Spring planting was months away. In the interim, their guns and bayonets were scythes and plowshares to fill their plates with the riches of the defenseless. On November 25, 1918, Petliura issued his instructions to the armed hordes, but there were very few willing or able to enforce his commands.

> Supreme Headquarters, November 25, 1918. Thereby I order the compliance with and the enforcement of the following decree of the Directorate of the Ukrainian National Republic.
>
> 1. The Armed Forces of the Ukrainian National Republic have been organized for the defense of the Ukrainian National Republic and for the defense of all working people of Ukraine.
>
> It has been the responsibility of every member of the military to protect every resident of Ukraine against any form of lawlessness and disorder and to prevent any such developments which have not been in accord with the decrees of the Directorate or might have disturbed law and order in Ukraine.
>
> All formations of the Armed Forces of the Ukrainian National Republic, including all privates and officers, must follow the orders of their superiors without any reservations and adhere to stern discipline. Anybody guilty of breaking discipline will be subject to judgment in the military courts. . . .
>
> 4. Any military or civilian person who commits any crime of robbery, rioting, or any other lawlessness of that kind on the territory of the Ukrainian National Republic will be subject to judgment by military courts.
>
> > Signed: S. Petliura, Commander-in-Chief
> > of the Republican Armed Forces of the
> > Ukrainian National Republic[19]

His command of the army, such as it was, gave Petliura more of the reality of power than was possessed by Vynnychenko, who had been named chairman of the directorate of the reconstituted Ukrainian National Republic. Vynnychenko held only the illusion of power and governed in accordance with an abstract ideology. The real instrument of power, the gun, belonged to his rival, Simon Petliura.

On December 12, Petliura arranged a truce with the German Command in Kiev. In exchange for the surrender of the city and their military materiel, Petliura gave the withdrawing occupation forces peaceful passage through his lines. Disguised as a wounded German soldier and a nurse, Skoropadsky and his wife slipped safely away into exile.

On December 14, the Sich Rifles occupied Kiev. Five days later, as its liberator, the generalissimo entered the capital. By making his grand entry into the conquered city, he had stolen the thunder from Vynnychenko and had widened a rift at the highest level of the government.

In the armistice agreement that ended World War I, the Austrians and Germans had been required to maintain order over their occupied zones in Russia. More than an outbreak of anarchy, the Allied Powers feared the development of a power vacuum that Vynnychenko and Petliura would fill. According to French reports about the Ukrainian leaders, they were another form of Bolshevik. From his headquarters in Jassy, General Berthelot instructed representatives of the puppet Skoropadsky Hetmanate to continue to rule until Allied Power troops could assume control.

French intelligence reports came primarily from men in the Skoropadsky government in the Ukraine and gave General Berthelot no warning of what was to come. When the first units of French forces landed in Odessa on December 18, 1918, the city was under siege. White Russians and supporters of the deposed Skoropadsky, with a unit of Poles, were holding the city.

Rather than a solution to the problems, the French were just another contribution to the chaos. They were too weak to impose order and too strong to be ignored.

Ukrainian commanders and politicians were confused, uncertain whether to fight and thereby incur the wrath of the Allied Powers or to submit and to abandon their control over their territory. At the last moment, they backed away from a conflict with the French.

A massive intervention was the only solution. Thousands of troops would be needed, but that was beyond French ability, unless there was support from the other Allies.

As London viewed the situation, the White Russians were the best means to restore the empire, although the British were not enthusiastic supporters of the restoration of the czar. Britain preferred France to withdraw her troops from the midst of the madness and to shift French support to the White Russians. In that way, the British hoped to reduce French domination of the region.

The French did give lip service to the White Russians, but they refrained from giving substantive aid. Behind French postwar policy was the spread of their influence into the resource-rich region, where France's economic interests were already significant. Despite France's declared policy of one Russia, it was prepared to make the Ukraine a protectorate of Poland, which was under French influence, or so they imagined.

Meanwhile, President Wilson believed that within every Russian was a caged democrat who would at first opportunity fashion a system similar to that of America. Like the other leaders, Wilson was convinced that Bolshevism was a momentary aberration that would pass without the need for the Allied Powers to act.

All that was needed for the natural course of history to end the red menace and to bring democratic rule to the collapsing Russian Empire was precious time. In order to give the situation the time to turn events in the proper direction, the independence movements had to be stopped. The Liquidation Commission, the sales office of the United States Department of War, in order to hinder the independence movement, was instructed not to sell war surplus equipment to the Ukraine. A sale of $12 million of medical supplies, blankets, and transportation equipment was made in April 1919, but cancelled in December by order of Secretary of State Robert Lansing.

Britain and the United States expected history to act without their participation. In January 1919, none of the Allied Powers was willing to help France secure a hold over the Ukraine. With the war over, the interests of the different members of the Allied Powers diverged and it was not in the interest of others to see the French dominate the region.

The French held a vulnerable enclave around Odessa. Only six thousand French, two thousand Greek, and four thousand

Polish troops had been landed. A major Bolshevik or Ukrainian offensive could have driven them into the Black Sea. Aware of his dangerous position, the French colonel, Freydenberg, turned to diplomacy to compensate for military weakness. He opened negotiations with the Ukrainians and the White Russians.

Freydenberg's proposal was to divide the Ukraine into two zones. One would be under Russian administration; the other under Ukrainian rule. France would function as policeman and mediator until the Ukraine was reunited into a reformed Russian Empire. The French agreed to grant diplomatic recognition to the Ukrainians for the transition period.

French cooperation did not come without a price. For their services, the French demanded from both parties economic concessions in the reconstituted, united Russia. Colonel Freydenberg added to his proposal the condition that the politically offensive Petliura and Vynnychenko be removed from office. Their reputations as Bolsheviks made any agreement of economic concessions useless.

To give himself a less radical image, Petliura resigned from the Social Democratic Party, while retaining command of the army. His old rival, Vynnychenko, was forced to resign from the government, a victim of his own dedication to his radical socialist ideology. Vynnychenko had supported negotiations with Lenin. While Vynnychenko talked, the Bolsheviks overran Kiev, which fell on February 5, 1919. Fault for the defeat was fixed upon Vynnychenko, and political power passed to Petliura, who thus supplemented his control of the military with that of the other institutions of the struggling Ukrainian state.

Despite his trappings of authority, however, circumstances had changed for the generalissimo. In December, he could claim to command an army of a hundred thousand citizen soldiers. By March his army had dwindled to twenty thousand. The Sich Rifles remained his only effective fighting force. Thus, while he gathered more power into his hands, there was in reality less power to exercise. He had become "the strong man" of an impotent state.

Loyalties were as fluid as the blood flowing throughout the Ukraine. Entire units of peasants defected to the Bolsheviks with their slogan of "Land, Peace, and Bread." Behind the advancing Bolshevik soldiers, followed the agents of the Cheka, the Bolshevik secret police, imposing Lenin's policy of "terror and starvation." The terror was to break psychological resistance. Starvation was to break physical resistance.

If a man wished to eat, then he would have to join the Red Army. The army was fed by the plundered grain taken from the peasants. During 1919, the Red Army grew from 3.0 million to 5.5 million. Despite the overall growth of the Red Army and the free use of terror, peasant rebellions weakened the Bolshevik grip over captured territory. As Petliura experienced, commanders revolted against the central authority of the Red Army and took their units to another flag or became independent gangs of marauding bandits.

Those days of turmoil in the first half of 1919 were the worst days of the pogroms. Jews were prey for every marauder, whether he claimed allegiance to the Bolsheviks, the White Russians, the Ukrainians, or no one. Folklore had it that every Jew had a store of gold under his bed, and the peasant soldiers believed it. During attacks in the towns of Balta and Proskurov, fifteen members of Schwartzbard's family, including his father and his stepmother, were killed.

Commanders knew better than to interfere with the lust of their men. For an ataman to keep his command, he had to condone the pogroms through silence or actively support them. Generalissimo Petliura chose silence. A word against violence, until the worst of it was spent, would have isolated him further. He kept his silence until August 26, 1919.

The sinister men of the "Black Hundred" and the "Red Hundred" are but one band. They are assiduously weaving the spider's web, provoking pogroms of the Jewish population, and on many occasions they have incited certain backward elements of our army to commit abominable acts. They thus succeeded in defiling our struggle for liberty in the eyes of the world and compromised our national cause.

Officers and Cossacks! It is time to know that the Jews have, like the greater part of our Ukrainian population, suffered from the horrors of the Bolshevik-Communist invasion and followed the way to the truth. The best Jewish groups, such as the "Bund," the "Unified" [United Jewish Socialists], the "Poale Zion," and the "Folks Party" [People's Party] have willingly placed themselves at the disposal of the sovereign and independent Ukraine and cooperated with us.

It is time to learn that the peaceful population, its women and children have been oppressed in the same way as ours and deprived of national liberty. This population has lived with us for centuries and shares our pleasures and our sorrows.

The chivalrous troops who bring fraternity, equality, and liberty to all the nationalities of Ukraine, must not listen to the invaders and provocateurs who hunger for human blood. Neither can they remain indifferent in the face of the tragic fate of the Jews. He who becomes an accomplice to such crimes is a traitor and an enemy of our country, and he must be placed beyond the pale of human society.

Officers and Cossacks! The entire world is amazed at your heroism. Do not tarnish it, even accidentally, by an infamous adventure and do not dishonor our Republic in the eyes of the world. Our enemies have exploited the pogroms against us. They affirm that we are not worthy of an independent and sovereign existence and that we must be enslaved once again.

Officers and Cossacks! Ensure the victory by directing your arms against the real enemy, and remember that our pure cause necessitates clean hands. I expressly order you to drive away with your arms all who incite you to pogroms and bring them before the courts as enemies of the state. And the tribunal will judge them for their acts and the most severe penalties of the law will be inflicted upon all those found guilty.[20]

Early during the epidemic of anarchy, the fever had reached the French Army. On April 2, 1919, to avoid mass mutiny, Paris ordered the evacuation of the expeditionary force in Odessa. Four days later, it departed, abandoning the White Russian allies to the mercy of the advancing Reds, to whom the French troops gave their stores and their blessings. With the withdrawal of French forces, the Allied Powers admitted their unwillingness and inability to manage the situation in the chaotic region. The indigenous players would be left the entire field on which to play their strategies for two more bloody years.

8

The Third Enemy

While the French abandoned their allies and their honor in Odessa, General Jozef Haller entered the chaos. With French supplies his troops reached Poland, where the French had lost control of their Polish ally. Although their mandate limited them to combatting only the Bolsheviks, Prime Minister Jozef Pilsudski of Poland had his own secret plan for the fresh, untested army.

To win the support of the Allied Powers, Pilsudsi had offered to march to Moscow to crush the socialist regime. The price: a mere $2.5 million. After his offer was ignored by the four powers in Paris, Haller's arrival on Polish soil gave him the chance to establish a plan to form a Greater Poland with satellite states around her. The destruction of the Ukrainian interests in Galicia and the seizure of the petroleum installations was the first step.

General Haller was made the executioner of Ukrainian independence. On May 14, 1919, his army, supported by other Polish units and their Romanian allies, opened an offensive against the combined Ukrainian and Galician armies. Galician forces numbered seventy-five thousand; Ukrainian troops under Simon Petliura had fifteen thousand. The combined force was short on supplies and officers. They were no match for the attacking force, which overran all of Galicia.

From Paris the Allied Powers protested the Polish assault

into a territory still under consideration by the Armistice Commission. Pilsudski pressed on; he was certain there would be no real opposition. As he viewed the geopolitical situation, the levers of advantage were in his hands. Allied troops were gone, leaving a power vacuum that Poland alone could fill. Pilsudski possessed the sole military force in Eastern Europe able to check the Bolsheviks. His one vulnerable point was his dependence upon the Allied Powers for arms. The destruction of Ukrainian resistance and conquest of West Galicia had to be achieved before shipments were curtailed and stores exhausted.

Pilsudski's gamble paid off. On June 25, 1919, the Peace Conference gave West Galicia to Poland and made East Galicia a twenty-five-year mandate. Polish aggression had been sanctioned by the Allied Powers. Over a one-year period, Jozef Pilsudski had taken Poland from a nonexistent state to an imperial power.

Ukrainian and Galician forces were in full retreat. The Ukrainian-Galicians were men without a country, and the Ukrainians saw theirs being overrun by the Bolsheviki and White Russians. Their last hope was to capture Kiev or some other city to give them a capital.

Before the Ukrainian army reached Kiev from the west, the city fell to the White Russians, who were advancing from the east. Freshly supplied by the British, the reconstituted White Russian army was a formidable force of 150,000. Rather than turn toward Odessa to gain access to a port and to possible foreign supplies, the Ukrainians moved toward Kiev. Trapped inside the Ukraine without sources of supplies, they were doomed orphans. More than a strategic plan, they needed hope. That could be found in Kiev, where the White Russians waited to repel the anticipated assault.

Representatives of the Allied Powers intervened at Kiev to prevent a battle between the armies. According to the British plan for the White Russians, Anton Denikin's White Russian Volunteer Army was to be employed to defeat the Bolsheviks and not to be consumed in senseless battles. Denikin became military commander of the army on March 31, 1918.

General Myron Tarnavskyi, commander of the Galician army, was persuaded not to engage the White Russians in a bloody fight for the city. As he saw the world, his real enemy was Poland, which had seized his country of West Galicia. An alliance with the White Russians was his last hope to recapture his occupied homeland. On August 31, 1919, an agreement between the Galicians and the White Russians was signed. Simon Petliura was left to make his own arrangements.

On September 1, 1919, Petliura did, when he signed a separate agreement with Pilsudski. The generalissimo declared himself hostile to the White Russians and ended any hope of support from the Allied Powers. Petliura was the commander of an exhausted starving band of poorly armed men who had no chance of victory and no real allies. They needed no other enemies, but they had one. In the autumn, his army was decimated by an epidemic of typhus. The epidemic raged across the Ukraine, Poland, and Russia. Combined with the influenza, which spread around the world, countless millions died, and Petliura's misery-burdened troops were among the casualties.

War, famine, and now pestilence besieged them. In a letter to Jean Pelissier, the French diplomatic agent who had helped organize the anti-Bolshevik uprising in the Ukraine, Petliura made a vain appeal for aid.

Mon cher ami Pelissier,

I rejoice at the opportunity of sending you my ardent salutations and of thanking you and all the supporters of our just and sacred cause for the powerful aid which you give our people in its struggle for liberty. . . .

I should have every reason to rejoice profoundly if the incessant efforts which you exert for the Ukraine are crowned with success and if, after having triumphed over all the obstacles and broken all the bonds, we should see you in the capital of Ukraina as representative of the real interest of your glorious country. . . .

An epoch has passed since I last saw you. Since then we

have undergone many ordeals, and many a white hair marks on our heads the grievous stages of the road we have traveled. We have many enemies, but they make the unity of our national will and arouse in us the ardent desire to conquer the sovereignty of our fatherland.

At the present hour, our most dangerous adversary is General Denikin, who, instead of fighting the Bolsheviks, has turned against us the artillery and rifles which he has received from the Allies and thus has weakened the anti-Bolshevik front. We have every reason to believe that Denikin, while receiving money of the Entente, also receives some from Germany, and his officers announce openly that after having defeated the Ukrainians, their chief will begin the strife against the Poles and Rumanians.

We have had no aid from anyone: neither munitions nor technical apparatus, nor sanitary products, nothing. Friend Pelissier, what tragic hours we have lived in our abandonment! It often happens that our soldiers are without cartridges. Then they charge with the bayonet against the Bolsheviks. The examples of heroism which they give, the bloody sacrifices which they make, are unique in military annals.

Three-quarters of our men lack shoes, clothing, everything; but their esprit is not impaired. We have no medicine; typhus decimates our army; many fighters die for lack of medicines and blankets. Alas, the Powers of the Entente, which proclaim such sublime principles, do not even permit the Red Cross to come to us.

We are dying, the allies wash their hands like Pilate, there remains for us only to say, "Morituri te salutamus." ["We who are about to die salute you."][21]

Ukrainian support in the United States had never been of sufficient importance to sway political opinion there. In an interview Simon Petliura made his last appeal for aid that would never come.

We have been terribly misrepresented abroad as Bolsheviki. We are not that, but a land of peasant proprietors, the strongest imaginable bulwark of a petty bourgeoisie. Why does not the

Entente drive Denikin against Moscow, instead of against the
Ukraine? We would join him and, at any rate secure his rear.
But while we fight him, and we will fight him, the Bolsheviki
will regain the initiative and all will be lost. That will not dismay
us. We had hardly anything left last year, and now see how
we have grown. The fight will go on indefinitely. We do not
ask for any gratuitous help from the Allies. We only want our
frontiers opened so that we can trade our products for manu-
factured articles and equipment. Let them open Odessa. We do
not ask them to pour in supplies free of charge to us as they
do to Denikin. And above all, for the sake of humanity, why
won't they let us have some medicines? I beg of you to explain
to the American people how we stand. I am sure they will in
that case not fail to respond.[22]

An alliance with Pilsudski was Petliura's last and only chance,
but the agreement was an act of suicide for the Ukrainian effort
to create an independent state. The Polish leader was making
agreements with every side. During November 1919 Pilsudski
made a secret peace treaty with the Bolsheviks that enabled them
to concentrate their attacks against General Denikin and his newly
acquired Galician army. At the same time, Pilsudski had an
arrangement with Denikin to conduct a joint offensive against
the Bolsheviks, although he never got around to setting a date.
By springtime, the Bolsheviks had broken the White Russians
and the Galicians. Pilsudski by sheer cunning had destroyed his
main opponents for the control over Galicia. For Pilsudski, the
road to Kiev was clear, and Simon Petliura was to be used to
lead him to another jewel for the Polish empire.

By April 21, 1920, the truce of September, 1, 1919, between
Petliura and Pilsudski was expanded into a treaty. For Polish
military aid and diplomatic recognition, Simon Petliura acknowledged Polish ownership of Galicia and renounced Ukrainian
interest in the territory.

The combined Polish and Ukrainian armies attacked the
Bolshevik-occupied city of Kiev. The capital fell. Again, Petliura
entered as its liberator, but there was not the celebration of

December 19, 1918. His inglorious return was as the Polish puppet, which cost him his last public support. Shortly after the last victory, his armies were defeated and driven back into Polish territory.

The Allied Powers had tired of the war. Like it or not, they accepted the inevitability of a Bolshevik victory. Lloyd George expressed his dissatisfaction with the Ukrainians, Poles, White Russians, and French. Britain was done with the mess! France clung to her illusions for a little longer.

By early autumn, the Poles, White Russians, and Petliura formed a new alliance. White Russians and Ukrainians mounted their last assault into the Ukraine. It went badly. As they retreated into Poland, the Poles disarmed them and interned them. Simon Petliura became a prisoner of the Poles, until he left to join the other exiles.

On October 12, 1920, the Poles signed an agreement with the Bolsheviks. The Poles recognized Soviet control over the Ukraine; the Soviets accepted Polish control over Galicia. Under the agreement hostile Ukrainian and Russian forces were to be neutralized.

As the Bolsheviks secured control over the old Russian Empire, Samuel Schwartzbard emerged. He had been the "ataman" of his unit of volunteer Jews throughout much of the chaos. From Bessarabia to Kharkov, they had fought Romanians, Poles, White Russians, Ukrainians, and an assortment of local gangs of bandits. Before it was over, he had seen Red troops loot, rape, and murder Jews, and seen his own men become bandits. The revolution had not made men better. Instead, it had been for many an opportunity to plunder and pillage. Once again Schwartzbard left. He returned to France to find the perfect man, for whom he had long been searching.

9

An Eye for a Thousand Eyes

Seven years after World War I ended, Paris, the City of Lights, the center of Western culture, had revived. Artists from around the world debated philosophies and compared fantasies in the cafes. A new age had come, of which the aeroplane and the radio were the technological symbols, while the flappers were the social expression of the modern liberalism. Buried in the mud-filled trenches, the old order and morality were left to decay and be forgotten. Among the abandoned refuse were the segmented portions of the abolished Austrian and German Empires and a region of the Russian Empire.

While Paris was soaring on its own enthusiasm, other areas of Europe were seething in the postwar chaos. Violence and assassinations became commonplace. During the decade of the 1920s, forty-four political leaders were shot or bombed to death.

Mixed with the artists of Paris were the refugees from Eastern Europe. Like refugees everywhere, they were restless, waiting for the signal that would send them home to wherever they looked for permanence. They had brought to their temporary home the baggage of their distant conflicts. Together in their transposed nationalist and ethnic spheres, they refought old battles, regenerated ancient hatreds, and plotted for the time when they could enjoy the glories of new victories.

After a brief stay in Switzerland, Simon Petliura arrived in Paris in October 1924 with his wife, Olga, and their daughter, Lessia. Soon after he arrived, he began publishing an exile newspaper, *Trident*, taking the name from the symbol of the nation he had led for a brief, bloody time. Petliura was the leader of Paris's Ukrainian exiles, and he kept their eyes focused upon the future nation. Daily he went with his family and friends for their midday meal at the inexpensive Chartier Restaurant in the Latin Quarter. In spite of his place at the center of the nationalists, exile in the foreign capital was a plunge from the center of power into a low-rent, cramped, two-room apartment without bath or kitchen facilities.

A constant circle of comrades around him gave Petliura an opportunity to talk about conditions back home. More important still, their presence gave him a degree of protection from the always possible danger of an assassination. Among the exiles, it was believed that many potential enemies were awaiting an opportunity to strike. The Soviet secret police, the Cheka, was said to be sending out agents to eliminate threats to the still-unsecured power of the Bolsheviks. As it had been in the Ukraine at the time of the chaos, numerous factions battled for power and carried their rivalries into exile. Other Ukrainian factions would have applauded the assassination of Petliura.

Then, there were the Jews. During the brief rule of Simon Petliura from 1919 to 1921, between 50,000 and 150,000 Jews were murdered in numerous villages across the Ukraine. Most of those lost lives were charged by Jewish survivors to the soul of Simon Petliura. To the Jewish refugees, the name Simon Petliura was the name of the ruler of Hell.

Samuel Schwartzbard knew well that name. Fifteen members of his family had been killed in the pogroms. Even if Petliura himself had not killed them, Schwartzbard had absolutely no doubt where to affix the charge for murder. Schwartzbard had a small watch repair at boulevard de Menilmontant 82, but his real interest, like Petliura's, was the written word and politics. Under the pseudonym "the Dreamer" (Baal Chalomoth), he wrote a weekly column for the Jewish labor newspaper in New York and Philadelphia, *Die Fraye Arbeiter Shtimme* (Free Workers' Voice), and he helped to organize labor unions in France. His remaining interest in the Ukraine was to resettle in Israel the Jewish survivors of the pogroms.

Within weeks of Petliura's arrival in Paris, Schwartzbard learned from a Russian language newspaper that the hated man was nearby. "When I heard that he [Petliura] was in Paris, I made up my mind to kill him. All of my compatriots, Jewish or not, could scarcely believe he was in Paris. They were unanimous in telling me, 'It isn't possible that this dog is here.' "[23]

Yet, *Trident,* full of anti-Semitic invective, was being published in Paris by Simon Petliura. Later, Schwartzbard's wife, Anna, recalled her husband's transformation: "I remember that his depressed mood dated from the time Petliura started his Ukrainian weekly, *Trident,* in Paris. My husband read this periodical regularly, and the after-effect was terrible excitement and despondency."[24]

Schwartzbard asked his friends to help him uncover the whereabouts of the former leader.

> Many people thought my inquiries about Petliura peculiar, and some even mocked me, inquiring whether perhaps I planned to kill him. The futile searches and the ironic comments often brought me to tears. Sometimes I just became sick at petty comments of friends who suspected something, who tried to dissuade me, saying that I should leave his punishment to other hands, not ruin the livelihood that I had.[25]

Despite the lack of support, Schwartzbard began the hunt for the man upon whom he focused his hatred. Acting as a lone avenger simply strengthened his determination. Always alienated, he had looked inward for his reasons. Killing Petliura was no different to him from leading a band of Jews through the chaos and slaughter of the Ukraine to forward his vision of the revolution.

Schwartzbard's only guide to identify the prey was a sketch from *L'Encyclopedie Larousse,* but the vague image was not good enough to provide a positive identification. Finally, after months of futile searching, Schwartzbard believed that he had sighted his prey near the Museum Cluny. Unnoticed, Schwartzbard was able to approach near enough to hear the supposed Simon Petliura speaking Ukrainian to a number of companions.

In spite of the threat to his life from assassins, Simon Petliura was an easy man to stalk. He lived in an unguarded apartment on rue Thenarde, ate at the same restaurant every day, and walked openly on the Paris streets. Schwartzbard began the tedious task of tracking his target. Each day, he carried his loaded 9-millimeter automatic pistol, in case an opportunity to strike presented itself. But there was never a moment when the believed former ataman was alone; additionally, there remained the haunting question if the man was in fact Simon Petliura or just a likeness of a poor sketch.

Nouvelles Ukraniennes (The New Ukrainians), another exile newspaper, provided the positive identification in a May 1926, issue. A clear photograph of Simon Petliura was enough for the final fatal act. Only by personally killing the leader of the pogromchiks did Schwartzbard expect to exact any justice for the murders of thousands of forgotten victims of an ignored "holocaust." No government in Europe showed an interest in the crimes, and no other Jew seemed to be concerned about exacting retribution from the man upon whom Schwartzbard and many of those very same indifferent Jews placed blame for the mass murders.

On the morning of May 25, 1926, Schwartzbard was ready to run his quarry to ground. He awakened early, dressed in his work clothes, concealed his fully loaded Browning automatic pistol under his shirt, and placed two letters into his pocket.

One letter was addressed to Anna. He told her,

> I am performing a duty for our poor people. I am going to avenge all the pogroms, the blood, the hatred of the Jews. Petliura was responsible for the misfortune of our people. He must pay with

his blood. As for you, conduct yourself heroically, hardily. I would never forget it if you were courageous. Accuse no one. I alone am responsible, but I could not live without avenging that great offense.[26]

The second letter was addressed to Maitre Henri Torres, a young Jewish lawyer who was among the most successful practitioners of the law in France. Already his name had been associated with celebrated cases. Torres was the best choice Schwartzbard could have made if he intended to escape martyrdom at the guillotine; and there was nothing in his character that pointed to a man with a martyr complex. Schwartzbard had taken up arms and fought in the uniform of France and as a revolutionary. During numerous battles he had proved his skill as a soldier and as a survivor. No, nothing in his character revealed Samuel Schwartzbard's eagerness to sacrifice himself. He intended to kill Simon Petliura and not Samuel Schwartzbard.

There was good reason for Schwartzbard to anticipate a favorable court decision. On March 15, 1921, on Hardenberg Strasse in Charlottenburg district of Berlin, Talaat Pasha, a former grand vizier and a war leader of Turkey, was assassinated, and his wife was injured by Solomon Teilirian, an Armenian student. The killer justified his action as retribution for the murder of six hundred thousand Armenians and the expulsion of six hundred thousand others. Among the dead were members of Teilirian's family.

No one doubted the guilt of the former grand vizier. Even the Turkish government wanted him for crimes against the nation. During the trial, Talaat was condemned. Teilirian explained why he had to act.

I am not guilty, because my conscience is clean. A fortnight before this deed the scenes of the massacre of Erzerum reappeared to me. I saw my mother, brother, and ravished sisters lying as corpses. Suddenly, the dead body of my mother stood up, placed itself before me, and said: "You know that Talaat

Pasha is here. You are utterly indifferent. You are therefore not my son." I then became suddenly awake and reached a decision to kill Talaat.[27]

True or not, the German court acquitted Solomon Teilirian. An editorial in the *New York Times* foresaw serious consequences.

The fact remains, however, that he was assassinated, not put to death with the judicial formality that is the right of even such as he, and to hold, as the German jurors did, that his taking off was "morally right" both reveals a queer view of moral rightness and opens the way to other assassinations less easily excusable than his or not excusable at all.[28]

Twenty-six months later, on May 10, 1923, Maurice Conradi, a Russian emigre and former soldier in the White Russian Army, ate supper in the dining room of the Cecil Hotel in Lausanne, Switzerland. He finished his meal with two glasses of brandy, after which he approached the table of three Soviet diplomats and started shooting. His first bullet hit Vorovsky in the head and killed him instantly. Arens and Divilkovsky, the other two diplomats, were wounded.

Like Teilirian, Conradi made no effort to conceal his crime. In his case, he justified it by the death of his Swiss father and uncle, after their property in the Soviet Union had been confiscated by the Bolsheviks. None of Conradi's victims was held individually responsible, but the jury could not hold the assassin guilty of murder.

Both Teilirian and Conradi were considered victims of injustice because they had been denied any recourse under law. If they were to receive justice, then they had to exact it for themselves. Thus, two courts in two countries had declared violence to be justice.

Samuel Schwartzbard had found his defense and justification. Because no state authority was prepared to act to give justice to the forgotten dead, racial dignity and his personal loss required him to execute Simon Petliura.

10

The Hunter and the Hunted

Morning after morning, Schwartzbard went out to kill. Each evening, he returned to his apartment to contemplate for another night the gravity of murder and to consider in what countless ways his plan could fail. The stress had become too much to conceal.

"Are you ill?" Anna asked him on the morning of May 25, 1926.

"No. My nerves are shot," he disclosed.

"Then stay at home. Have breakfast and rest," she urged him.

"I can't. I have an important appointment," he told her.[29]

At one o'clock, Samuel Schwartzbard arrived at Chartier Restaurant, to keep the fatal appointment. Inside, Simon Petliura was eating his midday meal. After waiting and watching for weeks, Samuel finally saw the opportunity. For the first time, Simon Petliura was alone.

Shortly after two o'clock, the former prime minister of thirty million Ukrainians finished his meal and came out into rue Racine. He was still alone.

Samuel Schwartzbard pushed through a group of university students. A moment later, he was face to face with the man who had been for so long his obsession.

"Are you Simon Petliura?" he asked in Ukrainian. Even then,

at the last moment, there remained the unquelled fear that this forty-seven-year-old man was the wrong one.

"Are you Simon Petliura?" he repeated in French.

The man hesitated, but he did not reply with words. Instead, he raised his heavy walking stick as if he were prepared to strike. Schwartzbard drew his pistol from beneath his clothes. As he squeezed off five rapid shots from the weapon, he shouted into the distorted face of the crumpling man, "Assassin! This is for the massacres! This is for the pogroms!"

At his feet lay the gravely wounded Petliura. Then, Samuel fired two more shots. Those two shots would echo through his trial and leave a doubt in the minds of even his supporters. Witnesses claimed that they were the coups de grace, applied by a cold-blooded professional killer who showed no mercy to the pleas of the dying man. A witness claimed to have heard Petliura utter "assez," French for "enough," but Schwartzbard said that he had heard only the moans of pain. In his own defense, Schwartzbard claimed to have been emptying his weapon into the ground, to avoid an accident. Whether a plea for mercy or a moan of pain, the sound was the last one ever uttered by Simon Petliura. He had become another casualty of the madness that had engulfed postwar Eastern Europe.

"Why did you do that?" asked Reginald Smith, an English school teacher who had left Chartier Restaurant a moment after Simon Petliura. Everything had occurred in front of his eyes. Almost before events were over, he grasped Schwartzbard's arm and spoke to him.

"He was a great murderer," Schwartzbard told the stranger. The assassin made no effort to flee the scene or to injure the interfering Englishman.

For a few moments, the sudden outburst of violence had driven back the crowd. As the individual shock passed and the fear ebbed, the crowd merged into an angry mob. The newly born beast found its courage and advanced toward the assassin with an empty gun in his hand.

"Lynch him!" the cry started from one of the many voices in the mob. The wall of anger closed, like an avenging vise.

At his post further along the street Police Constable Roger Mercier heard the series of shots. He had no doubt what he had heard. Up the street he saw the afternoon passers-by unite into an attacking mob. With his partner, Constable Munier, he assaulted the tightening wall, broke through, and reached Schwartzbard, who surrendered the empty weapon to him.

"Did you do this?" Constable Mercier asked.

"I killed a murderer," Schwartzbard admitted.

There was no time to discuss the right or wrong of the killing. Already, the mob had begun to strike, and the policemen were just as much threatened as the assassin.

Roger Mercier pulled his prisoner through the mob to a taxi, pushed Schwartzbard into the rear seat, and ordered the driver to go to police headquarters. Constable Munier was left to send the victim to the hospital and to gather witnesses.

"They're a wild bunch," Mercier told Schwartzbard.

The taxi was surrounded. Fists beat on the steel barrier that separated the mob from vengeance.

"Lynch him!" a voice ignited inside the pressing mob.

"Hang him! He's a foreigner!" another voice urged.

"We have courts for these matters! Leave him alone!" Constable Mercier shouted back at the deafened beast.

Slowly, the driver pushed his way through the wall. When he broke free, he accelerated the taxi and raced for the police headquarters.

"Go to Hell!" Mercier shouted at the screaming mob far behind.

During those moments in the midst of the mob, the two men, policeman and assassin, had been united by their common fear. The killing of Petliura seemed less important to them than their survival. At police headquarters neither the arresting officer nor the arrested killer felt any hostility toward the other.

"What did he do?" a clerk asked Constable Mercier as he was escorting Schwartzbard through the main office of the headquarters.

"Murder," Mercier replied with a casualness of normality.

The announcement did not pluck the noses of the bureaucrats from their folders of police reports on their way into swelling archives. In their papers those clerks had seen everything, noted the entire catalog of human mischief. Nothing could impress or disturb them.

Constable Mercier made his preliminary report to the police inspector on duty. For the inspector the murder was an inconvenience. He was at the end of his tour of duty for the day and eager to get on with other matters. To begin the investigation would delay him. So he instructed the arresting officer to keep charge of the prisoner, until Inspector Mollard came on duty. The wheels of French justice had to be delayed for a short time to await someone without a more important personal agenda.

While the French legal machine slowly began to turn, Schwartzbard's defense machine had been started. Already, the letter to bring Maitre Henri Torres into the case had been posted, but the public was not to know of it until long after the trial, when the knowledge could no longer harm Schwartzbard—the preparation to notify Maitre Henri Torres of the case demonstrated Schwartzbard's preplanning. He had not left his survival to chance. If he had not sent the letter before his arrest, he could have been denied legal counsel.

Before the new inspector came on duty, Schwartzbard was taken into a detention room. Several police constables gave the prisoner a visual examination.

"What did he do?" one inquired.

"Murder," Mercier informed his colleagues.

"Oh. Murder is it?" another commented. "Who did you kill?" he asked Schwartzbard.

"He was a great murderer. He was a Ukrainian general," Schwartzbard informed the curious group.

"Oh, well. Generals should learn how to die," the officer commented.

Constable Mercier had explained that the prisoner had been cooperative. Once that had been revealed, the other police constables seemed quite agreeable. How he behaved toward them defined his character as far as they were concerned.

A little later, Schwartzbard was summoned into the office of the new inspector. Already, Constable Mercier had made his report.

"Why did you shoot the man?" Mollard asked.

"Because I am a Jew," Schwartzbard replied. He wanted to instruct the inspector about two thousand years of persecution, of pogroms, and hatred, but the man behind the desk cared only about one murder on the corner of rue Racine and boulevard Saint Michel. None of those other horrors were in his jurisdiction or of interest to him.

"Are you sure that you shot the right man?" the inspector asked.

Over many weeks, Samuel had been stalking a figure who resembled the picture in his pocket, but no one who had seen Petliura face to face said to him, "He is your man." Now that the deed was done and the murder could not be retracted, the doubt lingered and tortured. His violence might have been a futile effort inflicted upon an innocent man.

A police constable interrupted the interrogation. The officer had just arrived from the emergency hospital, where the still unidentified victim had been taken. Since the shooting, the gravely injured man had not regained consciousness and had died. In his pocket the police found his identity papers, which bore the name "Simon Petliura." At that report, Samuel Schwartzbard leaped from his chair to embrace the messenger of such wonderful news. The executioner of the accused killer of thousands was ready to face the law.

The trial required months to prepare. It did not begin until October 18, 1927. While the case was being prepared, Schwartzbard was held in La Sante Prison in Paris. From his cell he wrote to the outside world.

A letter to his wife celebrated Petliura's destruction.

My Dear Anna,

It is something that has not been possible for me to do. I wish to have carved on my father's grave in Ananiev* an inscription:
"Yitzhak, son of Moishe Schwartzbard, Sleep in peace, great Jewish soul! Your son Shalom has avenged the sacred blood of your Jewish brethren and the martyrdom of all the Jewish people."
Control yourself. Compared to the unhappiness world over, your unhappiness is but a child's play. Be cheerful. Have a good time.
Take walks, and spend some time among friends. I will be happy, if you don't feel despondent and calm down again.
Your Shalom[30]

Schwartzbard wrote to his surviving family on Rosa Luxemburg Street in Odessa to tell them that he had avenged their common loss. A form of violent justice had been exacted in the streets of Paris.

I greet you, my near and dear relatives.
Proclaim it in the cities and villages of Balta, Proskurov, Cherkassy, Oman, Zhitomir, Enaniev, Krivoe-Ozero, Goloskov, Kiev, Kremenchug, Poltava, Triplie, Khrestinuka, Fastov, Vassilikov, and numerous other cities and towns where the blood of Jews has been spilled, their property has been looted, their holiest things have been profaned and destroyed. Spread the inspiring message—an outraged Jew has had his revenge.
The blood of the murderer Petliura, spilled in the eminent city of Paris, will awaken the world from its lethargy and remind it of the vicious crimes committed so recently upon the poor and abandoned Jewish people.
The ritual blood libel at Damascus, at Vienna, at Kiev, and other cities on this accursed terrestrial sphere; the persecutions, the massacres, the pogroms in Imperial Russia, and at this very moment in Rumania and in Poland; the fear of Jewish

---

*the Ananiev cemetery

advancement, the doors that are closed against the Jews; all this must cease for all time.

We are the people who have given the world a god, the Bible, morality. We have the great mission to promote universal emancipation and liberty.

We are the sacred martyrs, martyrs who want to free the world from its enslavement and decay.

We are ones who have protected the vineyards in foreign lands and abandoned our own.

Enough of that! First we must free ourselves and then think of others later.

I want you, my dearest ones, who live in that unhappy land of Ukraine, to find my father's grave in Ananiev and inscribe these words: Sleep in peace, great Jewish soul! Your son has avenged the innocent blood of your brethren and of the blood of Israel.

> Shalom, Son of Yitzhak, Son of Moishe Schwartzbard,
> Cell 7, Division 5, Prison of La Sante, Paris

Die Fraye Arbeiter Shtimme (The Free Workers' Voice) gave Schwartzbard the means to speak to an audience far beyond the walls of his cell and the borders of France. Through his pen, he wrote on the hardened memories of refugees from pogroms and persecution in many lands. To those accustomed to the burden of endurance, he demonstrated that a gun in a Jewish hand spoke with as much force as one in the hand of a persecutor.

To my dear comrades of the *Free Workers' Voice*:

I am writing from my cell and greet you cordially.

Having been a faithful soldier, devoted to the idea of revolution and class struggle for many years during which I had but one goal: to alleviate the grievous conditions of the impoverished and oppressed members of humanity. I came to realize that before being able to free the world, one must first free himself, which means to free the Jewish people from all the persecutions, murders, brutality, violence, and slanders which never cease to strike these abandoned people who are oppressed everywhere.

On a clear, beautiful day in the center of city of Paris I performed the first act in front of the entire world. I was too kind to this murderer under whose command thousands, tens of thousands of Jews, infants at the breast, old white-haired men, men and women, were exterminated; and bands under his command raped, pillaged, extorted, and burned.

These same haidamaks,* the descendants of the bandit murderer Chimielnicki, have not ceased even to this day to spill Jewish blood and bathe in it.

They spared the bullets; kikes aren't worth the price of the bullets. They had to be put to the sabre, so went the order of the ataman-bandits. Well, I didn't spare any bullets for this murderer. I fired five shots into his ugly body.

At last, I was able and I am happy to have been able, as a faithful soldier, to render a service to my poor, forlorn, and oppressed people. I have opened a new chapter in our sombre and bloody history of the millennium.

Enough of slavery, enough outpouring of tears, an end to imploring, crying, bribing. With our heads raised high, and with our chests stuck out, we demand from now on to live in equality with all. We demand it from the humanity which is drowning in the sins and crimes of the rotting twentieth-century civilization which is fast on its way to extinction.

My cordial greetings to all.

> As ever, yours with deep affection,
> Shalom Schwartzbard
> Cell 7, Division 5,
> La Sante Prison, Paris[31]

---

*Haidamaks were paramilitary bands that disrupted the social order in Polish Ukraine in the eighteenth century.

11

You, the Jury

Judge Georges Flory cautioned the audience to remain orderly and quiet, or he would clear the courtroom. Extra police guards stood by for the command to drive out the spectators who had been permitted to crowd into the room. Eight hundred sat or stood in a room suited for three hundred. Pressed together, the crowd provided the powder for an explosion that could be ignited by the sparks of the controversy.

Over the seventeen months since Samuel Schwartzbard had shot Simon Petliura, there had been a public debate about the right of a man to assassinate another. The major newspapers condemned the act as another sign of the violent anarchy that was spreading across Europe. The public view was fluid, driven one way by a surge of sympathy, pushed the other way by a current of revulsion. As the members of the jury took their places and were sworn in, no one could read by what infectious bug they had been bitten.

Journalists from around the world jotted notes about the courtroom. Flappers and rabbis, Ukrainian nationalists and students of law sat shoulder to shoulder to watch the legal drama.

There would be real drama. The best courtroom thespians were on the stage. Foremost among them was Maitre Henri Torres. His huge form in his black judicial robes was an impressive physical presence that could generate a cannon voice able to silence a crowded room. Torres stood over six feet in height and had the physique of a wrestler.

Representing Olga Petliura was Maitre Cesar Campinchi. The Corsican could match Torres shout for shout, gesture for Latin gesture. Maitre Albert Willm, who represented Oscar Petliura, Simon's younger brother, and Maitre Reynaud, the public prosecutor, had well-established reputations as practitioners of law, if not as true masters of the telling grimace or offending snarl.

On October 18, 1927, the Court of Assizes for the District of the Seine convened. Charges were read to the defendant. Schwartzbard was charged with violations of articles 295 through 298 and article 302 of the criminal code. To these he pleaded, "not guilty."

A court clerk read aloud a lengthy indictment of Schwartzbard, while being careful to exonerate Simon Petliura of any fault, as if he were being charged for having been a victim of murder. During the pretrial publicity, the defense had made it clear that Petliura would be put on trial for his many crimes against the Jewish people, and that strategy had not been missed by the court officials.

> After the fall of Kerensky and the victory of Communism, the general mobilization threw onto Ukrainian territory an enormous number of men who had been freed from the army. Left without discipline and without funds, they began to pillage. They were the real culprits in the massacres in which both the Jewish and Christian population suffered. The Red Army and the Denikin Army were not above such practices, and no doubt the regiments of which Petliura was the official head, and which were known as Petliurians, also engaged in them. It was very difficult for the Hetman who lived far away, and whose orders were frequently disobeyed, to control these activities which were really caused by the circumstances of the moment.[32]

The legal formalities had been completed. Judge Flory, the sixty-nine-year-old president of the court, addressed the defendant. He described the nature of the crimes and urged Schwartzbard to speak clearly in his own defense.

Here was the moment for which Schwartzbard had been rehearsing for seventeen months. The Court of Assizes was to be the ear of the conscience of Western civilization. The killing of Simon Petliura would have been a meaningless act of revenge if it could not be understood by others as a plea for another world, a shot to jar awareness of countless persecutions that had to end. Simply stated, the execution of Petliura was the execution of anti-Semitism.

Here also was the moment Torres dreaded. His client was a loose cannon. Once the platform was given to him, the legal counsel had no control over his tongue. His abrasive words could easily hone the blade of the guillotine that awaited him. All of the charges were capital offenses.

Torres had advised Schwartzbard to "stick to the facts." The defense counsel did not imagine that the jury would care about the centuries of persecution. They had not heard the shrieks of the dying nor had they seen the mutilated corpses. Their perception stopped with one corpse lying bloodied on a Paris street.

An argument had raged between the lawyer and his client. When Torres insisted upon determining the course of the defense, Schwartzbard had tried to dismiss him. The defendant would have preferred Gerard Rosenthal, Torres's assistant for his legal counsel. The aide to the famous attorney was more sympathetic with the volatile assassin.

Now, Schwartzbard had his platform, and a dam of unspoken despair burst. Schwartzbard described the torrent of blood flowing out of the middle of the seventeenth century, when the Zaporoghian Cossacks attacked Catholic Poles and Jews. Five hundred thousand were slaughtered; their torn corpses were scattered across the Ukraine, after which the horsemen swept into Poland itself to kill in the foreign lands. Less than a century later, another uprising soaked the land in Jewish blood.

The Haidamaki butchered and maimed as their grandfathers had done.

Schwartzbard rocked to and fro as though he were at prayer as he relived the anguishes of the blood-stained history of the Jewish people. At the end of the road of misery, he came to Simon Petliura, whom the assassin saw as the willing heir of the tradition of slaughter. Those ancient killers were praised in the stories and verses of Ukrainian writers. They were the inspiration for Ukrainian nationalists.

Judge Flory asked the defendant whether or not he had murdered Simon Petliura. Schwartzbard replied willingly that he had and described to the court just how he had avenged the killing of Jews.

"I asked him, 'Are you Petliura?' He didn't answer. He just lifted his heavy cane. I knew it was him. I shot once! twice! three! four! five times! Yes, five times! And then two more because I could not stop! I had an automatic pistol. My aim was good. After the fifth bullet, he fell to the pavement, all sprawled out."[33]

"Yes, he demanded mercy and you continued to fire," Judge Flory accused.

Schwartzbard insisted, "He didn't speak. He didn't say a word. All the time I spoke, he didn't respond. He didn't say one word. Only some cries of pain—'Aiee! Aiee!' There were cries, but not words. He fell immediately and was convulsive when he had fallen. My bullets struck well and I discharged my revolver into the soil only from a desire not to hit an innocent bystander accidentally."[34]

Witnesses at the scene charged Schwartzbard with a callous lack of mercy. Those last two shots, they claimed, were the coup de grace, a mark of a professional assassin. What Samuel explained were sounds of pain, "Aiee! Aiee!"; another said it was the word "enough" (assez).

Only one witness claimed to have heard Petliura say, "Enough." He was an Armenian refugee, Paul Bougdadjan. Torres seized the challenge. Why would a Ukrainian speaking man utter his last word in French?

The coroner, Dr. Paul, supported the witnesses. His examination of the body revealed that most of the injuries had been inflicted upon a prostrate victim. The fatal bullets came from a hand without mercy.

More than the murder of Simon Petliura, it was the public view of Schwartzbard that worried the defense counsel. A killer, driven by overwhelming passion, could be understood and excused. A cold-blooded murderer who could fire his gun point blank into a seriously wounded, prostrate, helpless victim was unforgivable.

Maitre Henri Torres approached Dr. Paul. Suddenly, the defense counsel drew a Browning automatic from beneath his judicial robes and thrust the muzzle into the face of the terrified coroner. Through a dramatic pantomime Torres demonstrated to the stunned jury how it would have been impossible, based upon the trajectory of the bullets through Petliura's body, for the shots to have been fired downward into the prostrate man. His conclusion to the jury was that Paul did not know what he was saying and that Samuel Schwartzbard, by discharging his weapon into the ground, was in fact proving to have been a conscientious assassin, worried about the safety of innocent persons.

Three psychiatrists, Drs. Claude, Marie, and Turel, had examined Schwartzbard. Claude, who testified in court, reported that the assassin was a self-educated, intelligent man who was obsessed with the single mission of assassinating the one figure, in whom he placed the blame for the deaths of thousands of Jews, including fifteen members of his own family. His deed was "automatic," which is to say that he did it without needing to think to do it. Torres considered the testimony support for his assertion that Schwartzbard was a driven man who had suffered immeasurable pain as a result of the pogroms. Schwartzbard was not a terrorist, not a professional assassin. He was a lone avenger.

It was vital for Torres to have him seen as a lone avenger, possessed by an obsession. If a conspiracy could have been proven, then Torres would have escorted his client to the guillotine.

The prosecution had a witness who was to be used to put the defendant into the midst of a cabal of conspirators. Dr. Koval's deposition was read into the trial record. Prior to his death from natural causes in July 1926, he had given evidence to Examining Magistrate Peyre. Koval had testified that he had seen the assassin twice. Both times, Schwartzbard was not alone.

During the first episode, Dr. Koval was with Petliura and Mr. Levitzky in a restaurant. At an adjacent table he saw Schwartzbard with a male and a female companion. They were eavesdropping on the conversation. During the second event the assassin and a friend followed Petliura along a Paris street. Despite his two encounters with the assassin, Koval could not recall the color of Schwartzbard's light brown hair. The witness did remember that he was "a man of dark Jewish type."

Schwartzbard denied that either episode had occurred. The deposition was not the real threat. That came from the letter he had mailed to his wife from the post office at l'Hotel de Ville. The message and the time stamp gave Torres reason to worry and reason to conceal the letter sent to him from the same post office at the same time. How cold-blooded the defendant would appear to have been to have employed his lawyer before the corpse had ceased writhing in the street!

"Accuse no one. I alone am responsible," the message to Anna said. If there had not been anyone else involved, then why did his supposedly uninformed wife need to be told to not accuse another?

The prosecution hammered the point. More deadly to the defense was the time stamp, which placed the assassin at two places at the same moment.

Although Samuel Schwartzbard insisted that he had shot Simon Petliura at 3:00 P.M., the actual time of the killing was 2:10. Samuel claimed that he had confirmed the arrival of his quarry at Le Chartier Restaurant. Then, he hurried to the post office to mail the express letter. A round trip between Le Chartier Restaurant and the post office at l'Hotel de Ville takes thirty minutes. According to his testimony, based upon prior observations, the assassin expected Petliura to take forty-five minutes to finish his midday meal.

If Petliura had been shot at 3:00, then there would have been enough time to make the return trip. The letter bore the time stamp 14:35. If the death of Petliura occurred at 14:10, then there had to have been a second person involved in the killing. By 14:35, Samuel Schwartzbard was a prisoner of the Paris police.

Maitre Regis de Trobriant who was having his meal on the balcony of a nearby restaurant, Le Soufflet, testified how he had noticed the assassin who had been standing across the street from Le Chartier. The witness told the court that for a full hour Schwartzbard had not left his post. What had attracted the attention of the witness to Schwartzbard was the prolonged period of his stay in one place.

In a major effort to destroy the argument of a conspiracy, Torres noted that it was the requirement of the post office to adjust the time stamp every five minutes. He then suggested that some clerks find this to be a bother. So, they make the adjustment in hourly periods. This, he argued, was the case at the l'Hotel de Ville office.

Schwartzbard, he insisted, had mailed the express letter at 1:35. He supported his statement by showing the two subsequent time stamps, 3:50 and 5:50, from substations through which the letter passed. If it took two hours, he argued, for a letter to go from station B to station C, then it should take a similar period from station A to station B. A time stamp of 1:35 made for a handling time nearer to two hours than one of 2:35.

Either through laziness or by a simple, innocent mistake, Torres theorized, the incorrect time was marked on the letter, and a false impression was created. To support his argument, he presented his passport to the jury. The document had been issued in 1926, but it bore the erroneous date of 1936. The error on a valuable document proved, he suggested, how easily an error on a letter could be made. No, there was no fellow conspirator. There was only a mistake.

In spite of the crucial relationship between the letter and the establishment of a conspiracy theory, the prosecution did not call anyone from the post office to challenge Torres's assertions. Neither did anyone ask why it was so important for the defendant to send the letter to his wife, who would have learned in short order of the assassination.

Schwartzbard had said that he had not wanted to involve his wife in such an act, as though violence was foreign to her. In 1917, he had taken her into the thick of the chaos and the revolution in the Ukraine. Here was no fragile flower, whose petals would wilt in the face of difficulty. That, however, was another point the prosecution did not challenge.

Years later, just in passing, Torres revealed the existence of the second letter to retain him to defend Samuel Schwartzbard. "I would never have known about him, if he had not also scribbled a few lines to me, to ask me to defend him."[35] Under the French legal system, a suspect in the hands of the police is not assured legal representation. By making an early contact with one of the most prominent defense counsels in France, Schwartzbard was protecting his legal position. Because of the silence of Torres and Schwartzbard, the prosecution did not know of that letter. If the prosecution had known of the message to Torres, one can only speculate as to how much harder the prosecution would have pursued the case. As it was, vulnerable points in the defense were left to stand.

During the trial Schwartzbard revealed with how much determination he sought and stalked his quarry. Then, after such careful effort, he jeopardized everything by leaving the scene of the pending killing to post a brief note to his fragile wife. If Petliura had left early, if a visitor had joined him for lunch, if there were a delay at the post office, if numerous other unforeseen eventualities had arisen, the opportunity would have been lost. Not only would he have lost his opportunity, he would have exposed his secret plan.

Schwartzbard's wife, if she had been as innocent as Schwartzbard claimed, might have protested such a scheme. What would Torres have done? He would have been given prior knowledge of a serious crime. Failure to act to prevent it would have made him a party to it. Schwartzbard's dash to the post office indeed was a gamble, and Samuel was not a man who took senseless gambles. Even his surrender to the police made tactical sense. It had been the willingness of Teilirian and Conradi to face the justice system that demonstrated the effort to exact justice from a world that did not otherwise provide justice. It, therefore, was the assassin who was the victim.

Although the prosecution failed to develop these critical arguments exposed by the letter, it did seek to establish the existence of other participants. The prosecution did not limit its contention to a union among a few Jewish refugees to kill a commonly hated former persecutor. The prosecution linked Schwartzbard with Moscow and the Cheka. Chief witness was Ellie Dobkovsky, whose deposition was read into the trial record. Although he was available, he was not called to testify.

Dobkovsky was a man of many philosophies, which shifted freely with the winds of opportunity. He had converted from Judaism to the Eastern Orthodox faith and joined the Ukrainian nationalists. From the nationalists he transferred his loyalty to the rising power of the Bolsheviks, who made him the commissar for Jewish affairs in the early Soviet government. Time brought another transformation. Dobkovsky moved to Paris, where he worked on Ukrainian nationalist newspapers, to alert the readers to the menace of the spreading Red revolution.

The adaptable Dobkovsky revealed that he was party to secret plans that had been discussed at the January 9, 1926, conference of the Comintern, which was the international arm of the Soviet Communist Party and its vehicle for the promotion of global revolution. From a few seeds of knowledge, Dobkovsky raised a forest of myths. Foremost on the agenda of the Comintern, he claimed, was the liquidation of Simon Petliura, who was said to possess great influence over the people of the Ukraine.

Dobkovsky explained how conditions in Poland made the assassination urgent. Pilsudski, who had an alliance with Petliura and had betrayed him in October 1920, was planning to unite with the former ataman to recapture the Ukraine. Pilsudski, however, did not return to power until May 1926. The conference occurred in January. Dobkovsky attributed to the Bolsheviks great foresight.

The witness of variable ideologies did not explain how Pilsudski intended to conquer the Ukraine. Poland was in economic and political turmoil. Her former French ally was not agreeable to another war. Regardless, he said that the Bolsheviks lived in profound fear of Petliura, though he had failed earlier to arouse his people to fight for their independence.

To eliminate the former ataman, Dobkovsky told the examining magistrate that Schwartzbard had been recruited. The prosecution had information to demonstrate the political history of the assassin. His moderate stands as a member of the League of Human Rights and the Committee to Aid the Victims of the Pogroms were not the whole picture.

Austrian police provided the French with the arrest record of Waltzburg, which they said was an alias for Samuel Schwartzbard. In 1908, he had been arrested for housebreaking.

"French law forgives you," Maitre Torres declared.

Schwartzbard did not wish to be forgiven. As far as he was concerned, he had committed no crimes for which he needed to be forgiven. Although Austrian police had charged him with housebreaking, he claimed that they were arresting him because of his association with anarchists. His politics was the true motivation.

"Are you an anarchist?" Judge Flory inquired.

Schwartzbard claimed that he was. The prosecution refuted him, labeling him a Bolshevik. Their proof was his leadership of the volunteer Jewish brigade, Rasala, which had fought in support of the Bolsheviks. This, the defendant insisted, was a union of convenience and not a marriage of believers.

General Shapoval, another witness for the prosecution, suggested otherwise. The former commander of the Ukrainian army had fled to Paris where he published *L'Ouvrier Ukranien* (Ukrainian Worker). His brother published *La Nouvelle Ukraine*

(The New Ukraine). Shapoval introduced a mysterious Mr. Volodine, who could have been made less mysterious by being summoned to testify. His address was known.

Volodine had worked for both of the Shapoval newspapers. The former general told the court that his employee had come from the Soviet Union to organize a hit team to assassinate prominent personalities. The former general reported how the mysterious Volodine had tried to extract information about the activities of the former ataman. On the day of the shooting Volodine was excited and told Shapoval how Petliura had been shot by Schwartzbard and how he had stood watch for Schwartzbard, who was to allow himself to be arrested so as to use a French courtroom to discredit the Ukrainian nationalist movement. General Shapoval gave to the assassin a fanatical dedication to his Marxist or anarchist cause that could have cost him his head. His crime carried the death penalty.

Despite the denunciation of the mysterious Volodine, the Paris police were not sent to arrest the co-assassin, nor did the Ukrainian nationalists hunt him down as they might have done a Cheka agent. Three months after the accused agent was supposed to have aided in the murder of Simon Petliura, he posed with General Shapoval for a photo. The general explained his continuing association with the murderer of his friend as an effort to penetrate the operations of the Soviet secret police.

Decades later, the testimonies of Dobkovsky and Shapoval provide the foundation for the still widely accepted belief in the Ukrainian communities that Simon Petliura was a victim of the Soviet Union, which viewed him as a danger to its control of the Ukraine. Samuel Schwartzbard remains in many minds a Cheka agent.

The main thrust of the defense strategy was to prosecute Petliura for crimes against the Jews. While Petliura was to be resurrected as a devil, Schwartzbard was to be presented as a true and noble avenger. A petition with the names of two thousand neighbors, Jews and Gentiles, was introduced to demonstrate his popularity. Character witnesses were called and letters submitted to the trial record to certify the courage of the defendant, who had fought heroically for France. On his chest, for the jury to see, Samuel wore his Croix de Guerre. His former commanding officer, Captain Rousset, testified about Schwartzbard's courage in battle and dedication to the French cause.

Torres brought into court a series of witnesses to fill the minds of the jury members with horrors that not even men who had gone through the horrors of the battlefield had not seen. Corpses of men, women, and infants were heaped before their tortured imaginations. Torres continued to reveal the grotesque scenes until the jury could absorb no more. Even the witnesses for the prosecution added vivid descriptions to the images of carnage. Whereas the witnesses for the defense placed responsibility upon Simon Petliura, witnesses for the prosecution blamed the Bolsheviks, the White Russians, the numerous bands of marauders, and the madness of the times. They insisted that the ataman had sought to stop the barbarism. Maitre Campinchi had a book of two hundred orders that had been issued by Simon Petliura. These, the defense declared, were empty gestures that came after the pogroms had passed. A Ukrainian historian, Dr. Tcherikover, remarked bitterly, Petliura's appeals were "comparable to a physician's medicine administered after the death of the patient."[36] The prosecution noted that there had been efforts by the Ukrainian government to give aid to devastated communities. These were "crumbs for the stolen loaf," Torres responded.

Witnesses explained how Petliura's men destroyed a community. First, an officer or an official accused the Jews of supporting an enemy, usually the Bolsheviks, or of murdering an Eastern Orthodox priest. Compensation was demanded and was usually paid. Then the troops attacked to rape, rob, and murder. Often, it was done on a Friday evening, to trap the people in their synagogues. When the pogrom ended, the leaders said that it had been a spontaneous expression of outrage.

The witnesses were certain that the men were from Petliura's army, because they carried banners with the trident, and they shouted the slogan, "Kill the Jews and save the Ukraine!"

When Petliura went to Kamenetz-Podolsk, the former ataman's defenders announced, the Jews praised him.

"Because he had the guns," defense witnesses replied.

As much as the defense wanted to place full responsibility for the pogroms upon Simon Petliura, none of the witnesses could claim that the ataman had ordered a single attack upon a community.

"Petliura was responsible! Even Ukrainian officers said so. His soldiers killed our people, shouting his name. One regiment had a band; and it played, while knives fell on the heads of innocent babies. Petliura could have stopped it, but he wouldn't listen to our pleas," Haia Greenburg, a nurse who had lived through the worst of the horrors, explained.[37]

Dr. Ilytch Tcherikover reported a conversation with the leader of the Ukraine, when Petliura said, "I can not do anything to stop the pogroms and maintain discipline in the ranks."[38] Whether or not Petliura was an anti-Semite did not matter. The corpses were just as dead.

One hundred and twenty-six witnesses had been scheduled to testify or to have their depositions entered into the trial record. By October 26, only a fraction had appeared or had their depositions entered. After the deposition of Colonel Alexei Boutakiv, the testimony called "the infamous words" by Torres, it was agreed by the prosecution and the defense to end the trial. More description of the horrors would not further enlighten the fatigued jurors.

In 1919, Colonel Boutakiv had been an artillery commander at Proskurov, where some of the bloodiest crimes had occurred. The pogroms he called "divinely inspired."[39] Torres could add nothing more than those words to defend his client. It was time for the lawyers to make their final pleas to the jury.

Maitre Albert Willm began the series of summations. For two hours he discussed the events, but the briefer, more merciful summation by Maitre Cesar Campinchi was the statement aimed directly at the core of the question. Legal niceties were less important to him than the question of a murder and what was to follow.

I condemn the pogroms. I consider the Jews a noble race who
have suffered from the time of the Babylonians right up to the
time of the Russian Tsars. But Schwartzbard in his desire to
avenge the pogroms mistakenly killed an innocent man. . . .

Countless documents have been introduced in the discussions. No one meanwhile has been able to supply a shadow
of a proof which could stain the pure memory of the de-
ceased. . . . Do not, therefore, seek to judge Simon Petliura. But
a man has been murdered. That is a fact. . . . You should have
brought proof that Petliura was responsible for the pogroms,
and you have not done so. You [Schwartzbard] pretended to
have killed because he was a hangman. But in reality, you killed
because he was a national chief desiring the independence of
his country. He was a good man, just and courageous, who
desired the respect of the minorities, notably of the Jewish minority. His declarations constantly established this. . . . If
Schwartzbard is acquitted by you [the jury], what will prevent
your successors from acquitting this young man [Oscar,
Petliura's brother] if he were to track down Schwartzbard and
shoot him in vengeance? Gentlemen, I say this to you with
the greatest respect, with the deference that I have for jurors
before whom I have so often pleaded. There is only one
alternative—on the one side serene justice, on the other blind
fanaticism.[40]

Throughout the trial Torres sought to fight the case on moral
grounds. By making Simon Petliura into a wholly responsible
evil leader of the Ukraine, Torres justified the killing, as though
his client were ridding the world of a dangerous virus.

Prior to the summations, Judge Flory had instructed the jury
that they had to confront five critical questions: (1) Was the
accused, Samuel Schwartzbard, guilty of willfully inflicting injuries upon Simon Petliura on May 25, 1926? (2) Did the inflicted
injuries cause the death of Simon Petliura? (3) Did Schwartzbard
intend to cause the death of Simon Petliura? (4) Did Schwartzbard act with premeditation? (5) Did Schwartzbard strike from
ambush?

Torres cautioned the jury: An affirmative answer to the first question would mean death for the defendant. Before the jurors were released to answer that critical question, Maitre Torres took them through the days of testimony in a thirty-minute summation:

I have just spoken about the passivity of the Jewry, which did not know how to organize a gendarmerie of its own [and] which Petliura did not even begin to discuss until tens of thousands had been killed, assassinated by his soldiers, as they let themselves be exterminated in the village squares . . . because a Jew who would lift a stick to defend himself was an unknown phenomenon. So submissive was the Jewish race to ancestral domination that they had become accustomed to this organized terror.

Well! I say that when one becomes a French citizen as did Schwartzbard, when one experiences the freedom, full of life, among the Parisians, when a French soldier in a trench has held a hot steel in his hand, a new soul, ardent and trembling with excitement, then is awakened within him, that one strikes out for the sake of justice.

Ah! He waited, you have heard. Schwartzbard, you have been almost rebuked because you have waited. He waited. Why? Because even those obsessed by one idea, even those with apostolic zeal, upon their return to Paris of 1920, are taken in by the charming, gentle, relaxed way of life among us, because their return means rediscovery of the fireside, family, habits, work, friends, lectures, committees, chats. All this because there is more discussion of how to organize assistance for the victims of the pogroms than conspiring to strike out at those responsible for those crimes.

And Schwartzbard, if he had not heard one fine day that Petliura had returned, would have become accustomed to all this, in the company of a poor woman for whom he is the life itself as she is the only family he has. . . .

No, it is no longer you, Schwartzbard, who is the cause here; it is the pogroms. . . . Gentlemen of the jury, to condemn the pogroms of yesteryear is to prevent those of the future. Not just Schwartzbard's attorney is speaking. With him there are the multitudes of the tortured and with those the voices of Abbe Gregoire, Rabaud Saint-Etienne, Mirabeau, Gambetta, Victor Hugo, both the dead and the living, plead with you to acquit him, this man who bears on his forehead, like a terrible seal, all the tragedy of a people.

Gentlemen of the jury, I have reached the end. Answer "no" to the first question. Because you have compassion, you must acquit Schwartzbard. Gentlemen, you are responsible today for the prestige of our nation and for thousands of lives which depend on the verdict of France.[41]

At 5:40 P.M., the jury retired to consider the week of evidence. Twenty-five minutes later, they returned to court to pronounce sentence: "Not guilty."

Pandemonium swept the courtroom. The spectators shouted, "Vive la Republique! Vivent les jures français!" (Long live the Republic! Long live the French jury!) A few Ukrainians in the crowd disagreed with the verdict. Their protests provoked fist fights that spread into the corridors.

That night was a night for celebration. There were dancing and singing in the streets. A French jury had declared, as had German and Swiss courts, that violence could deliver justice. Later, the National Assembly passed new laws to make it easier for refugees to enjoy the privileges of French citizenship. In the spirit of the victory Judge Flory granted financial compensation to the widow and to Oscar Petliura. Each was granted one franc.

12

A Thousand Eyes for an Eye

Celebration of the courtroom victory was a brief episode that was tainted by the nearness of reality. If Samuel Schwartzbard could seek redress of a grievance through violence, so, then, could others. Oscar Petliura had reason, Ukrainian nationalists had cause, and they could cite three precedents to uphold that right. Teilirian was acquitted by a German court, Conradi was freed by a Swiss court, and Schwartzbard was applauded by a French court. Three courts in three sovereign states had approved the private use of violence to obtain a personal retribution. Why not a fourth?

Faced with that inescapable reality, Schwartzbard went into hiding. In spite of his seclusion, he had acquired a louder voice and more listeners. In 1933, he toured the United States to promote his two Yiddish language books, *In krig mit zich aleyn* (At War with Myself) and *Inem loif fun yoren* (Over the Years). His audience was mainly refugees from the slaughters of the Russian Empire. They had heard the anguished calls, and saw Schwartzbard as a demonstration that one Jew could make a difference, that one Jew could strike back and succeed.

During the trial, Schwartzbard had received support from Jews in the United States. A defense fund had furnished four thousand dollars to bring witnesses to Paris to present the court with visions of the horrors that had cost so many innocent lives. In the United States, Schwartzbard had found broad sympathy.

If he was a hero to these survivors of the madness, he was something less heroic to others. As always, Schwartzbard was an outcast from the mainstream. He was a blend of unresolved contradictions that provided enough friction to alienate the majority. Perhaps Dr. Claude had summarized it correctly when he described Schwartzbard's thinking as "an immaturity of ideas."

As a young revolutionary in the Spark movement, he had aroused the hostility of the others who saw his clinging to Judaism as a rejection of Marxism. As an orthodox Jew, he had been denied by Jews, who considered his propensity for violence to be contrary to the principles of the faith.

His triumph in court did not end the alienation. In his memoirs, Schwartzbard denounced his friends for failing his cause. While he imperiled his head by telling the French court that he had had the support of friends, later, in his writings, he denied that they had cooperated. The later version described a lone assassin on a private mission for a greater cause.

Schwartzbard's mission did more than just place his life in jeopardy. The assassination closed to him the one door to the place a Jew could go to find the preservation of the ancient traditions and the protection of a united people. The British government of the Palestine Mandate refused to grant him residency. To the British, the self-confessed assassin was not the kind of a citizen wanted in a volatile environment.

There was no one to plead his case. The various Jewish agencies bringing Jews to the ancestral land wanted nothing to do with Schwartzbard. He had to be content with aiding others to find sanctuary in what was intended to become Israel.

For a brief time, the French expressed their sympathy for his cause of justice from persecutors by altering the citizenship laws to enable refugees from Eastern Europe to acquire the prized French citizenship. A decade later, that sympathy would fade, when economic conditions made life more difficult and the outrages of National Socialism sent thousands of Jews in search of safety to France, just as the pogroms of czarist Russia and the pogroms of Petliura had.

Schwartzbard continued writing. In 1938 he had gone to Cape Town, South Africa, to report on the Jewish communities where numerous refugees were fleeing. He contracted an illness there and died on March 3. As a mark of their respect for the still wandering Jew, the Jewish community gave Samuel Schwartzbard a hero's funeral.

During his fifty years of life, Schwartzbard had seen the spread of the pogroms from Balta across the Ukraine. For just a brief moment in history he had seen a flowering of French liberalism, but then he saw it wilt as the French abandoned their principles for the hatreds of Nazism. He had seen the cycle come and go. Always hate flourished in the fertile lands of Europe, where it had so often before grown and spread.

A few years later, his deed was recalled in Jewish blood. On July 1, 1941, the German-led Nightingale Batallion of Ukrainians marched into Lemberg. Seven thousand Jews were apprehended, humiliated publicly, and murdered. One year later, the same troops returned and added two thousand more corpses to the catalog of the murdered. Lemberg, which had been so important to so many twenty years earlier because of its petroleum became important to a new generation as a place of the pogroms. Those slaughters were dedicated to the memory of the fallen atamen, Simon Petliura. The massacres commemorated sixty years of violent death. Over those years, only the method and the extent of the pogroms had changed. However the Nazis would apply technology to the process of mass murder, the reality was the same as it had been in hundreds of Ukrainian towns and cities. It was still a pogrom, the legacy of the Narodnaya Volya and the Black Hundred.

Part Two

The Enemy Within

13

The Nest of the Hawk

Once the railway line was built into the high Alpine valley of the canton of Grisons, Switzerland, the town of Davos was no longer isolated. People could come to enjoy the mountain remoteness, the quiet slow life, the clear brisk air. Iron mining and dairy production soon became secondary industries, replaced by tourist resorts and health sanatoriums that provided employment for hundreds of new residents. Over the sixty years from 1860 to 1920, the population multiplied fivefold.

Two of the hotels and two of the sanatoriums were owned and operated by Germans, for German guests and patients. Located in a German-speaking region, Davos was for the Germans a home away from their homeland.

When Wilhelm Gustloff's doctor order him to take the Davos cure for tuberculosis, he was following a well-established treatment. If all went as expected, the young man would be cured in a few years and free to return to Mecklenburg in northern Germany to pursue his career as a bank clerk. By then, though, World War I was certain to have ended, and he would have missed his appointment with one of the greatest events of human history.

In 1916, when he was sent to Davos, Gustloff was twenty years old. He wanted to offer his life in service to the Kaiser, to seek his manhood on the battlefield, but his own body had betrayed him by its weakness. Instead of the glory of war and the challenge of the battle, he was confined to the ignominy of Davos, where war was far beyond a neutral border.

Although the tuberculosis was too serious to permit him to serve in the armed forces of imperial Germany, Gustloff's illness was not serious enough to require confinement in a sanatorium. As long as he did not exert himself, he could work and live a normal life. A job at the meteorological post in Davos was made available for him. Drawing weather maps was just the type of work that would not strain his lungs. Although the weather station was on Swiss soil, it was a part of the German meteorological service. Gustloff would be serving his Kaiser and being paid by Germany.

About the time that Gustloff was settling into Davos, thousands of other Germans were arriving in Switzerland. They were beneficiaries of "Operation Internee." The program was a Swiss humanitarian effort that had the side effects of filling thousands of empty hotel rooms and giving the Swiss extra leverage over the battling powers around them.

World War I devastated the Swiss tourist industry and isolated the small, landlocked state within a circle of warring powers. For the most densely populated nation in Europe open borders were vital. Half of Switzerland's food and all its coal and other resources had to be imported. To pay for the country's imports, the Swiss built their country into the most industrialized nation on the continent.

War was profitable for the chemical, machine tools, and machinery manufacturers, who sold to anyone. The export sector prospered, while food prices rose and scarcities multiplied. By housing thousands of disabled officer prisoners from the Central Powers, the Swiss secured guarantees for food shipments and access to essential resources. In turn, the warring powers were able to place into Swiss hands at bargain prices sixty-two thousand disabled prisoners. Some of Gustloff's countrymen arrived in Davos. From them he learned about the war he would never have the opportunity to experience.

Toward the end of the war, the German government could no longer afford to maintain the weather station and transferred it to the Swiss. The employees were retained. Wilhelm Gustloff was among the rare few with a secure position. At the end of the war, the disabled prisoners were repatriated. Former officers of the imperial army returned to a devastated country that was in turmoil. Gustloff remained behind, continuing to draw weather charts for his new employer, the Swiss government.

Europe entered the peace with their economies as battered as their armies. Switzerland was no exception. Unlike her imperial neighbors, Switzerland did not lose vast territories and a monarchical form of government, but she did lose most of her foreign capital. The value of investments, due to losses in Russia, Austria, and Germany, shrank from 8 billion to 2.5 billion francs. At the same time, Switzerland had lost much of her export market, and tourism had not recovered. Switzerland needed investment capital to build new industries in order to absorb the unemployed and to finance essential imports.

Neutrality had saved the Swiss from the bloodletting of the war, but the peace brought a more dangerous enemy, one that did not recognize neutrality. Bolshevism had seized control of Russia and was threatening to engulf Germany and Hungary. When general strikes spread through Switzerland, a deep fear of the Red menace gripped the Swiss as it had the Americans and British, who had sent troops to Russia.

Davos was no longer a remote haven. In the new political climate, danger lurked right at the foot of the mountains. From his secure home in the eastern Alpine valley, Gustloff observed the transformation of a familiar world into the postwar chaos. Germany had been stripped of her empire, of her monarch, and of her dignity. The economy was plagued by unemployment and galloping inflation.

In 1923, Gustloff descended from the mountains to travel to Munich, where he was among the earliest members of an infant movement of which few had heard, the National Socialist Party. Their leader was an expatriate Austrian, Adolf Hitler. National

Socialism pledged to restore Germany to her former place of importance, and the party provided an explanation for the defeat and for the chaos that were continuing to emasculate the once great nation. Underlying German defeat was not a flaw in the nature of the German people or in the system. Defeat and humiliation were due to an insidious global conspiracy of Judaism and Marxism.

Hitler offered a simple solution. Find and destroy those elements, and Germany would take a major step toward the restoration of her greatness. Gustloff carried that message to Davos. Whenever Germans came to the sanatoriums for medical treatment or to the resorts for relaxation, Gustloff awaited them with the message from Munich, until, among Germans, Davos became known as a place to avoid. But Gustloff was confident that the tide of history was flowing toward the eventual triumph of his cause.

If Germans were not interested in hearing his message, some Swiss were. They had seen their economy devastated, and they had little hope that it would recover. They, too, were in search of someone or something to blame. Gustloff had just what they needed.

Although he operated separately from Gustloff and had his own view of the world, Heinrich Rothmund saw the same danger from the Jews and the Communists. In 1920, he was named director of Switzerland's police and given the power to implement his personal philosophy. Among his most important acts was the organization of the *Fremden Polizei* (Foreigners' Police). The Fremden Polizei became a separate force that answered to Heinrich Rothmund, who had his personal policy of keeping out the foreigners, especially the Jews, who he considered to be one of the main sources for the spread of Communism.

Government immigration policy did not change. It did not have to. By constructing an insurmountable barrier of red tape, a type of Great Wall of Switzerland, Rothmund set out to halt the advance of the Jewish-transported red menace into the confederation. During the 1920s, Jewish immigration came mainly from Eastern Europe: Russia, the Ukraine, and Poland, where Communism was most virulent.

Heinrich Rothmund concluded that Jews, except for a rare few, were the people least capable of adapting to Swiss culture and one of the greatest threats to national stability. How effective his policy of exclusion was is revealed by the numbers, which show that the Jewish population between 1920 and 1941 fell from 20,979 to 19,429. Rothmund's policy worked smoothly. If the public noticed what was happening, no one criticized loudly. Thus, the foundation upon which Wilhelm Gustloff was to build was laid.

Economic hardships continued until 1927, when the prosperity of the Roaring Twenties reached Switzerland. Tourism recovered and Swiss exports revived, although the traditional ribbon and embroidery industries had disappeared. Enjoying their new prosperity, people forgot the red menace and the concerns about Jewish immigration. Extremists had problems attracting audiences. Regardless, up in Davos Gustloff continued to draw weather charts and to proselytize among German patients in the sanatoriums and to tourists in the hotels.

Then came the Wall Street stock market crash of October 1929. The brief flirtation with prosperity slid back into unemployment and stagnation. A hundred thousand Swiss lost their jobs. By world standards the number was not high. For the Swiss the rate was uncomfortable. They had the highest wages in Europe and were vulnerable to the increasing economic Balkanization of the world, as each country tried to save itself behind barriers of tariffs and regulations.

During October 1930, Hans Vonwyl consolidated all of the anxieties of the suffering petit bourgeois into a political movement, the National Front. It was just one of many new political organizations at a time when extremist groups on the left and on the right were flourishing in the climate of economic hardship.

The National Front opposed Free Masons, Marxism, Jews, monopoly capitalism, and the inheritance tax. The party membership of small businessmen suffered from the competition of supermarket chains, department stores, and large corporations. Of all the businesses that threatened their economic survival, the small businessmen found one particular business was their worst enemy: EPA, a Jewish-owned department store.

After developing his own movement, Hans Vonwyl in the autumn of 1932 transferred control of the organization to the newly named *Landesgruppenleiter* (district group leader) of the National Socialist Party for the district of Switzerland. This was the organization of Wilhelm Gustloff. Vonwyl went to edit *Iron Broom*, the newspaper of the Iron Broom Movement, which was the violent arm of the National Front, the "Grey Shirts," who had been preceded in Italy by the "Black Shirts" and in Germany by the "Brown Shirts."

Later, Hans Vonwyl left the editorship of the *Iron Broom*, to edit *Alemannen*, a newspaper published across the border in Freiburg, Germany. The Gestapo arrested him and held him for a year. Upon his release, Vonwyl returned to Switzerland. His experience at the hands of the Gestapo cured him of his fascination with National Socialism, but he had done the damage by providing Wilhelm Gustloff with a vehicle to seize control of Switzerland.

Still in Davos, Wilhelm Gustloff was riding a political wave to certain triumph. Around Switzerland the red menace that drove the frightened into the embrace of the extreme right was marching and demonstrating. On November 9, 1932, Communists and Socialists in Geneva stormed the police and a unit of troops. Eleven rioters were shot to death. If anything confirmed the warning from the right that the country was being engulfed by Communism, these violent outbursts did.

On January 30, 1933, many Swiss were relieved that Adolf Hitler had come to power. His objectives were to crush the Reds and to take away the power of the international Jewish conspiracy. Among the celebrants was Theodor Fischer, whose League of National Socialist Confederates was the nearest Swiss organization to the Nazi Party in Germany. In a demonstration of solidarity with their parent movement, Fischer addressed National

Socialists in the nearby German city of Freiburg: "Switzerland is a vassal state of France and a Jewish protectorate. . . . Germans! Be thankful to that mother who has produced that German hero, Adolf Hitler, who will deliver us from our greatest peril!"[42]

In April 1933, to celebrate the coming of their savior, Wilhelm Gustloff brought together the separate movements into the *Kampfbund* (Battle Union) for a day of solidarity, *der Frontenfrühling* (the Front Spring). Step one, to unite the separate fronts into a single formidable force, had been taken. From his headquarters in Davos, Gustloff could claim proudly to be their "Führer," but he was colliding with a force as durable as the very mountains themselves. The many different organizations appeared to be united by a common ideology. But in spite of their common philosophy, they remained divided by their stronger attachment to their regionalism. *Der Volksbund* from Basel, for example, drew its members from that area, and preserved its distinctions from others in Zurich or Appenzel.

National Socialism advocated a strong central government that would destroy the regionalism. Such a policy provoked opposition from every corner of the confederation, especially from the Italian and French minorities, who comprised 30 percent of the population. As seen by the general public, regionalism was best preserved by a weak central government and autonomous cantons. National Socialism could not overcome the Swiss aversion to outside control, whether from another canton or from a foreign country.

Swiss Minister of Finance Jean-Marie Musy, a member of the Catholic Conservative Party and the French minority, reflected the regional fear of National Socialism. On May 10, 1934, he told a cheering audience, "Switzerland will either remain a democracy or cease to be Switzerland."[43]

Across the European continent there were many politicians whose loyalty was shifting in the political winds. Musy was among the trend followers. His dedication to Swiss democracy seemed to have been conditional upon the strength of the Nazi movement. Shortly after his speech, he collaborated with the

National Front to produce propaganda films such as *Die rote Pest* (The Red Plague) and published the Fascist newspaper, *La Jeune Suisse* (Young Switzerland). After a few more years, in 1944 and 1945, when Germany was near defeat, Musy, working in cooperation with the Jewish Joint Distribution Committee, traveled to Germany to arrange the release of prisoners from Theresienstadt and Bergen-Belson. By that time, the destruction of National Socialism was a certainty. For Musy and other such men, the wind had shifted.

14

Hitler's Missionaries

Glory was for Wilhelm Gustloff a fleeting joy. What had seemed in April 1933 to be a plum to be dropped into Adolf Hitler's hand had diminished into a faded dream. Destroying all of Gustloff's efforts to recruit the Swiss for his Führer was Adolf Hitler himself. On August 23, German troops crossed the frontier to arrest a Czech, Weber, who had escaped from Germany. Several German soldiers pursued him into Switzerland, captured the refugee, beat him severely, and dragged him back across the frontier. As a result, a diplomatic furor arose and continued until Weber was returned to Switzerland. Many similar episodes convinced the Swiss that their giant neighbor was dangerously aggressive. Such a threat was the cement that reforged the Swiss into a solid force against National Socialism.

In May 1933 the Swiss government outlawed the wearing of Nazi uniforms and insignias. During the September elections for local offices in Zurich, the heart of the Swiss fascist movement, the National Front, captured only 10 out of 120 seats. On October 12, Minister of Defense Rudolph Minger requested the first installment of a 120 million franc appropriation for the improvement of the military. He informed the Federal Council that Germany had a secret plan to invade the country. Twenty million francs ($5.9 million) started the rearmament program. That made

Switzerland the first nation to identify the true nature of the Nazi regime and to prepare to deal with it. A German advocate of Nazi imperialism, Dr. Ewald Banse, described the nature of the mountainous neighbor. "This anti-German feeling is so strong that even in peacetime the German tourist is worse treated in German Switzerland than the British, the French and now the American tourist. This childish dislike needs to be taken very seriously indeed and is an important fact fraught with possible military consequences."[44]

More than anything, what separated the Swiss from the Germans was Swiss nationalism, which instilled an automatic hostility toward the threat to overrun their country. There was a good deal of sympathy for the anti-Semitism of Adolf Hitler, but the Swiss were reluctant to impose restrictive laws and to practice overt defamation. German Ambassador Ernst von Weizsacker noted in an official report:

> If one examines the Swiss banks, press, Parliament, and the medical and legal professions, not to speak of governmental officialdom, one will find Jewish persons playing a role only in very exceptional cases. The idea that a Jew might sit in the government would only meet with a smile here. Switzerland actually does indulge in anti-Semitism, but not in words. Serious Swiss people readily admit in conversations that it is only the form they dislike in the German procedure in the Jewish question.[45]

The Swiss were willing to tolerate a Heinrich Rothmund, the director of the *Fremden Polizei*, the Foreigners' Police, but not a Josef Goebbels, Germany's minister of propaganda. Field Marshal Hermann Göring ridiculed the Swiss as "Alpine Jews" and "shit heads."

As the Swiss became more alarmed about an invasion and turned more hostile, other methods had to be employed to take control of their country. In keeping with the dictates of *Ausland Organisation*, the international arm of the National Socialist

Party, Gustloff's strategy shifted from recruiting the Swiss to the enlistment of the one hundred thousand German residents of Switzerland. *Ausland Organisation* had outlined the role that was expected of Germans in foreign countries. "Each party member who goes abroad becomes a fighter for the New Germany and a missionary for the Führer's ideas."[46]

During the early summer of 1934, Gustloff and the other representatives of *Ausland Organisation* met in Berlin to learn the strategies that Adolf Hitler had fashioned for them to follow. Their group had been formed before National Socialism had come to power in Germany. Offices had been established in eight zones around the world. *Ausland Organisation* was operated by the party and kept separate from the state institutions. Through the party the Führer could operate without the problems of bureaucratic interference or the inhibitions of diplomatic niceties.

Less than a year and a half earlier, he had been named chancellor, but Hitler was not secure in his office. Strong opposition was continuing. At home, he was using the SA and the Gestapo to break his opponents, while internationally he employed *Ausland Organisation* to soften other countries in preparation for the eventual seizure of power. In the early pages of *Mein Kampf* Hitler described the first phase of the conquest of much of Europe and the incorporation of the lands into his Third Reich. "One blood demands one Reich. Never will the German nation possess the moral right to engage in colonial politics until, at least, it embraces its own sons within a single state."[47] All of the Germanic peoples were to be merged. Austria and portions of Switzerland, Poland, Czechoslovakia, France, Holland, Luxemburg, and Denmark were to be included. Ewald Banse prepared the maps for the Third Reich and explained the objectives.

One is indeed filled with shame that there are offshoots of German blood who do not consider the fact that they speak German as proof that they belong to the German people! Quite naturally we count you Swiss as offshoots of the German nation (along with the Dutch, the Flemings, the Lorrainers, the

Alsatians, the Austrians, and Bohemians). And I hope that you will one day see fulfilled the prophecy of our K. F. Meyer (I say "our," because you are not worthy of him): Patience: the day approaches when a single tent will shelter the German people. Patience: one day we will group ourselves around a single banner, and whosoever shall wish to separate us, we will exterminate![48]

Ausland Organisation was vital to the policy. Overseeing it was Rudolf Hess, who reported directly to Adolf Hitler. Commands originated from the Führer himself and were passed down the chain to the Wilhelm Gustloffs. Hitler himself told the representatives what was expected of them and how the strategy would be applied:

My first demand from you, therefore, is blind obedience. You are not the judges of what is to be done in your district. Neither shall I always be in a position to explain to you in detail what my intention is. Your obedience is the fruit of your trust in me. . . . As the front line of our German fighting movement, you will make it possible for us to complete the occupation of our positions, and to open fire. You have all the functions that we, the older men, carried out in the last war. You are the army's outposts. You will have to prepare definite enterprises far in advance of the front.

You will have to mask our own preparations for attack. . . . It is a good idea to have at least two German societies in every country. One of them can then always call attention to its loyalty to the country in question, and will have the function of fostering social and economic connections. The other one may be radical and revolutionary. It will have to be prepared to be frequently repudiated by myself and other German authorities. I want to make it quite clear, too, that I make no distinction between German nationals and Germans by birth who are citizens of a foreign country. . . . It will depend on you, gentlemen, whether we reach our goal with comparative ease and without bloodshed. You must prepare the ground. Germany will spread its might far beyond its borders in the east as well as in the south-east. . . . We do not seek equality, but mastery. We shall not waste time over minority rights and other such ideological abortions of sterile democracy. . . . If you succeed, then you too will be called to leadership, unhampered by agreements and legal red tape. . . . You shall be my viceroys in the countries and among the people who today persecute and oppress you. What has been our handicap—splitting, the century-long impotence of the German Reich, having millions of the best Germans to emigrate and become the cultural fertilizer for other countries— this is now our pride.

Just as the Jews became the all-embracing world power they are today only in their dispersal, so shall we today, as the true chosen people of God, become in our dispersal the omnipresent power, the masters of the earth.[49]

Austria was among the first targets for seizure. On July 25, 1934, National Socialist assassins killed Prime Minister Engelbert Dollfuss. The assassins were captured and executed. In Germany they were memorialized as heroes and martyrs for the cause.

Violence had been a key instrument in the rise of Hitler. Brown Shirts had been highly effective as a means of silencing the opposition, either by beating or murdering the stubborn. What had worked in Germany was applied internationally. In Bavaria, near the Austrian frontier, the Austrian Legion, composed of expatriate Austrians, paraded and trained. Eventually, they were the vanguard who seized power. Erich Maey led a similar force of Swiss expatriates who were preparing to incorporate the 2.8 million German-Swiss into the Third Reich. Like the Austrians, they paraded in their uniforms. When the Swiss government objected, Hitler ordered them to remove their uniforms. Later in 1935, after the United States complained about Nazi support for National Socialists in the United States, Hitler instructed the American imitators to disband and to cease evoking his name. When some disobeyed, the Führer feigned helplessness. Everyone understood the charade. It had been described at the *Ausland Organisation* conference.

15

Heal Thyself

Out in the streets of Germany the heavy boots of SA (*Sturm Abteilung*) troopers were trampling down the remnants of Weimar democracy. Shouts of *Heil Hitler!* saluted the birth of the Third Reich, while few mourned the passing of liberty, such as it had been.

From the window of his hospital room David Frankfurter was an indifferent observer of the momentous historical events occurring around him. Imprisoned by illness in his hospital bed, his own private despair, his personal anguish, scarcely left space in his thoughts for politics, especially the politics of a foreign country.

After years of strenuous effort and family opposition, Frankfurter had come from Yugoslavia to study medicine in Germany. His foremost concern was to eventually master the scourge of cancer, not to waste his life debating the trivial subjects of National Socialism versus corrupt Weimar democracy. Before transferring to Frankfurt University, where he had been confined to a hospital on January 30, 1933, he had studied at Leipzig University.

Despite his own anxieties and the apprehensions of his parents, he had survived the demands of a medical education, had gone further than anyone had expected, and had overcome his lifelong battle with tuberculosis of the bone. Then, when he was in sight of his goal, his body betrayed him. Once again, the disease surged from its cage, took control of his life, and sent David into the hospital for his fifth major surgery.

David had been a child of six in 1915 when a Croatian doctor made the diagnosis. After seventeen years of both painful and useless treatment, the illness had not been defeated. At most it had been restrained, and the outcome had been postponed, until he was a twenty-three-year-old student in the medical college at Frankfurt University.

As far as Frankfurter was concerned, his presence in the university had been ordained by the place of his family in society. Every male member of his family was born with the shackle of obligation and with the crown of prestige. For five generations, they had contributed physicians, scholars, and rabbis to their community. To do so was as natural as the changing of the seasons, the passing of day into night. Upon his birth in 1909, the obligations had been bequeathed to David, who welcomed his inheritance.

For his duty, David, as had his older brother, chose the practice of medicine. Who better than he could understand the meaning of pain and suffering? The severe treatments had made pain and suffering an inescapable part of his life. Still, he was expected to endure in silence, to accept from God whatever gifts he chose to give. Whether riches or poverty, whether pleasure or misery, each thing was a gift of equal worth that only an ungrateful human being, or, worse, an unbeliever, would not accept. For David, the son and grandson of prominent rabbis, showing deep gratitude for his suffering was his duty, and he did not shirk that fated duty.

As with all of the members of his family, David had been taught to see himself as someone special and apart from everyone else in their community. They were an Austrian island in the midst of a Croat land. Five generations earlier, Frankfurter's ancestors had moved from Vienna at the heart of the Austrian Empire to the backwater of Daruvar in Croatia. Among the people of the hinterland the family was a beacon of wisdom. Christians and Jews alike came to the house to seek the opinion of his father, as others had come to gain the knowledge from the bygone generations. If Jews in the Ukraine and elsewhere in the Russian Empire were dying in the pogroms, the Frankfurter family was as remote from all of that as though they lived on a different planet. In their separate world apart from the turmoil elsewhere, the family enjoyed the riches of honor and dignity. David had no knowledge of anti-Semitism.

During much of the time, the Frankfurter family was a part of the majority Croat society. They spoke the language, involved themselves with the community and participated in the progress of the land that had become theirs. Inside their home they preserved a separate society. They continued to speak German and to cling fiercely to the culture of their long ago abandoned city of Vienna. Each generation sent out sons to study in Austria and Germany to return with a fresh infusion of their valued substance.

While they were Austrians with deep roots in the culture, they also saw themselves as Jews. Their Jewishness, though, did not rely upon a constant infusion of the distant cultural roots. It had survived eighteen hundred years in the Diaspora (the dispersion of the Jews after the Babylonian captivity) and showed no sign that it could not continue for another eighteen centuries.

Confined for prolonged periods to the house, David was immersed more deeply in the Austrian and Jewish aspects of the family's culture than were his two brothers and two sisters. While they attended school with their peers, he was tutored by his parents and surrounded by the library with its volumes of religion and philosophy. Alone with a society of books, the youngster learned little of the outside world. Not taught by his books was the ability to cultivate relationships with other human beings. Illness alienated him from the world, except for whatever could be created privately within himself.

As far as his parents were concerned, illness had exempted David from his family obligations. God had chosen not to give him a long life. So his parents gave little thought to his living a full one. Although they sentenced him to a brief fruitless existence, David had not accepted their view of his future. Like other young men, he was making plans for his life and looking ahead to the time when he would have the right to call himself a physician. Despite his uncooperative body, David continued his education, mastered was what needed, and was ready to step into adulthood. Whatever God had given him as a body, he intended to turn it into a medical doctor, even if that had to be in defiance of his parents. David's parents did concede that their son had achieved more than had been expected, but medicine, they believed, was an impossible dream. Regardless, David dreamed it. He would not, as his parents urged, accept the secondary career as a dentist, which would have taken less strenuous training in Vienna.

However difficult had been the struggle to achieve his success, the effort had not lessened David's confidence or dulled his determination. As so many others before him had done, David left home to pursue his dream for a full life. That meant nothing less than to be a doctor.

Frankfurter's effort to move from dreamer to medical student took him to Leipzig University and then to Frankfurt University. There, the dormant reality awakened, seized him, and inflicted upon him more pain and doubt than he had ever before known. The disease attacked his mastoids, parts of the skull bone. As a result of the surgery, he lost total hearing in one ear and had a serious reduction in the other. Morphine became necessary to control the surges of pain. Often sleep could be found only by the use of sleeping tablets.

In the university hospital in January 1933, Frankfurter had awakened from the anaesthetic to a new society that had no place for such as he. Adolf Hitler's accession to the chancellorship of Germany was for the armies of Brown Shirts license to make dogma into policy. Mobs were the instruments of the still-quavering dictatorship.

At Frankfurt University, which had been funded extensively

by Jewish supporters, the faculty was purged of Jews. Jewish students were harassed and driven into isolation. Books with ideas unacceptable to the National Socialists were burned. With little resistance, the educated elite of the academic world joined the barbarism of the mob.

From them Frankfurter got no sympathy. He was doubly damned: damned for being Jewish and damned for being less than perfect. Hitler had already assigned him to his place. "If the power to fight for one's own health is no longer present, the right to live in this world of struggle ends. This world belongs only to the forceful 'whole' man and not to the weak "half' man."[50] Frankfurter was an easy problem for his examiners. They needed no excuse to fail him, to rid the university of a Jew.

After winning so many battles against his own body, Frankfurter had to confront the unfamiliar battle of anti-Semitism. But not all was lost. There was a hope in Switzerland, where the toxin of National Socialism had not yet poisoned the soul. While he applied for a place at Bern University, he lived in Frankfurt with his uncle, who was a rabbi. Those weeks of waiting were the longest days in his life. When he was accepted, the news was a summons to a struggle for survival.

In the autumn, Frankfurter traveled the few hours to Switzerland to begin his last battle. If he failed again, then the dream would end. He would be half a doctor, which is to say not a doctor, and half a man, which would mean in the real world not a man. In Bern, Frankfurter took a room at the Jewish boarding house of Linnie Steffen and concentrated on his studies; the last critical battle to fulfil himself had started. Everything else in the world was put aside. Although he had seen in Germany the ferocity of the SA, he ignored the tramping feet of the Swiss Grey Shirts while he studied the growth of cancer.

By the end of 1933, the vigor of the Nazi movement in Switzerland had ebbed. Even in Germany, the fury of the SA had been brought under control and the political climate had warmed. Enforced order allowed delusions of safety to blossom in the regulated calm. Frankfurter found it simple to enjoy the delusion that to see nothing meant that there was nothing to see. Politics was for others and not a subject suitable for a serious doctor in pursuit of a cure for a killer disease.

16

The Fifth Column

Once Adolf Hitler came to office, the stature of Wilhelm Gustloff underwent a change. Because of the increasing number of
conflicts between Germany and Switzerland, he lost his per-
suasive powers over the Swiss. At the same time, he increased
his intimidation powers over expatriate Germans. *National
Zeitung* of Basel labeled him the "Dictator of Davos." Among
the German expatriates he was named the "Hawk of Davos,"
one who observed everything. Ernst Alfred Thalmann, a member
of the *Bundesrat* (Federal Council) from Basel, commented, "It
is notorious that the majority of the Germans who live in
Switzerland are under unbearable pressure from the *Gauleiter*
[Gustloff] and from the leaders of the auxiliary groups. They
are fearful that one of these people will denounce them, and they
will not be able to return home."[51]

As a *Landesgruppenleiter,* Gustloff was a power unto himself.
The German ambassador who had to answer for Gustloff's
misdeeds had no say about his conduct. Ambassador Ernst von
Weizsacker wrote,

> I sought to ensure that, on the model of Fascist Italy, Party
> officials should be dependent on the Legation and Consulates,
> but unfortunately I had no success in bringing this about. I

131

should like to have had some authority over these officials so that I could have controlled them and prevented excesses. Egged on by Party instructions from home which were concealed from the official German representatives, the Party functionaries carried on their mischievous activities among the Germans in Switzerland. They attacked old German societies and individual Germans, and distinguished themselves by their presumption. To come into conflict with Swiss authorities was for them a proof of courage.[52]

Wilhelm Gustloff concentrated his recruitment efforts on the one hundred thousand Germans in Switzerland. At most, he was able to bring five thousand into his National Socialist family circle. These were not permitted to be "halfway" Nazis. Once in the movement, each was expected to give his entire life to the cause. Each believer was expected to participate in more than one of the thirty-five separate organizations and the three hundred auxiliaries. Most were scarcely more than social or educational clubs with heavy doses of political indoctrination. Boys were placed into *Hitlerjugend* (Hitler Youth). Girls were enrolled in *Bunddeutscher Mädle* (League of German Girls). Women were part of *Frauenarbeitsgemeinschaft* (Women's Work Society). Every aspect of professional, personal, and family life was involved. When called, one had to be ready to serve by appearing at meetings, by participating in demonstrations, and by maintaining a close watch over other National Socialists to assure no one deviated from the straight and narrow.

Among the various organizations *Deutsche Turn und Sportverein* (German Sports and Athletic Club) had broader purposes. Cloaked within the athletic activities was military training. From these members the foundation of an armed underground fifth column to seize Switzerland from within at the appropriate moment was being prepared.

As with any military operation, an intelligence network was essential. The network across Switzerland was built from the *Landesverband der Deutschen Studentenschaft* (Overseas

German Students' Association). German students in Swiss universities kept a close watch over their countrymen. Any German student or professor who was too outspoken against Hitler was subjected to intimidation. Lists of enemies of the Third Reich were prepared. Jews were identified and located in preparation for the spread of German policies into the new territories. Although Gustloff had no legal standing as a representative of Germany, the Swiss government understood from whom he took his orders. No one in Bern wanted to provoke Adolf Hitler, who held an economic noose around the nation.

During the few prosperous years of the 1920s until the Wall Street crash, Swiss bankers had returned to invest in their traditional German capital market. Faced by the collapse of their own economy as a result of the situation in the United States, the Weimar government froze all foreign investments. Suddenly, the Swiss bankers were unable to withdraw their capital to meet other obligations which brought the entire system near to a state of financial collapse.

A dangerous financial predicament was made perilous by the loss of other banking assets. Between October 1929 and 1936, Swiss banks suffered from a net outflow of deposits. Swiss diplomats kept the pressure on Germany to release Swiss funds, but it was not until 1937 that the Swiss managed to restore their financial stability. Meanwhile, the policy required the Swiss to appease whenever necessary and to manipulate the Germans whenever possible. While the Swiss sought to preserve the soundness of their banking system, they dared not provoke the Führer. One of the humiliations that the Swiss felt they had to endure was Wilhelm Gustloff. Up in his headquarters in Davos, the leader of the Nazi movement in the confederation enjoyed the sense of his immunity. If any man could claim special status as one above and beyond the law, he could.

The Germans understood the crucial role of Swiss banking in the economy and struck at the vulnerable heart of the Swiss economic foundation. Far more than could be accomplished by military threats, the Germans held their leverage through economic means, but they could press their advantage only so far. They discovered the limit in 1934, when the Swiss willingness to tolerate Wilhelm Gustloff was made unbearable by the encroachment of the Gestapo into Swiss national pride. The Gestapo (*Geheimestaatspolizei*) had been organized by Hermann Göring in April 1933.

In January 1934 Georg Thomae, an agent of the Gestapo, arrived in Zurich. An early objective of the secret police was to learn who in Germany, Jew or otherwise, had money hidden in Switzerland. In 1936, possession of such undeclared assets was made a capital offense. Because of his experience as an employee of a German bank, Georg Thomae was selected to conduct the investigation.

Thomae's parents had apprenticed him to a banker. For a while, he worked in the profession, until he tired of the formalities and stiffness. In 1928, he left to be a vagabond and wandered from job to job and from city to city. The Wall Street crash soon filled the streets with thousands of other men without jobs or destinations. They were an angry pack in search of an easy solution and someone to blame for their troubles. National Socialist missionaries had what they wanted. Thomae liked what he heard, hated what they hated, and joined the party.

When he enlisted in the Gestapo, he was an enthusiastic recruit. Here was an opportunity for excitement and access to the advantages that the members of a privileged group enjoyed. Assignment to Switzerland was an opportunity to establish himself in the organization and to savor the pleasures of sanctioned spite.

Through bribery, trickery, and the sexual seduction of a bank clerk, Thomae was able to get lists of Swiss account holders. Their names were forwarded to Berlin, and the depositors arrested. Bankers had no way to know that requests from depositors to transfer the contents of the accounts to Germany came from victims of the secret police, and the funds were seized on their arrival. The depositors vanished into concentration camps for a prolonged misery or into a grave. When eventually the bankers realized what was occurring, they faced a dilemma of how to handle the crisis. Not only were they obligated to protect their clients, they were also facing ruin. If it became known that Swiss bank secrecy was being violated regularly, then their worldwide reputation would be destroyed.

Violation of the tradition of bank secrecy occurred at the same time as the failure of the Swiss Discount Bank. Two serious scandals required immediate action to preserve the system. A bank reform act was passed, and Article 47 of the Swiss Criminal Code was added. For the first time, a federal law to assure bank secrecy was enacted. Preservation of the banking system was a necessity for national security. While the Swiss tolerated many other assaults upon their national dignity and sovereignty, an attack upon the banks was seen as an act of war. The activities of the Gestapo were stopped; Georg Thomae fled from Switzerland.

Article 47 of the code stated:

> Whosoever as agent, official, employee of a bank, or as accountant or accountant's assistant, or as a member of the Banking Commission, or as a clerk or employee of its secretariat, violates the duty of absolute silence in respect to a professional secret, or whosoever induces or attempts to induce others to do so, will be punished with a fine of up to 20,000 francs, or with imprisonment of up to six months or both. If such an act is due to negligence, the penalty shall be a fine not exceeding 10,000 francs.[53]

The scandal created by Thomae revived public interest in the conduct of Wilhelm Gustloff, who was still leading the Nazi movement from his "Hawk's Nest" in Davos. Both men were serving the same master, as was Hans Wesemann, who in 1935 struck another painful blow at Swiss national pride. Each episode added to the public desire to remove Wilhelm Gustloff by one means or another.

Hans Wesemann had been a journalist with a number of German newspapers and a longtime socialist who had been expelled from the Social Democratic Movement. Before Adolf Hitler came to power, he had left Germany to wander throughout Latin America. By 1933, he arrived in London, from where he observed the rise of the National Socialists. In April 1934 he made an offer to the Gestapo.

Thousands of political refugees were fleeing from the Nazis. Wesemann's reputation as a socialist journalist gave him ready access to their inner circles. Who better than liberal journalist Hans Wesemann could keep the Nazis informed about the activities within the groups of refugees? He was hired.

Wesemann moved to Switzerland, where thousands of refugees had gathered. Once there, it was simple for him to be accepted into their innermost circles. In October 1934 the Gestapo placed on their list of wanted enemies Berthold Salomon, a Jewish journalist. By wonderful good fortune, Hans Wesemann included Salomon among his friends. They had been colleagues on *Die Weltbühne* (World Stage).

Berthold Salomon, who wrote under the pseudonym Jacob, had been an old-fashioned muckraker. He had acquired many dangerous enemies within the Weimar government. In 1928, he had been imprisoned for uncovering too much corruption. During 1932, to avoid arrest by the tyrannical von Pappen government, which came to power at the end of the Weimar Republic, Salomon moved to Strasbourg, France, from where he operated his Independent News Service. Well-placed informants in Germany kept him supplied with confidential news. When Hitler came to power, Salomon's information alerted readers to a secret plan to rearm and to Nazi preparations for a European war. Such disclosures placed him at the top of the Nazi enemies list.

From Strasbourg to Basel is less than two hours by train. Wesemann invited his old friend to come to celebrate the Fastnacht spring carnival. For seven centuries, the people of Basel have dedicated their spring carnival to several days of partying. During those days of celebration, when people wear strange costumes and concern themselves with having a good time, many strange events can occur unnoticed.

Hans Wesemann introduced his old friend to two men, Manz and Krause. A moment later, they dragged Salomon into their automobile, chloroformed him, and drove him the few miles to the German frontier. When Salomon regained consciousness, he was a prisoner of the Gestapo. A list of confidential informants had been removed from his pocket. On that list the Gestapo found many well-placed enemies whom they arrested and murdered.

Swiss police learned about the kidnapping. Shortly afterwards, Wesemann was arrested, revealed everything, and ignited a new diplomatic battle between Switzerland and her violent neighbor. Having their sovereignty trampled upon outraged the Swiss government and its public.

The first response from the German ministry of foreign affairs stated, "There is no proof that Salomon entered Germany voluntarily."[54] It was an example of the right hand not knowing what the left hand was doing. As with the *Ausland Organisation,* the Gestapo was not subject to the authority of the Foreign Ministry, which was often surprised by the problems thrust upon its diplomats.

Unable to do much to curb the conduct of the aggressive German government, public anger turned immediately toward Wilhelm Gustloff, who had heightened the fury by publishing in his party newspaper, *Reichsdeutsche,* instructions for National Socialists to boycott any Swiss business that did not sell German products.

The *National Zeitung* described Gustloff as "warden of the state of Switzerland" and "the oppressor of freedom who fills the air with pestilence."[55] Members of the National Assembly demanded from the ministers of the Federal Council a reason why Wilhelm Gustloff was permitted to remain in Switzerland. Dr. Gaudenz Canova from the canton of Grisons (*Graubunden*) demanded on April 3, 1935, an explanation from Minister of Police and Justice Johannes Baumann:

Is the Bundesrat [Federal Council] aware of the following?
1. that Wilhelm Gustloff, a German citizen, also a former

official of the Swiss Meterological Institute in Davos and currently the *Gauleiter* of the National Socialist Party for the District of Switzerland, is insolently provoking the democratically minded Swiss and also is threatening and harassing foreigners who come for medical and recreational purposes?

2. that Wilhelm Gustloff has established in Switzerland German support groups which are military in character and whose leaders obligate the members to swear allegiance to Hitler?

3. that Wilhelm Gustloff displays Hitler's banners during the rallies and that the members wear Nazi uniforms?[56]

Although the issuance and revocation of residency permits came within the jurisdiction of Heinrich Rothmund's *Fremden Polizei,* he in turn was answerable to Minister Baumann, who declined for nearly six months to reply to the questions about the deportation of Wilhelm Gustloff. His reply came on September 25, 1935, after Salomon had been returned: "Applause of the people is a matter of total indifference to me. Nevertheless, I must not pander to them against my conscience and judgment. My duty is to watch over the security and welfare of the country and at the same time, serve the cause of justice. Everything else is secondary."[57]

Beyond his concern about the reactions of Germany, Baumann had a personal interest in the subject. The German ambassador, Ernst von Weizsacker, revealed a conversation between the Swiss minister and the German *Landesgruppenleiter.*

The Minister of the Interior, Baumann, once received Gustloff in the Bundeshaus, which is situated high above the Aare. Gustloff, the Minister told me, declared in the course of this visit: "If the Führer were to order me to throw myself out of this window into the Aare, I should do so without thinking." Such fanatical devotion made Baumann feel rather at a loss. But when Gustloff was slandered in the Swiss Parliament, Baumann behaved in a correct manner and spoke in his defense.[58]

In spite of the furor that the Swiss government raised with the German authorities over Salomon's kidnapping, human rights were not a consideration. The Swiss government did what it believed to be in the "national interest." Salomon was a dispute over Swiss national sovereignty and nothing else. Upon Salomon's return he was deported to France. He had been an unwelcomed problem to the politicians and the diplomats in Bern. Foreign Minister Giuseppe Motta told questioners in the National Assembly:

> The Federal Council made use of Article 70 of the National Constitution to justify Jacob's expulsion, based on the following grounds: when Jacob entered Switzerland, 1. his entry was in gross disregard of existing rules and regulations; also, the purposes of his entry were not those permitted under the law; 2. his intention was to obtain a false passport under another name; 3. he intended to engage in intelligence work. As far as he was concerned, getting political asylum has never been the issue.[59]

Berthold Salomon was returned a broken man. Before his arrest, he had been physically frail. Months of torture had ruined his health and destroyed his will. Throughout his journalistic career, he had never refrained from speaking. That had changed. The Gestapo had silenced him. *L'Avanguardia* reflected the view of the Swiss press. "It is an appalling injustice that Jacob, a fighter for humanity, is arrested in Switzerland, while the propagandists for German barbarism, the 'Gustloffs,' can spread unhindered their anti-democratic poisons."[60]

As far as the Swiss government was concerned, the Salomon matter was closed. Bern could resume normal relations with Berlin. As far as the public and the press were concerned, the problem was not over. Wilhelm Gustloff remained in Davos. The newspapers continued to campaign for his expulsion. The police considered the temper of the public to be high enough to justify police protection, which the *Landesgruppenleiter* declined. Despite the daily barrage of threatening mail, Gustloff did not take such messages seriously.

> Baden, 22 May, 1935
> The undersigned organization has unanimously passed a death sentence against Gustloff in Davos. We give you until 15 June, 1935, to get out of Switzerland. After that the decree will go into effect.
>> Wilhelm Tell

> Away with you! Your time is up. You won't damage our land any more. Since our authorities don't dare to hunt down the insolent messenger from Hitler, we take to defending ourselves. Note this . . . marksmanship is not a forgotten art here.
>> Your special friend[61]

17

A Cure for Society

In the summer of 1934 Frankfurter was called from Switzerland to be present at the death of his mother. During his years of illness, he had become closer to her than he had to his stern father or his brothers and sisters. Her death was to the introverted young man the end of his one strong human bond.

Without his mother to mediate between him and his father, a conflict could not be avoided. Rabbi Frankfurter had an unchangeable image of his disabled son. Eventually, David's father expected the strain of medical school to defeat the sickly boy. That meant that everything would have been for nothing. Why then should his ill child persist in inflicting suffering upon himself and distress upon the family? Did it make sense, when the outcome was so certain?

For David to reject his father's vision of him was seen by the inflexible rabbi as an act of filial defiance he could not tolerate. Once the young Frankfurter stepped onto the train to return to his medical studies in Switzerland, he had taken an irreversible step and had burned all of his bridges home. Only as a doctor could the rebellious son return. To achieve less would mean being crushed by total humiliation after useless defiance.

Linnie Steffen worried about the student who had returned from Yugoslavia. The death of his mother, the trouble with his

141

family, and the constant torment of his ailing body made the year 1934 a difficult one. Steffen was haunted by the fear that Frankfurter would harm himself in order to escape from the torment that forced him to rely upon morphine to deaden the pain and sleeping tablets to rest.

Instead of struggling through the muffled lectures and attending to his duties as an intern, Frankfurter went to the cafes to talk about the politics of their violent world and to smoke two packs of cigarettes a day. Outside events had captured his attention. While he had been dedicated exclusively to his study of medicine, he had ignored world events as if he were immune from the impact of tyranny and violence.

During the latter half of 1933, that had not been difficult for him. A brief, deceptive calm had spread across Germany and into Switzerland. If one tried, it was possible with little effort to imagine that Hitlerism and anti-Semitism had become stains upon a turned page in history and that the future would be peaceful.

But 1934 brought an end to the respite, just when Frankfurter was seeking an escape from his personal struggle for fulfillment. Politics grew into an addiction that separated his mind from his specific situation to the general plight of the outside world. There was much to discuss. Georg Thomae had just invaded the sanctity of the banks; the Iron Broom Movement and the National Front were circulating copies of "The Protocols of the Elders of Zion."

"Protocols" seized the interest of the entire nation. At the end of October 1934, officials of the Nazi groups were tried in a Bern court for distributing the inflammatory material in fifteen languages. For the first time, Jews and Nazis confronted each other in the court, and the public was there. The people came to observe the sensational trial that converted the Palace of Justice into a stage on which Nazism and Judaism were scrutinized and judged. Behind the National Front and the Iron Broom Movement was Wilhelm Gustloff, whose arm seemed to reach throughout Switzerland. Watching from amidst the crowd, Frankfurter absorbed the excitement of the moment.

Mocking the upsurge in National Socialism across the continent, Frankfurter gave a copy of *Die schlimme Juden* (The Evil Jews) to friends. Inside the work by Carl Albert Loosli, who discussed the view of the "evil Jews," Frankfurter wrote:

> Here is an account of how bad we are, and the greatest of our crimes seems to be that we are not so black as we are painted. The chosen method of those who hate us is to see our crimes and our errors while they shut their eyes and hearts against what is good in us.
>
> To honest and unprejudiced observers, we have always appeared substantial and even honorable. Hope, therefore, remains that God will gain a victory over the devil in the human heart. Another of the bad ones,
> D.F.[62]

As each week passed, the times worsened, giving Frankfurter a steady diet of fresh problems to devour. *Der Sturmer* (The Storm Trooper), the private voice of Julius Streicher, filled Frankfurter with horror and hatred of the Nazism. The paper was published in Nuremberg and combined the bitterest anti-Semitism with pornographic illustrations. When Streicher began the paper in 1921, it had been a local hate sheet with a small, regional audience serving as the symbol of his new political movement, *Deutsch-Sozialistische Partei* (German Socialist Party), which was a rival of the National Socialism of Adolf Hitler. In 1922, Streicher merged his party with the Nazis and acknowledged the leadership of Hitler. Through *Der Sturmer,* Streicher by outdoing Hitler in his expressions of anti-Jewish hatred, maintained the attention of a dedicated following. By 1935, the paper was being distributed nationwide and in nearby German-speaking countries. Frankfurter had no problem finding the hate-permeated journal.

The Hans Wesemann affair gave Frankfurter another reason to worry. If the Swiss frontier did not stop the advance of the National Socialist machine, then no one was safe. Jews in Switzerland heard about the lists that were being made in preparation for their arrest and imprisonment in one of the German concentration camps, about which the Swiss newspapers kept the people well informed although German newspapers censored such news.

There was always some new horror to distress Frankfurter, but September 1935 was an exceptionally terrible month. In Nuremberg the new anti-Jewish code, the Nuremberg Laws, took the last liberties from the Jews of Germany. The two new articles of law denied citizenship to all Jews, which stripped them of their civil rights, and prohibited mixed marriages.

The Swiss did not need to look too far to find signs that the confederation, too, seemed to be in danger. In Switzerland the open sympathy of Minister Johannes Baumann for the National Socialist cause convinced many that the Nazis had taken control of Switzerland. Those with that opinion held the view that Wilhelm Gustloff was the secret ruler of the confederation.

Late in 1935, Frankfurter and a student of philosophy were discussing the political trends. The student of philosophy removed a revolver from his pocket and placed it in the middle of the table. "If they come for me, this is what they'll get," he told David. The gun was to be his dialogue with his would-be executioners.

Contained within the cylinder of the gun were six statements of strength, resistance, and equality. The gun made the helpless powerful, the frightened courageous, and the oppressed formidable. There was so much contained in that machine of destruction. Frankfurter, who had never had any experience with firearms or with brutality, was converted in that moment to a practitioner of violence. A gun could cure injustice and the sense of personal failure.

For days he held the steel image in his mind. Time made the weapon feel more comfortable in his thoughts. He was still standing on the threshold between thought and deed when he went to peer into the windows of the gun shops on Aarbergergasse in Bern. Once beyond the threshold, who could know where his new power might transport him? Frankfurter was just a window shopper, checking what was available. As he entered a shop, he still had not decided to buy one of the many instruments of death on display. To the novice, the lack of knowledge made it difficult to decide what weapon would be appropriate for the killing of a *Landesgruppenleiter.*

The woman clerk was pleased to show him the selection of arms. Finally, one did capture his attention. It was a short-barrel Browning revolver that fitted snugly into his pocket, in which he could conceal it easily until he chose to kill. For ten Swiss francs, the price of an expensive shirt, the gun and a handful of ammunition were his. The clerk didn't even need to see any identification or ask his name. Ten francs was his only proof that he had the right to possess the means to kill. It was all so frighteningly simple and exhilarating.

At the boarding house Frankfurter exhibited his new toy to Steffen. To the young man, who had never held such an instrument before, the gun was a novelty to be twirled on his finger and brandished, as if it were a child's plaything with no other purpose than to amuse. Sight of the weapon made Steffen uneasy. Often, she had seen her troubled boarder sink into a deep despair. She imagined that during some future time he might turn it upon himself to free himself from the burdens of his life. Now that he had a gun nearby, depression could easily be turned into death. Following his return from Yugoslavia, Steffen had feared that he might destroy himself. Sight of the gun revived the fear and kept it lurking always somewhere in the back of her mind.

Toward the end of 1935, Frankfurter began thinking of his personal future. His own body was failing him; the world was crushing him. Much of his life had been dedicated to the creation of a physician, a healer of the sick. As 1935 passed, Frankfurter had come to accept the inevitable failure of his life. His body would not support the demands of the profession. Facing him was the humiliating prospect of returning defeated to his less-than-merciful father, who would not hesitate to tell him, "I told you so." After that, it would be a life of physical pain and endless despair. What kind of future was that for someone who had been so determined and had come so close?

An idea that had been growing steadily just below the surface began to break through Frankfurter's protective shell. If he could not heal the diseases of the human body, then he might treat the ailments of the society. In his drawer he had the necessary medicine for the treatment of the malady of Nazism, a six-shot, short-barrel Browning revolver. As he saw it, Frankfurter was better prepared to apply the treatment than were most. His life was over, destroyed by his own failing body. He could lose nothing else.

Nearby, Germany was growing stronger. As each day passed, the likelihood that Switzerland would be absorbed appeared to increase, and few were preparing to repel the menace. The manifestation of the Nazi disease was Wilhelm Gustloff. Newspapers were demanding his expulsion. Regardless, from his headquarters in Davos he continued to rule. He had powerful friends in the Swiss government and cowering opponents. To deal the movement in Switzerland a fatal blow, it would be necessary to crush the head of the Nazi Party, and the heart would cease to beat.

Frankfurter weighed the possibility of going into the heartland of National Socialism, to strike directly at Adolf Hitler or one of the other members of the Nazi pantheon. A bullet into Göring or Goebbels would be heard around the world, but the Jews of Germany would pay a terrible price. Worse beyond calculation was the likelihood that he would fail. Humiliation would make the failure unbearable.

Gustloff was the only choice. He was near, and he was vulnerable. A bullet into him would certainly alert the Swiss, who were already aware of the menace on their frontier. Such a blow would be applauded by the public. The assassin would die a hero who had slain the enemy as David had slain Goliath. Frankfurter's sling would be a revolver. His stone would be a lead bullet. After he had felled Gustloff, he would proclaim the justness of his action by sacrificing himself. He would not be a skulking killer striking from the shadows. Frankfurter decided to confront Gustloff face to face, Jew to Nazi, and execute him for his crimes against humanity. A message was to be heard in Berlin, "Enough!" When he spoke that word through the muzzle of his revolver, it would be the first act by a Jew to exact from the Nazi regime a taste of justice through violence.

To prepare for his assignment, Frankfurter went to practice at Ostermundingen Shooting Range and returned to his room to consider when and how to act. Time slipped away on catlike feet. Days matured into weeks. Weeks aged into months. Then, it was the end of January 1936, three years after he had been dismissed from Frankfurt University. "Enough" needed to be spoken.

18

Because I Am a Jew

For many of her student boarders, away for the first time from critical parental eyes, Linnie Steffen was a substitute mother with the privilege to scold but without the authority to command. She worried about her young men, especially about David Frankfurter. Each came to her with his share of problems, but Frankfurter was burdened by weights heavy enough to break the backs of most men.

Although amiable and eager to be engaged in an intellectual discussion, Frankfurter was inwardly alone. Ideas served as a barrier that separated him from everyone else. While he discussed politics and philosophy freely, the real person remained concealed. There were no close friends in whom he confided, no young women with whom he shared his hidden feelings. Occasionally he received a letter or a telephone call from a brother in Yugoslavia. Periodically his father sent without comment money to help finance the objectionable medical education David was neglecting.

On Friday, January 31, 1936, Steffen found a brief note from her worrisome boarder.

Dear Linnie,
I will not be back tonight.
Details, later.
Cordially yours,
David[63]

Immediately Steffen checked his dresser drawer. As she had feared, the Browning revolver was missing, which to her worried mind could mean only one thing. Of course, he was going to kill himself. She had feared just that from the moment the weapon had been brought into the house. Why else did he disappear as though he were a thief?

Through the day, Steffen waited to hear that the body of David Frankfurter with a bullet in the head had been found somewhere around the city. She contemplated going to Rabbi Messinger to ask what to do, but she hesitated, embarrassed by the prospect of telling her fears to the rabbi just to have Frankfurter return in a day or so after a brief holiday. With nothing more than apprehensions to support her fears, Steffen waited and waited for any news.

Early that morning, Frankfurter had placed the revolver, six bullets, and a bottle of sleeping tablets into a briefcase and taken the train to Zurich. There he changed for the second leg of the trip to Davos. On a winter Friday, he was not likely to be noticed. Weekend vacationers were going to the mountains for the winter sports.

"Tickets," the conductor called, passing from carriage to carriage. For the conductor it was another day of punching tickets and giving information. At the end of the line in Chur, he would turn around and return to Zurich, as if his life were an endless circle.

"Ticket," he said to Frankfurter. The conductor punched the piece of paper and paused. After years of studying the characters of travelers, he had learned to read what thoughts were behind the masked faces. Here was not the usual weekend traveler. The man in his mid-twenties was withdrawn, detached from the laughter and preoccupied by some grave matter. What burden the stranger carried, the conductor could not imagine.

The conductor himself bore a weight, and he had no one with whom to share it. For just a while, he unloaded his anxieties upon a stranger who would soon be gone. Little did he know that the young man was bearing the same heavy trouble, which was called National Socialism. On the previous day, Adolf Hitler had celebrated the third anniversary of his accession to power. "Judge us in four years," he had advised the German public in 1933. After three years, the conductor had passed judgment upon him and condemned the Führer as a mad tyrant who would bring to Europe another bloody war and immeasurable destruction. The prophetic railway conductor envisaged German madmen swarming across the nearby frontier to engulf Switzerland in the catastrophe. Despite the clear and present menace, which he perceived vividly, the others on the train were indifferent to the peril and content to amuse themselves, except for this distressed young man.

Alone with his private doubts in the swaying carriage, Frankfurter's resolve had been fading. Again, as he had done from the day that he had purchased the gun, he was seeking excuses to delay performing the act of murder. From the time of his birth, his father had taught him that nothing was so grave as to justify the use of violence. Yet he had assigned to himself the duty of executing a threat to the Jews in Switzerland only to abandon that very same self-imposed duty.

During the brief conversation with the obsessed conductor Frankfurter recovered his courage. At first, he had intended to save only the Jews, but he had been shown the need to preserve Switzerland, which had given him her hospitality. He would serve the Jews and the Swiss. Both were being threatened. Both needed someone to strike a fatal blow, to stop the advance of the Nazis.

Refired by the chance meeting on the train, Frankfurter completed the trip. Toward the late afternoon he entered the Hotel Metropol-Lowen. Amidst the laughter, no one even noticed that he had arrived without any luggage, save for a briefcase. As far as others were concerned, if anyone noticed him, David Frankfurter appeared to be one of many weekend visitors who had come from the city to enjoy a few days of amusement in the Alpine snow. Nothing about the betrayed his true reason for his visit.

Never having planned an assassination, Frankfurter intended to keep his method simple. After a brief rest, he would telephone the house of Wilhelm Gustloff to make an appointment to see him immediately, walk the short distance to the house, kill him, and kill himself. By evening, the news would be heard around the world. In an hour or so, Hitler would know that there was at least one Jew who was prepared to take a stand. Once others saw how easily it could be done, that one man with one gun could shake the foundations of Nazi tyranny, an army of angered Jews might rise up. Frankfurter offered himself to give the courage and the signal. In this one way, his futile life and his insignificant death would have had some purpose.

Outside, evening was canopying the town. It was after four o'clock. Back in Croatia, his father would have begun the celebration of the Sabbath: "This was the hour of grace, when Princess Sabbath, the bride of Israel, is greeted in all the synagogues, when the angels of peace are invited to the festive board, when the candles flicker, and bread and wine stand in readiness for the blessing. . . ."[64] Throughout his life the Sabbath had been an honored day. To have violated it would have brought down his father's wrath. Now, what would his father think when he learned that his son had violated the Sabbath by murdering another man? It would make no difference to his father what this man represented. In the philosophy of the rabbi, murder was against the law of God.

Frankfurter knew that. The son of the rabbi, the young man who had studied with his parents had always known that simple and unyielding law, "Thou shalt not kill." What Frankfurter had not decided was whether murder on the Sabbath was somehow more wrong than on other days.

Such ideas had to be considered. In the hotel room the debate raged between David, the son of a rabbi, and Frankfurter, the assassin with a mission to preserve Jewish life and Swiss independence. Should he kill on the Sabbath? Should he kill on any day? When finally, the debate subsided, it was too late to act. Night had settled over Davos, and everyone was going to bed.

Yes, it had happened again. As soon as the time came to act, Frankfurter found himself procrastinating, arguing himself into inertia, as if he were a mountain with little more to do than to see time pass. He had allowed his studies to be neglected by inaction, by finding excuses. Then, he was allowing Gustloff to continue to spread his web of tyranny over Switzerland, while he, Frankfurter, continued to live in pain and anguish.

Shame made his own company unbearable. Again, as he had done so often, David submerged into a deep well of depression that drowned him in hopelessness. To escape from himself, Frankfurter swallowed several sleeping tablets. Posed against an inward-turned anger, the pills were impotent, overwhelmed by the virulence of his despondency. Frankfurter was left to suffer through the creeping hours of the night, until morning came.

Through the night of torment, an ironic comedy had been played. David Frankfurter had inflicted unnecessarily upon himself hours of merciless torture that the telephone call to Wilhelm Gustloff would have ended. The third anniversary of the Third Reich had been a day to celebrate for National Socialists. *Landesgruppenleiter* Wilhelm Gustloff had gone to Tunersee, near Bern, to speak to a crowd of true believers. He had been just a short distance from Frankfurter's boarding house. Gustloff did not return to Davos until February 3. If Frankfurter had prepared his mission more carefully, he could have struck at Gustloff without the need for a long trip into the mountains. His night of self-doubt and anguish would not have needed to be suffered, but he would not learn how the fates had played with him until long after, when the knowledge would be another mockery.

In the morning, the urgency of his mission had eased. During Saturday, Frankfurter, the assassin of the previous night, wandered through the resort village. Several times, he passed a sign that invited him to Kurpark 3. "Director of the National Socialist Party for the District of Switzerland" the sign declared, revealing to Frankfurter the power of the *Landesgruppenleiter,* who was permitted to proclaim his position so openly. If anything could prove the rightness of the assassination, then it would have to be this open display of Nazi arrogance.

Saturday passed without an attempt to kill Gustloff, and Sunday arrived. Around Davos the other visitors amused themselves in the snow. The important event of their day was a skating race. Wives and girlfriends cheered their racing husbands and boyfriends to a meaningless victory. Frankfurter felt a surge of disgust at their frivolous contest. Not far away, thousands were living in terror; thousands were facing uncertain futures. Their suffering was being mocked by the triviality of the tourists in the home of Wilhelm Gustloff. That sign continued to summon Frankfurter to fulfill his assignment, but he held back to consider further the approaching end of his time on earth. To enjoy just a few more hours of precious life, Frankfurter allowed the weekend to pass.

On Monday, when he left his hotel, Frankfurter did not walk toward Kurpark 3 to strike the fatal blow at Nazism. Instead, he went to the Jewish sanatorium, Ethaniya, where he introduced himself to the director, from whom he requested a few minutes of time. Frankfurter disclosed that he was to graduate in a year from Bern University, after which he would require a residency. They conversed as though Frankfurter, the assassin on his mission to kill and to die, had a future to discuss. Consumed by the meaningless charade, Frankfurter allowed Monday to escape unused. The wheels of their fates were carrying the two men toward the fatal collision. At Kurpark 3, Wilhelm Gustloff had returned from the celebration.

Back in Bern, Linnie Steffen was no longer able to wait for news of her armed, troubled boarder. She told Rabbi Messinger her fears. He urged her to inform the police, who began to search for Frankfurter. Thus, the assassin was being sought before he had gone to kill Wilhelm Gustloff.

Tuesday morning arrived. Frankfurter welcomed the day. Tuesday was Ki Tov, the Jewish day of good luck. Anything attempted on Ki Tov was certain to succeed. It was not the thinking of a scientist or the son of a rabbi. Regardless, the idea pleased and assured the would-be assassin. Tuesday, February 4, 1936, was to be the killing and the dying day. The decision was fixed in Frankfurter's mind. Soon his family would learn about his violence toward Gustloff and toward himself. To his father and his brothers and sisters, Alfons and Joseph, Ruth and Naomi, he wrote:

My dearly beloved father,
I have always given you much sorrows and worry and little joy. I cannot go on. Forgive me; it is not hard for me to leave this life, knowing that you will never doubt my boundless love for you and my blessed mother. Be strong and trust in God as you have always done. You have Alfons and Joe, Ruth and Naomi, who will still give you much pleasure. I have lost my faith in myself and mankind. I cannot go on. My last wish is that you say Kaddish* for me. I hope soon to be united with my dear mama before God's judgment seat. Be strong, you and the children. May God in his mercy give you and all Israel a better fate. Farewell.
     Your unhappy son,
     David

My dear beloved brothers and sisters,
For the last time I send you greetings, with a prayer that God in his mercy may keep our dear father and you healthy and strong. You alone shall know what moves me to depart from you and the world. I can no longer bear the sufferings of the Jewish people; they have destroyed my joy in living. May God avenge all the wrong that has been inflicted upon us Jews. I myself hope to be an insignificant tool in His hand. Farewell and forgive me, I could not do otherwise. Even in death,
     Your faithful brother,
     David[65]

---

*a prayer for the dead

His future decided, all questions resolved, Frankfurter the assassin revelled in the delight of absolute certainty. He said the prayers for the dead, consigned himself to a grave, and sapped every nutrient from his last feast of time, until it was 7:30 in the evening.

Frankfurter had loaded six bullets into his revolver and placed the gun into his coat pocket. On a package of cigarettes he had written the step-by-step plan that would end in Gustloff's death.

> The sentence must be carried out on Monday 3/2, at 9:30 A.M. First call up and ask if he is home. If he does not come out and cannot be seen, attempt to escape; otherwise, go through with the suicide. One or two shots in the chest. Revolver in righthand pocket of jacket, not of overcoat, ready to fire. As soon as I am in the room, suddenly pull it out, fire three shots at his head or chest.[66]

When early in the evening Frankfurter left the hotel, the plan had been abandoned for the simpler strategy of a ring on the door bell and a face-to-face meeting. Outside, the weekend visitors had thinned in number, and most of the remaining visitors were in cafes for their evening meals.

"Herr Frankfurter," a woman called. Two women appeared from the darkness. They were Frau Kaufmann and her daughter, who had come from Bern for a few days in the snow.

"Would you join us for tea?" they invited.

"I have an appointment," he told them.

Their unexpected appearance reinforced his resolve to kill Gustloff. If those two wealthy Jewish women from Bern had been living a few kilometers further to the east, they would be worrying about their lives, not thinking about playing in the snow or having tea and cakes. Life was a bitter comedy that gave a line on a map the power to determine life and death.

Although those women seemed to be unaware of the nearness of their doom, the director of the National Socialist Party for the district of Switzerland intended to take away from them their casual amusements and their very lives. Right in front of their unseeing eyes, the sign pointed the assassin toward his objective at Kurpark 3.

David Frankfurter rang the door bell.

From upstairs a woman called down to him.[67]

"Is Herr Gustloff at home? And can I speak to him?" Frankfurter called back.

Frau Hedwig Gustloff invited him up. The plump woman in her late thirties seemed to be neither annoyed nor surprised to receive an unannounced visitor. Since her husband had risen to such a prominent position, surprise callers had become routine, a necessary demand of the office. Although the police had warned Gustloff that a real threat to his safety existed, no precautions had been taken. Up in Davos, apart from the troubled world, the remoteness bred a sense of security. Even those who were hostile to the movement were courteous and correct.

Nothing about Frankfurter stirred suspicion in Hedwig Gustloff's mind. He spoke politely in perfect German and looked as if he were a typical German or Swiss man in his mid-twenties, the Aryan type, who Hitler had said would raise the German nation to greatness.

"My husband is busy for a few moments, but then he will be able to see you," she assured Frankfurter. Frau Gustloff led him through the house.

"Please wait in his study," she said, directing the visitor into the room from where Wilhelm Gustloff controlled the strategies of the movement in Switzerland.

Frau Gustloff pointed to a chair and left Frankfurter alone. The room had the usual furnishings, except for the larger than life-size photo portrait of Adolf Hitler. Written on the bottom of the silver framed picture in the Führer's hand was the dedication, "To My Dear Gustloff, Adolf Hitler." Beneath the photo was the dagger of an SS officer with its inscription, "Blood and Honor."

Sight of the SS dagger reminded David Frankfurter of the song sung by SS troopers as they marched.

> When Jewish blood spurts from the knife,
> things will be twice as good.

The assassin had come to the right place. In a moment, Wilhelm Gustloff would enter the room, and David Frankfurter would be forced to draw the revolver from his pocket and kill. His finger fumbled with the steel instrument with its six words of protest. While he fingered the instrument of death, Frankfurter reconsidered his position. There still remained time to escape. If he fled, no one would know why he had come and how he had failed. Alone in the study, he had come as a Jewish fly into the den of the Nazi spider. How often did the fly devour the spider?

Wilhelm Gustloff had confided to friends that he often gazed into the piercing eyes of his leader to draw fresh strength. Frankfurter, too, looked and drew strength from those hate-filled madman's eyes. His strength was the resolve to fulfill his mission. If he could not reach the core of the Nazi body, Frankfurter would with a surgeon's skill cut off one of its extremities. Thus ended the brief debate whether to flee or to kill.

From another room Frankfurter heard the voice of the director. He was shouting into the telephone to overcome the static on the line. On the other end, Dr. Hubermann, who had organized the weekend celebration of the third anniversary of Hitler's rise to power at Tunersee, was straining to understand.

"The dirty Communists and Jews will have to be taught a lesson," Frankfurter thought his failing hearing had discerned through the closed door. Then the director hung up the telephone and came to meet his unannounced visitor.

"Here I am," he said to Frankfurter who had risen from the chair.

This was the image of the Aryan superman! Gustloff was taller and broader than Frankfurter. He was the real Nazi Goliath!

Frankfurter pulled the Browning from his coat pocket. He leveled the barrel at Gustloff's chest and squeezed the trigger. The revolver uttered a useless click.

Gustloff grasped his opportunity. In desperation, he charged his would-be assassin, and his fingers reached for Frankfurter's throat. Under the assault of the more powerful man, Frankfurter retreated across the small room. Already Gustloff's hands were around his throat. His strong fingers were choking Frankfurter, while the young man continued fumbling with his gun. Then he discovered the fault. Before Gustloff had entered the room, Frankfurter had been fingering the Browning revolver. Somehow he had released the cylinder and had rendered the weapon useless. Clumsily, Frankfurter pressed the cylinder back into place, a loose bullet tumbled out and rolled across the floor, but the gun had been returned to its role as an instrument of death.

During the brief dance of death, neither spoke. Gustloff did not shout for help or plead for his life. Frankfurter did not leave words for history. With the hands of the Nazi around his throat and the barrel of the weapon jammed into the chest of the *Landesgruppenleiter,* the assassin squeezed the trigger. This time, the Browning fired, again and again. Four bullets struck Gustloff. A fifth was lodged in the wall. Wilhelm Gustloff, the director of the National Socialist Party for the district of Switzerland, was dead on the floor.

The volley of shots reverberated through the house and into the quiet street. Gustloff's wife rushed into the study. She saw her husband lying dead and his murderer still clasping the smoking revolver. When she shrieked, the sound severed the frail threads of Frankfurter's self-control. Once the threads were broken, he panicked and fled crazed through the unfamiliar house. By some means unknown to him in his panic, he found the door and burst through it to seek his freedom in the darkness.

Outside, a barrier of curious bystanders had formed, blocking Frankfurter's escape. He waved the empty gun. "Make way or I'll fire!" he shouted. The wall yielded. The assassin hurled himself into the darkness and was soon lost in a field of snow. Animal terror fueled his legs, until he was exhausted. Then, he threw himself into the snow and bathed his burning face.

As Frankfurter reclaimed control of his mind, he realized a horrible truth. He had sunk from a man with a just cause to a creature of the jungle. In his fall, he had abandoned the justice of his act of violence. Flight and escape meant shame and disgrace. Others would label him a madman or a common murderer. Either way, the messenger would be the message, and Wilhelm Gustloff, the Nazi, would become Gustloff the victim of a Jewish murderer. Somehow, he had to rescue the nobility of his deed.

Frankfurter pressed the gun to his head to complete his assignment, to recoup his dignity. He, too, was to have died, but a second terrible truth was spoken by the silence. The gun was empty! His bullet, his statement of sincerity, his escape from his misery, had fallen from the revolver and had rolled away unspent.

Without another bullet to complete his assignment, a single option remained. Frankfurter had to surrender himself to the police, before they found and arrested him. Of his arrest, there was no question. The assassin had left a trail that an amateur could have followed.

On Friday afternoon, when Frankfurter had registered at the Hotel Metropol-Lowen, he had given his correct name and address. At the time, he had not anticipated his own survival. He was to die with Gustloff. Afterward, what did it matter whether or not the police knew who he had been and where he had lived?

Frankfurter turned back toward Kurpark 3. Out in the field of snow, he had lost all sense of time, but he was aware that enough of it had passed to return the quiet street to its customary calm and stillness. The police, the curious bystanders, and even the corpse had gone, as if nothing had occurred.

A light shone from the window of Kurpark 2. Frankfurter rang the bell and was greeted by an elderly couple who came to see what new excitement was stalking their usually dull avenue.

"I have some information for the police. May I use your telephone?" Frankfurter said, attempting not to alarm the couple. Any sign that they were looking into the face of an assassin might have terrified them.

They admitted the stranger and stood by while he telephoned

Figure 2—SIMON VASSILIEVICH PETLIURA

Figure 1—SAMUEL (SHALOM) SCHWARTZBARD

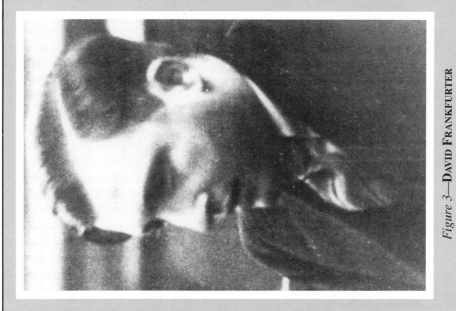

Figure 3—**David Frankfurter**

Figure 4—**Wilhelm Gustloff**

Figure 5—HERSCHEL FEIBEL GRYNSZPAN

Figure 6—ERNST VOM RATH

Figure 1—SAMUEL (SHALOM) SCHWARTZBARD was a self-educated, Ukrainian-born Jew, who was a revolutionary, labor union organizer, poet, and journalist. On May 25, 1926, he rose to international fame when he assassinated in public the former leader of the short-lived Ukrainian Republic. Samuel Schwartzbard was born in 1888 near Balta and died of an illness in 1938 in Capetown, South Africa.

Figure 2—SIMON VASSILIEVICH PETLIURA was a young revolutionary in the Ukraine and rose to become the leader of the Ukrainian Republic and commander of its armed forces. His brief rule over the chaotic state left him branded by Jewish survivors of the numerous pogroms as a mass murderer. On May 25, 1926, he was assassinated for the alleged crimes. He was born in 1879 and died in 1926.

Figure 3—DAVID FRANKFURTER was a twenty-six-year-old medical student in Switzerland, when he turned from the study of physiology to the study of politics through the barrel of a gun. Convinced that Wilhelm Gustloff was going to engulf Switzerland in German Naziism, he assassinated the leader of the Nazi movement and broke the grip of Naziism over the neutral state. He was born into a prominent Jewish family in Croatia in 1909 and died of natural causes in Israel in 1982. He was the only one of the three assassins to reach Israel.

Figure 4—WILHELM GUSTLOFF rose from a weather-chart clerk at a German meteorology station in Davos, Switzerland, to the leader of the National Socialist Party. He joined the Nazi movement in 1923 and became an active proponent of its international cause. In 1936, the man who had become known as The Hawk of Davos and a threat to Swiss independence was shot to death. He was born in Mecklenburg, Germany, in 1896.

Figure 5—HERSCHEL FEIBEL GRYNSZPAN was a seventeen-year-old teenager enjoying the amusements of Paris when he entered the German Embassy and assassinated the first diplomat that he was able to reach. He was born in Hanover, Germany, in 1921, and disappeared from history in a German concentration camp in May 1945.

Figure 6—ERNST VOM RATH was the Third Secretary in the Paris German Embassy and a man of scant importance when he welcomed into his office a special messenger, who had brought a secret document for the unavailable ambassador. Vom Rath, who was born in 1911, was shot and died of his wounds on November 9, 1938.

the police. Afterward, to escape their curious gaze and to cool his fevered nerves in the winter air, he went outside to await the constables.

Frankfurter the assassin was held by the tension of an actor about to step onto a stage. The thinking of his role was more frightening than the real performance after the curtain rose. While he waited for the drama to commence, his legs needed to move, to consume the surging tension. As if possessed by a force more powerful than his own will, Frankfurter walked away from the scene of the assassination. Instead of waiting for the police, who were taking too long a time to come for him, Frankfurter decided to go to them. Already, his impatient legs were transporting him toward the police headquarters near the city hall. On his way, Frankfurter passed the two plainclothes detectives who were responding to his telephone call.

When Frankfurter entered the police station, it was quiet as if nothing had occurred to disrupt the normal peacefulness of the remote community. A young police constable in uniform stood behind the office counter.

"I suppose you've heard what happened at Kurpark 3," Frankfurter said. "I'm the murderer."

From the moment the report of the anticipated assassination reached the police, a previously formulated theory guided their investigation. Wilhelm Gustloff had been classified as a high-profile target who was certain to draw an assassin. Warnings to him had been ignored. Offers to protect him had been refused. The police were just waiting for what they considered an inevitable event.

The police expected a team of professional assassins to make the kill. As soon as they struck, they would be running for an international frontier to get beyond the jurisdiction of Swiss police. More than an hour had passed. The police were watching the Austrian border. They were not waiting for the killer to walk into their office to confess. In the mind of the young constable, Frankfurter was a mentally unbalanced case in search of a moment of notoriety or a decoy who was to distract the hunters from their fleeing quarry. According to the police theory, he could not be a professional assassin. The carefully formulated theory had not taken into account the action of a lone Jew with a self-assigned mission.

"Can you prove that?" the skeptical constable inquired.

There was one way to prove his claim. The assassin removed his empty gun from his pocket and deposited it on the counter. With a sweep of his hand, the policeman snatched the weapon away and locked it into the drawer, before the confessing assassin changed his mind. Frankfurter was taken into custody and escorted into an adjacent office to await the return of the detectives.

It took time for Frankfurter to convince his interrogators that he was exactly who and what he was. Once they were satisfied, they escorted him into a conference room and gave him an hour to relax. Then, the president of the township of Davos, Salomon Prader, came to question him. He was followed by police and political officials who escorted Hedwig Gustloff into the chamber.

"He is the murderer!" she exclaimed, running to the assassin. The widow's eyes were red from weeping. Yet, she was remarkably calm.

She raised Frankfurter's face, to peer into his eyes.

"You look so kind. You have such good eyes. Why did you do it? Did you know Gustloff personally?" she asked.

"If you had known him," she continued in a soft voice, "you wouldn't have done it. Why did you do it? Did you have personal reasons?"

"No, not for personal reasons," Frankfurter replied to her questions.

"Why did you do it then?" she screamed in mounting agitation.

For a very long few minutes, Frankfurter could not respond to her appeal. He had difficulty swallowing and trouble finding words. When he did speak, it seemed to be someone else making the sounds that came from his mouth.

"I did what I did, because I am a Jew," Frankfurter exclaimed in a voice that he scarcely recognized.

Those words pierced the dam of Hedwig Gustloff's composure.

The reservoir of anger and hatred burst out, and she poured invective over him and the Jews of the world. In the Jews she saw every evil, everything foul. And now that vileness had come into her home and killed her husband. She continued her harangue until the police removed her from the room.

About eleven o'clock, the investigating magistrate, Herr Dedual, arrived. His preliminary inquiry continued until one o'clock in the morning. Then David Frankfurter, the assassin of Director Wilhelm Gustloff, was taken to a cell to be held until his trial.

19

An Inconvenient Martyr

At the beginning of February, thousands of foreign visitors were arriving in Germany to attend the Winter Olympics at Garmisch in the Bavarian Alps, just a short distance from the Swiss resort community of Davos. The games were to last from February 7 to February 16, 1936.

The entire country had prepared itself for those days of triumph and glory, during which Germans intended to demonstrate through the superiority of their athletes the supremacy of their race and philosophy. In consideration of the sensitivities of the foreign guests, overt anti-Semitic practices were curtailed. On January 10, the government ordered the removal of banners with anti-Jewish slogans and the withdrawal of *Der Sturmer* from public displays. Since 1935, the newspaper had been circulated nationwide, but what was normal for Germans was deemed too shocking for unaccustomed foreigners.

Then news reached Berlin that Wilhelm Gustloff had been assassinated by a Jew. Since the beginning of the National Socialist movement, Jews were claimed to have been responsible for the humiliating defeat of 1918 and every other subsequent problem. Suddenly, Hitler had a flesh and blood Jewish assassin to present to the German public.

Inside the ruling circle of Germany there had been an expec-

tation of a Jewish backlash. Three years of persecution was certain
to eventually provoke a reaction. If Germany did not respond
to the first sign of Jewish violence, then German officials feared
that it would encourage future attackers.

Worse than the danger from the Jews was the threat from
the Brown Shirts. Hitler had come to power through their violence,
and he needed them to crush the still-surviving resistance to
his totalitarian regime. They had been bred upon a diet of anti-
Semitism. If the visible Jewish menace were not eradicated
promptly and harshly, then their disillusionment with the government might turn them against their creator.

Waiting in the background to take command of the horde of
SA troopers was Julius Streicher. His ambition to seize control
of the movement had been moderated, but it was still there. Here
was his opportunity to take the troopers away from Hitler and
use them to carry himself into power.

In spite of the threat from within the movement, Hitler dared
not release his storm troopers to avenge the assassination. If
he did unleash them upon the Jews, thousands of foreign visitors
would witness Nazi madness and carry the message home. In
order to justify not freeing the Brown Shirts to attack the Jewish
enemy, the strategy had to be to play down the Jewishness of
the crime, to find another, less important, enemy.

The solution to the problem was to broaden the spectrum
of guilt to include the Swiss press, which was charged with the
crimes of anti–National Socialism and anti-Germanism. According to the accusations by the German propaganda machine, the
Swiss papers were said to be under Marxist or liberal socialist
influence. Outside of Germany, the theme found a receptive audience and was echoed by the foreign press. In the United States,
the Literary Digest presented Wilhelm Gustloff as the helpless
victim of a crazed German hater who had been aroused to violence
by the leftist dominated press.

Gustloff, a German physicist, attached to the Davos observa-
tory, for some time had irritated Swiss Socialists by organizing

Germans in Switzerland in support of Hitler. Because he gave assurances of his respect for Swiss neutrality, the authorities decided he could remain in Switzerland. The Leftist Swiss press, however, had long demanded his expulsion on the ground that he did not fulfil his promises to the Government.[68]

On February 5, the Foreign Ministry in Berlin sent instructions to the German Embassy in Bern to have the less inflammatory policy promoted through German journalists.

The German press has been directed as follows: The murderer was not committing an act of revenge, did not know the victim, arrived from Yugoslavia three years ago from whence he had derived no motive for his deed. The reason is rather that during a three years' stay in Bern he had been exposed to a Swiss press campaign. The victim was innocent. He had the care of the Germans in Switzerland; his behavior was always correct, as the Federal Council have attested. The campaign was not conducted by the Spd. [Social Democratic] press alone, but by the entire left-wing press which has for years exceeded the limits of the permissible.[69]

Although Wilhelm Gustloff had had no official standing beyond any other German resident of Switzerland, the Swiss government dared not ignore his death. His real power had been far greater than that of Ambassador Baron von Weizsacker. Immediately the Swiss moved to defuse the situation to avoid the potential diplomatic explosion.

Minister of Foreign Affairs Giuseppe Motta, a senior member of the Federal Council, filed an official statement of regret with the German ambassador. Then the two men met for forty-five minutes of serious discussion. During the talks, the outraged ambassador condemned the bigotry of the Swiss press and held it partially responsible for the assassination. Motta replied to the charges.

As regards the judicial investigation, Motta said that the Supreme Court of Grisons, which consisted of at least seven judges would, on the basis of the intensive investigation now in progress, ensure that the severest and most thorough punishment was meted out for the abominable crime. The investigation would naturally, in the interests of Switzerland, too, have to cover the antecedents of the crime. It was true that there was as yet no evidence of there having been a concerted plot. . . .

Motta tried to represent Jewish vengefulness as the primary motive. He pointed out that the author of the crime is of rabbinical descent and returned repeatedly to the Semitic perpetrator's hatred for the Third Reich. He also tried, by drawing attention to the perpetrator's poor knowledge of the German language, to cast doubts on his having been incited by the Swiss press.[70]

The Swiss eagerness to appease the Germans was demonstrated by the efforts of the government to abandon the policy of freedom of the press. On February 6, the Federal Council ordered two socialist newspapers, Le Travail and Le Droit du Peuple, to curb their anti-Nazi comments or to face closure. During 1934, the Swiss government had enacted a press law to control the political opinions of the newspapers, but not until Motta received a severe scolding from Ambassador von Weizsacker was the law enforced.

Behind the Swiss willingness to abandon press freedom and other civil rights was their effort to preserve their banking system and the economy that depended upon a healthy banking foundation. The Swiss were still caught by the same economic noose that had been tightened around them by the Weimar Republic. A portion of the two billion francs in loans and investments that had been frozen was being repatriated, but the agreements had not been completed. The Swiss remained vulnerable to German intimidation. While an effort was made to strengthen their bargaining position with their powerful neighbor, the Swiss followed a strategy of delay and appeasement.

The Swiss willingness to accept humiliation was seen in the unfavorable trade agreements they were prepared to tolerate. Germany was the largest foreign market for Swiss products, and Switzerland relied upon Germany for supplies of raw materials. To assure a continued flow of coal, the Swiss and the Germans agreed upon a barter arrangement. The Germans accepted credits at advantageous rates for their coal. The credits could be used to purchase Swiss goods or services. For loyal National Socialist Party members, one benefit was to be able to enjoy free vacations at Swiss expense in Swiss resorts such as Davos.

For economic reasons, the Swiss wanted to put behind them the problem of the shooting. The Germans, too, were satisfied to have the subject of the assassination pass. Just at that time, Gustloff's death was proving to be inconvenient. Still, Hitler had to maintain the facade that his missionary in Switzerland had been important to the movement. Frau Hedwig Gustloff, the widow of the newest National Socialist martyr, received a telegram of condolences from der Führer: "In the heavy loss you have suffered, I express to you, in the name of the whole German people, my sincerest sympathy. The nefarious crime that put an end to a life of a truly German man has created deep emotion and resentment in the entire nation."[71]

Gustloff's superior, Ernst Bohle, the director of *Ausland Organisation* and the second in command under Rudolf Hess, was dispatched to Davos to escort the body to the northern German town of Schwerin, where, on February 12, Wilhelm Gustloff was given a state funeral. Three thousand party functionaries attended. They lined the streets to salute Wilhelm Gustloff as his body was carried on a gun carriage through the town. Hitler himself delivered the eulogy, which did not stir the mobs to vengeance. It was a temperate speech, calmer than might have been expected for the canonization of a National Socialist saint.

Gustloff had not fallen in vain. The Jewish assassin had not foreseen that when he killed one, he awakened in the far-distant future millions and millions of comrades to a true German life.

Every foreign group of the National Socialist now had its
National Socialist patron, its holy martyr to the movement, and
its ideal. Everyone would carry his name in their hearts and
never more forget it. It is not Germany that is weakened, but
the power which committed this deed. The German people had
lost one of the living in the year 1936, but had gained an immortal
for the future.[72]

The speech was broadcast by radio across Germany. SA units
were ordered to their barracks to listen to their leader, who had
traveled from the Olympic Games in the south of Germany to
Schwerin in the north. Before and after, the troopers were warned
not to take into their own hands retribution for the murder. The
Führer would, in his own good time, and in his own way, retaliate.

In the meantime, the memory of Wilhelm Gustloff was to be
preserved by the renaming of Dernburgstrasse and Dernburg Platz
in the Charlottenburg district of Berlin to Wilhelm Gustloffstrasse
and Wilhelm Gustloff Platz. The former Jewish minister in the
old Weimar Republic was to sacrifice his brief glory for the glory
of the late *Landesgruppenleiter*.

A year later, in September 1937, a bronze plaque with the
martyr's name was attached to a bridge in Nuremberg, in the
domain of Julius Streicher. Hitler's major rival addressed the
crowd. When he spoke, there was no restraint, no worry that
the crowd would be remolded into a mob. "Look at the path which
the Jewish people has traversed for millennia: Everywhere murder; everywhere mass murder!"[73]

Because of the concern at the time of the assassination about
the presence of thousands of foreigners in Germany, the Brown
Shirts had to be restrained. Similarly, other punitive practices
had to be curtailed until Hitler secured complete control over
the country and Germany had established itself as a major power.

Among some of the government officials, the assassination
provided an economic opportunity. The Ministry of Finance,
always short of revenue, advocated a punitive tax against the
Jews. The Ministry of Justice, however, opposed the proposal

because it feared a similar tax would be applied by foreign governments against German residents abroad. Because of that danger of retaliation by other governments, the tax was not enacted, but the idea did not die. Two years later, another assassination of another German would resurrect the tax.

If the Jews were to escape the violence of an SA-directed pogrom and a punitive tax, they were not to be left untouched. Just a small sample of what was coming was introduced. Goebbels applied what was to become his pet tactic against the German Jews whenever he wished to punish them for one thing or another. All Jewish cultural organizations were to cancel cultural activities. For the moment, this was to be the worst punishment to be inflicted for the killing of Wilhelm Gustloff.

Meanwhile, in Switzerland, the Swiss government responded to increasing pressure to restrict the menacing behavior of the Nazi movement. On February 18, the Swiss government banned the National Socialist Party and enforced regulations that limited the political activities of foreign residents. The German government, as had been expected, protested. *Völkischer Beobachter* (The People's Observer), which was Hitler's voice, said,

> The action of the Swiss Federal Council is so contrary to the simplest sense of justice that it is hard to believe. . . .
> There can be no question that the government at Berne has struck at German-Swiss relations in a most painful fashion. If only for reasons of justice the question must be raised whether organizations of Swiss citizens in Germany must not be subjected to the same action that has been taken at Berne.[74]

The protest was just a gesture. As far as Hitler was concerned, Switzerland was low on his agenda for the amassing of power. Another more important issue was developing. Hitler planned, despite the opposition of most of his military advisors, to re-occupy the Rhineland. Under the Versailles Treaty, the region was to be controlled by French troops. Only German police were permitted to operate in the border region.

On March 7, 1936, Hitler announced to the Reichstag that four divisions of German troops were moving into the territory. Already in the Rhineland thousands of other regular army troops, who had been disguised as police, were taking up their positions.

Should the superior French forces have resisted the German reoccupation of the Rhineland, the Third Reich would likely have fallen, and Hitler removed from power. German commanders had been ordered to retreat upon meeting resistance, but the French ignored the invasion. A German bluff had won the bloodless battle and ended the restraints upon the chancellor. On March 29, the German electorate in a national referendum supported the successes of their Führer and gave him the legitimacy to crush more of his opponents.

German remilitarization of the Rhineland was only the first of many steps that made 1936 an important year. A new economic policy was begun to concentrate the industrial foundation of Germany into the source for the development of a massive military force to conquer Europe and beyond. In international relations, Hitler signed agreements with Italy and with Japan to present a united front against potential enemies. Compared to these events, the assassination of Gustloff was too unimportant to be permitted to detour the course of history.

By December, the more important matters had been resolved and Hitler could turn back to the unsettled question of the assassination of Wilhelm Gustloff by the international Jewish conspiracy. The trial of David Frankfurter began on December 9, 1936. There were no longer foreign visitors to bother German propagandists, and the next major events on the National Socialist agenda, the absorption of Austria and seizure of the Sudetenland, were far away. Wilhelm Gustloff had regained his importance to Adolf Hitler, who ceased to dismiss him as an inconvenience. To their immense discomfort, the Swiss had all of Hitler's attention and they dared not ignore his bluster and threats.

20

The Politics of Justice

The murder of a prominent Nazi by a young Jewish student will be sternly reprobated by the entire Jewish people. The crime is as alien to their mentality as it is intensely abhorrent to their feeling; and they will deplore and resent it. If anything, indeed, could add to the severity of their condemnation it would be the realization that the mad act in question was merely an aping of the violence which they have so fervently condemned when directed against one of themselves. Jews do not want to descend to such a level. They know that the right course, in the presence of oppression, is not to degrade themselves by retaliating in kind, and that their appeal is not to the pistol, but to the human conscience and the moral law. No more impressive exemplification of this attitude, in fact, could have been given than the dignity, the patience and consistent restraint with which the German Jews have borne themselves during the last three dreary years of unparalleled provocation and organized repression. We repeat, therefore, that we repudiate and denounce the crime just committed, and which must be laid at the door of one solitary and desperate youth. Let us add that any aggravation of the plight of the German Jews by reason of a misdeed on the part of a single individual who was not even one of their number would only be repaying crime with crime and would rightly shock the sentiment of the civilized world.[75]

Rejection by a broad spectrum of the Jewish community in forms such as this one, from the *Jewish Chronicle*, had less impact upon David Frankfurter than what he heard from his family. Nothing made clearer to him the gravity of his crime more than did the condemnation from his own father. The renunciation from the unyielding rabbi in Croatia reverberated from the stone walls of Frankfurter's cell. Each syllable lashed painful wounds across his conscience. The assassin sent a message to his unforgiving father. "Ask my father, in my name, to forgive me. I have been false to him, his teaching, our faith."[76]

Other men, all strangers, saw the bloody study at Kurpark 3 as a battleground over which to wage the war between National Socialism and human rights. Already, the collision course had been set, and Frankfurter's shots were seen as just the first volley in what was building into a major conflict. From Paris the famous civil rights lawyer, Maitre Vincent de Moro-Giafferi, offered his services. Members of the World Jewish Congress in the United States, South Africa, Switzerland, and France gave moral and financial support.

Outside of the WJC, few Jews supported David Frankfurter. The words of the article from the *Jewish Chronicle* represented the broad opinion of Jewish comment in Europe. In Germany the Central Association of German Jews, the only officially recognized Jewish organization, condemned the killing. "Those who believe they are justified in assassinating their opponents exclude themselves from the society of the human community."[77]

One of the first steps in preparation for Frankfurter's legal defense was the selection of an attorney. Rabbi Messinger's son, a student of law, urged Frankfurter to retain a lawyer without any connection to the Jewish community, in order to prevent the Nazis from turning the case into an anti-Jewish campaign.

When Frankfurter chose a Swiss lawyer, seventy-one-year-old Dr. Eugen Curti from Zurich, the Nazi machine claimed that the selection of a famous non-Jewish civil rights attorney was to mask the Jewish conspirators in the deep shadows. Moro-

Giafferi and the Dutch legal counsel for German emigres in Holland, J. De Vries, joined the defense as advisors.

They were optimistic about the outcome of the trial. By 1936, political assassination had achieved a level of legal legitimacy. Teilirian in Germany, Conradi in Switzerland, and Schwartzbard in France were all confessed killers, all self-proclaimed avengers who had sought a private form of violent justice, and three courts in three countries had upheld their right to kill. So then, his supporters argued, should be David Frankfurter. His cause was no less just than that of his predecessors. Even Article 65 of the Swiss Federal Constitution recognized, by exempting political murder from the category of capital crimes, the right of someone to kill for political cause: "No one may be sentenced to death for a political offense. To be political the crime must justify itself as an effective means for achieving a political end, or must be an item in a general political movement."[78]

Article 65 was unnecessary to protect David Frankfurter from the executioner. Under Article 88 of the criminal code for the canton of Grisons, murder was to be punished by a prison sentence of no less than fifteen years and no more than twenty-five years. Legal minds searched for the means to alter the charge of murder. Article 50 allowed for a killing committed during a time of "high emotion." Section 46 permitted self-defense. "Self-defense can be pleaded by one who has to avert an illegal onslaught on his own or another's life and limb, health, property, liberty, or honor, in circumstances when no adequate appeal to the help of the authorities is possible."[79]

The Germans, too, were considering the possibility that the assassin might be acquitted or given a mild sentence. Any such treatment would be a rebuff of Germany and an international humiliation. Dr. Josef Goebbels, the minister of propaganda and enlightenment, intended to make the courtroom in Chur a stage across which he would parade the faceless Jewish conspirators. If some Jews wanted to distance themselves from the assassination and downgrade the killing to a random act by an individual, the Nazis intended to develop it into a cause to support their programs of destruction of the Jewish community in Germany and beyond. One hundred and twenty German journalists were booked into the Steinbock Hotel to report home the daily developments. Long before the trial began, German newspapers prepared the public for the drama. Soon after Wilhelm Gustloff had been shot, Julius Streicher had set the theme for the propaganda spectacular, and Adolf Hitler could not ignore the course that one of his chief rivals for control of the Nazi movement had begun. As the New York Times noted, "The newspaper Fraenkische Zeitung, published by Julius Streicher, leading anti-Semite, asserted that 'an individual cannot be accused in this murder case. The whole Jewish race must be brought before the court, for Frankfurter acted for his race. . . .' "[80]

The press campaign vilified the Jews in Germany. The papers made it clear that they were to pay for the crime, as if half a million fingers had pulled the trigger of the Browning revolver. In an attempt to avoid arousing the anger of the German public, Jews were instructed by local leaders to cancel or curtail Chanukah celebrations, which were to coincide with the period of the trial.

Goebbels was not content just to have the journalists report the proceedings in Chur. He dispatched the legal counsel for the Ministry of Propaganda, Dr. Friedrich Grimm, to seek standing before the Swiss court in order to represent the interest of Wilhelm and Hedwig Gustloff. Goebbels hoped to direct the course of the events by having a German participate in the trial, but Grimm was refused recognition. Before the trial had even begun, Germany had suffered a public rebuke. In response, German newspapers warned the Swiss not to offend Germany by coddling Frankfurter.

While the issue was given central attention in the German and the Swiss press, the trial was for most of the world of scant importance, because Naziism was still not perceived as a threat to world peace or democracy. Because of their general indifference, Frankfurter's action was meaningless to most of the world population. As a consequence, little more than the outcome of the trial was reported in the international press and then only on the back pages.

Earlier, during the days when Frankfurter had been in the headlines, he had received little sympathy. Much of the press condemned and ridiculed him as just a mentally unbalanced fanatic, while his victim was presented as an educated, dedicated humanitarian, just as German propaganda had intended. What readers in the United States knew of the events were illustrated by the nearly fictionalized story in *Newsweek*.

Wilhelm Gustloff stamped the snow off his boots.

"There is a young man wanting to see you," said his wife. "Dull-looking fellow. . . . Didn't say what he wanted."

Somewhere in the white-clad valley, chimes struck 4. Dr. Gustloff went to his study. Seated at his desk he saw a stranger, a stranger pointing a gun at him.

Little groups returning from runs down the Weissfluh heard shots sharp and clear in the winter air 5,000 feet above the sea.

Dropping skis and sleds, they ran toward an apartment house on the Kurplatz, principal square of Davos.

A stupid-looking young man, clutching a pistol, brushed past them. From within came a woman's screams. . . .

He was born in 1910 at Vincovici, Croatia, son of a rabbi. He had failed to pass medical examinations at Leipzig and Bern. People called him mentally backward.[81]

Ten months later, David Frankfurter was stale news. When the trial began, only a small number of interested persons outside of Switzerland and Germany took notice.

At ten o'clock on the morning of December 9, 1936, the court for the canton of Grisons convened in the cantonal capital, Chur. Five judges in black robes sat. Seventy-one-year-old Justice Rudolf Ganzoni was the president of the court.

Attorney General Friedrich Brugger delivered the opening statement of the trial. He acknowledged the physical and psychological health of the defendant, but dismissed them as unrelated to Frankfurter's actions. "Frankfurter is suffering from both psychological and physical collapse. He is obsessed by persecutions he witnessed in 1933. The death of his mother seemed

to have undermined his desire to live."[82] Then, he disparaged Frankfurter's motivation and reduced him to a vain, self-seeking murderer: "Frankfurter intended to commit murder, not suicide. Therefore, his action was motivated by 'vain glory,' not sacrifice."[83]

The attorney general concluded that the full weight of the
law should fall upon the killer. He demanded eighteen years of
imprisonment at hard labor, loss of civil rights, payment of
compensation to the widow, and expulsion from Switzerland at
the completion of the sentence.

Frau Hedwig Gustloff in the black clothes of a mourning
widow took the stand. She was escorted by officials of the German
Embassy, Charge D'affaires von Bibra and Dr. Kordele, *Ausland
Organisation* representative in Bern. Officers of the SS in the
audience saluted her arrival and departure. On the stand, Mrs.
Gustloff described the events in the house on the evening of
February 4 and pointed out the already confessed assassin. Then
she reviewed the character of her husband.

The widow had become an important instrument of the propaganda campaign. At the funeral, she and Wilhelm Gustloff's
mother posed at the grave side, their arms raised in the Nazi
salute. The pictures of the defiant women were circulated throughout Germany. German propaganda presented David Frankfurter
as a demented pawn of a Jewish conspiracy and of the anti-
German, socialist-dominated Swiss newspapers. Press reports
referred frequently to his sickly appearance and to the physical
manifestations of his mental retardation.

Between the time of his arrest and the commencement of the
trial, David Frankfurter had undergone hours of psychological
evaluation by Dr. J. B. Jorger, a psychiatrist and the director of
the cantonal hospital.

German observers objected to Jorger's testimony as being "too
sympathetic" to the defendant. The psychiatrist had referred to
David's polite manners, a mark of his family upbringing, and
spoke of his intelligence. Jorger submitted a thirty-two-page report to the court and presented his testimony. Of Frankfurter's
health, Jorger explained:

No mental illness has affected the accused's actions.

However, Frankfurter is victim of a "weakly constituted nervous system" which must have influenced the accused through physical illnesses of which there are many.

His depression is the result of both physical and psychological illnesses which prevented him from achieving his life's goals. The force which was driving him to suicide by the end of 1935 became linked with the Jewish problem. Thus, the Jewish problem became secondary to the idea of suicide.

In Jorger's opinion, this prehistory, combined with the basic weakness of Frankfurter's psychological constitution, caused a reduction in his ability to take responsibility for his actions. "Frankfurter's attitude during the examination was always pleasant and correct. Never, at any time, did he refuse to answer questions."[84]

When Jorger reached the subject of suicide, he explained the failure: "That which has just exploded can not explode for the second time."[85] According to the doctor, the act of kiling Gustloff drained Frankfurter of the emotional force to turn the gun upon himself.

The most-awaited testimony was that of the assassin himself. Frankfurter had described for Jorger his deep affection for Switzerland which he sought to defend. He had "killed for the love of Switzerland. He had to kill Gustloff who was spreading pestilence throughout the air."[86]

Dr. Werner Ursprung, the public prosecutor, seized the opportunity to attack the defendant: "Any upright, thinking Swiss would be disgusted and not be appreciative of such shameless, worthless talk! . . . We find our police quite capable of preserving our independence and order."[87]

There was more than courtroom theatrics in the response of the prosecutor. Ursprung had been a friend of Gustloff and the legal advisor for the National Front, of which Gustloff had taken control in 1932. Thus, the Nazi cause had its own spokesman inside the courtroom. That gave the defense reason to worry.

David Frankfurter attributed to *Der Sturmer* the final push that took him to murder. He told the court, "I read *Der Sturmer,* that notorious anti-Semitic German organ, in which there are written things too revolting for any human being to endure whether he be Jew or Gentile."[88]

Late in 1936, the actions of the National Socialist Party added credence to Frankfurter's claim that *Der Sturmer* was more than could be tolerated. The party had bought the pornographic paper for $750,000 to take it out of the hands of Julius Streicher, who had demanded double the money to relinquish the national platform upon which he challenged the leadership of Adolf Hitler.

Defense Counsel Curti fought his case on the ground that Frankfurter had been subjected to a barrage of hatred from the Third Reich, which was openly persecuting the Jewish population. Reports of the persecution were submitted, but they could not be presented as evidence.

Before the trial Curti had sought to have Minister of Justice and Police Johannes Baumann provide Gustloff's dossier to confirm the breadth of his illegal activities, but the Federal Council had refused to release the files to the court and the defense was denied permission to discuss the character of the victim. This took from the defense the strategy of putting Wilhelm Gustloff on trial as Henri Torres had Simon Petliura. As a consequence, Frankfurter's trial had to be fought as a murder case without the political overtones instrumental in the previous trials of Teilirian, Conradi, and Schwartzbard.

At the conclusion of the trial on December 12, Curti delivered his summation. He appealed to the court to grant clemency to the defendant, who the counsel stated had been motivated by hatred of National Socialism. Frankfurter's deed, the lawyer noted to the court, had been made in error and could in no way serve to aid world Jewry.

Through his words Dr. Curti had accepted the terms of the trial that had been set by the court, and had abandoned the righteousness of the killing, which other supporters upheld. His action was seen by supporters as a betrayal of the cause and drove away many who had believed in the case. Emil Ludwig, the Jewish philosopher and writer, withdrew, angered that an effort to appease the court was made by casting aside the principles of justice.

In the end, Frankfurter was orphaned. His father had not forgiven the crime, the broad spectrum of the Jewish community renounced him, former supporters abandoned him, and the general public did not have much interest in his cause. It seemed as though his gun had spoken to a deaf world. What little support he did receive came from the Swiss press, which was aware of the menace on their border.

On December 14, the court reconvened to pronounce its sentence. Attorney General Brugger received everything that he had demanded. The sole sign of mercy from the court was to apply eight of the ten months already served to the overall sentence. President Ganzoni explained the sentence by remarking that the judges had taken into consideration the youth of the assassin and his "previously blameless life."

21

The Davos Cure

After the court rendered its decision and passed sentence upon David Frankfurter, a riddle summarized the general view with the question. "What is the difference between Conradi and Frankfurter?" The answer: "A common border."

During the trial of Conradi, the Swiss government left the prosecution and the defense in the hands of the local courts. Conradi had shot a Soviet diplomat, whose country had no means to retaliate. The Soviet Union had no economic control over Switzerland and could not send troops to the frontier to rattle their sabers.

Germany was a very different matter. Hitler held a large portion of the Swiss foreign investments and German troops were already on the border. In Bern, the Swiss could hear clearly the rattle of Nazi sabers.

Whether pro or con, the Swiss agreed that the trial of David Frankfurter had a strong dose of politics in the decision. This aroused Swiss resentment. In spite of the nearness of their dangerous neighbor, the decision did provoke protest, especially in the press. Critics condemned the lack of an independent judiciary, which was subject to the political interests of the state.

On Herr Hitler's side, the judgment will be celebrated with rallies in praise of Swiss honesty and integrity. Would it be greeted with the same feeling of satisfaction in the land of Wilhelm Tell? We are horrified by the judgment. . . .

Frankfurter will not live through the eighteen years. He is a sick man; he would not want to live. . . .

Worse than the personal side of the matter, which can be mitigated, is the moral victory of National Socialism. . . . The Jews in Germany who are already persecuted and so miserable will hear again Streicher's howl of triumph. And how about Gustloff's followers? They will certainly see in the judgment incitement to redouble their blessed efforts in Switzerland.[89]

On December 21, the International League to Oppose Anti-Semitism held a demonstration in Paris to protest the severity of the sentence. All appeals and demonstrations were ignored by the court and the political authorities. As far as Switzerland was concerned, the Frankfurter Affair was over and better forgotten. To continue to argue about the problem could only arouse more difficulties with bellicose Germany.

The sentence was in reality worse in its appearance than in its application. Once Frankfurter was placed into the jurisdiction of the prison authorities, he could seek exemption from the labor requirements on grounds of health, or he could serve out his term in a sanatorium or hospital. The final decision was for Dr. Jorger to make, and he was inclined to be lenient.

Sennhof, the prison for the canton of Grisons, was located in Chur. It was a modest institution staffed by four guards, a warden, and the warden's wife. She prepared the meals, mended the clothing, and nursed the ill. From seven o'clock in the morning until six o'clock in the evening, the inmates in their brown and white uniforms were free to wander at will within the walls of the prison. Exempted from the sentence of hard labor and freed from the strain of medical studies, the prison was for Frankfurter a sanatorium in which his weak body had an opportunity to strengthen itself. To make his stay a little more comfortable, Axel Anschel, a Jewish butcher from Zurich, kept Frankfurter supplied with kosher meats and chocolate. Others may have forgotten the assassin, but he had a small circle of loyal friends who stood with him.

Prior to Frankfurter's imprisonment, the Germans had expressed their concern that he would be given special treatment. But once he was confined, the Germans showed no interest in the real circumstances of Frankfurter's imprisonment. Like their Swiss counterparts, German authorities were eager to put the subject of Gustloff behind them. Conviction of Frankfurter was presented as a moral victory for National Socialism, and Wilhelm Gustloff had been given his place among the martyrs for the sacred cause. The German press proclaimed its satisfaction with the outcome of the trial. In Switzerland, the newspaper of the National Front proclaimed the decision to be a victory for the cause of National Socialism.

> The justice system did not let either [the] international or [the] domestic Jewish press influence it; the miserably constructed defense made no impression. Now, everything is back in place. The "hero" Emil Ludwig-Cohns of the World Jewry and his Liberal-Marxist vassals are drowning together in a sack. The morally and spiritually inferior being has now disappeared behind the gate of the prison. A real Jewish hero![90]

Once the Frankfurter Affair was resolved, there were for the Germans other matters to consider, such as the reestablishment of the National Socialist Party in Switzerland. On December 17, 1936, von Bibra discussed the matter with an official of the Ministry of Political Affairs, the ministry of Edouard von Steiger, who was sympathetic to National Socialism.

> For reasons of Domestic politics, the Federal Councillor could not at present put through a removal of the ban. On the other hand, he did not wish to worsen relations with Germany by declining the German request. If the question did not have to

be publicly discussed again and if the Landesgruppe were to be directed from the Legation, the Federal Councillor would leave us a completely free hand to expand and direct the Landesgruppe as we wished. Motta, whom I saw for a brief period immediately afterwards, confirmed the view Frolicher [deputy director of Ministry of Political Affairs, Foreign Office] had taken.[91]

The Federal Council was not prepared to revoke the prohibition against the Nazi movement. To have done so would have certainly aroused a general protest, but the Swiss government was equally unwilling to provoke the Germans. Their solution, therefore, was to instruct the Germans in how to violate Swiss law. If later the public was to learn that the Germans were exceeding their authority, then the Federal Council could feign outrage and demand German compliance with Swiss law. U.S. Ambassador to Germany William Dodd explained Swiss eagerness to accommodate their powerful neighbor. "Fear of Hitler is the cause of this, government feeling that to do otherwise might cause aggressive German action."[92]

During February 1937, von Bibra was made, unofficially of course, the Landesgruppenleiter for the district of Switzerland. As agreed, the Swiss did not notice. Von Bibra had powers Wilhelm Gustloff would have envied. While Gustloff operated through Ausland Organisation as a representative of the National Socialist Party, his successor's office had been combined with the powers of a state official. The new Landesgruppenleiter did not appeal to Germans to join the party. He commanded. He held the weapons to enforce his edicts. Thousands obeyed. If they did not join the Nazi Party and serve the Führer, their passports could be cancelled, their citizenship could be revoked, and relatives in Germany could be harassed.

Heinrich Rothmund of the Fremden Polizei wanted the expatriate Germans to comply with the dictates of the Landesgruppenleiter. He feared that if they lost their freedom to travel, then he would not be able to deport them whenever it suited his purposes, because as stateless persons no country would be obligated to receive them and Switzerland would have to hand over a group of people who were a potential source of trouble. "Switzerland has no interest in increasing the number of stateless people. Therefore, we should encourage the Germans in Switzerland to submit to the pressure and join the Party."[93] It made little difference to the police official that he was contributing to the violation of Swiss law. In his thinking and in the thinking of other Swiss leaders, political considerations took precedence. Nothing was sacred as long as it served what was called "the national security."

During the one-year presidency of Wilhelm Gustloff's friend, Johannes Baumann, in 1938, Heinrich Rothmund was sent as the Swiss representative to the Evian Refugee Conference, convened by President Franklin Roosevelt to discuss the problem of Jewish refugees. The issue had been made critical by the expulsion of fifty thousand Jews from Austria after Hitler's native land had been incorporated into Germany.

President Baumann would have had difficulty finding a less sympathetic man to send. During a conversation between Rothmund and Georgine Gerhard of the Relief Agency for Emigrant Children, a private organization in Basel, Switzerland, Rothmund told her, "If I had a check in my pocket for a hundred thousand francs from the Federal Council for your relief activities, I would keep that check in my pocket."[94] This statement demonstrated the depth of his concern, a view that he did not attempt to conceal. By leaving him in a position of authority, the Swiss government was assured that anti-Jewish policies would be implemented in fact and save the political leaders the need to expose themselves to condemnation by putting into visible law the codes to achieve what was being performed for them by their willing servant and his private force, the Fremden Polizei.

The Swiss government managed the refugee problem by establishing concentration camps run by the Ministry of Police and Justice. When the camps were criticized as harsh and substandard, Baumann responded.

Emigrants whose moral characters are not under major attack are interned in Witzwil or Bellechasse. They are subjected to a special discipline, of course go out to work together with the other inmates of the institution, and receive normal prison food; but in their leisure time and at night they are allowed to be together. They also enjoy certain privileges—for example, in entertainment, reading matter, mail, etc. . . . Naturally their internment is not made a matter of criminal record.[95]

Baumann preferred to halt the refugees at their source. Negotiations with Germany considered a variety of controls to prevent Jews from reaching the border. Finally, Rothmund devised the simple plan of having a "J" imprinted in Jewish passports. The mark closed borders worldwide to the Jews and assured their eventual extermination in the death camps, but that was of scant importance to Heinrich Rothmund. His job was to prevent them from entering Switzerland and he did accomplish that.

At the end of the war, when Switzerland was condemned for its refugee policies, Heinrich Rothmund took the full brunt of the attack. Whatever regulations had been applied to prevent Jewish refugees from seeking asylum in Switzerland or safe passage through it were created by the *Fremden Polizei*. Most orders had been given over his signature.

At the time, David Frankfurter was to the Swiss just a problem to be eliminated and that was achieved by imprisoning him and allowing the Germans to violate Swiss law. Jewish refugees, too, were just a problem to be eliminated by altering their passports. What was important was that the nation maintain its independence, even if that meant adopting many of the characteristics that made Nazi-controlled Germany a dangerous enemy.

By the spring of 1937, David Frankfurter had passed from public attention. Events elsewhere soon erased his importance, but Frankfurter's memory needed to be revived briefly late in 1938, when Ernst von Rath, a minor German diplomat in Paris, was assassinated by Herschel Grynszpan, another Jew.

Faced with a second attack by a Jew, Nazi authorities feared a widespread Jewish uprising. Suddenly, two years after the Gustloff assassination, Adolf Hitler was no longer satisfied that the international Jewish conspirators who were behind the killing of Wilhelm Gustloff had not been captured and brought to trial. The National Socialist machine had a ruthless and persistent memory. If Adolf Hitler was dissatisfied with the outcome of the Frankfurter case, eventually he was to have his revenge.

When the German Army invaded Croatia, the special SS units carried lists of enemies to be found and destroyed. On their lists they had the members of the Frankfurter family in Vinkovci. On Palm Sunday, April 6, 1941, SS troopers remembered David Frankfurter's father, Mortiz Frankfurter, who had denounced David's act of violence. He was captured, stood on a table on public display, and tortured. His beard was removed hair by hair. Then, the SS and their Croatian Ustashi allies embarked on a campaign of slaughter. Jews and Eastern Orthodox Catholics were murdered. Of the eighty thousand Jewish residents of Yugoslavia at the outbreak of the war, only twelve thousand survived.

In a Swiss prison Frankfurter watched the fortunes of war shift from the brief years of German glory to total defeat. Unburdened by the pressures of the world, his body grew stronger. A healthier man walked out of prison in 1945 than had entered Sennhof nine years earlier. No one protested his early release. A defeated Germany and Hitler's ghost did not frighten the Swiss. Regardless, the last of the sentence was imposed; Frankfurter was deported and banned for life from Switzerland.

Frankfurter turned toward Palestine. When the state of Israel was created, he became an employee of the Ministry of Defense and wrote the memoirs of his meeting with Wilhelm Gustloff, *Nakam* (Revenge).

Late in life, he married and fathered two children. In 1969, Switzerland cancelled the banning order to permit Frankfurter a visit to the land for which he retained fond memories. A 1976 Swiss film, *Confrontation, the Assassination in Davos*, recalled the evening in Davos when Jew met Nazi. On July 19, 1982, at the age of seventy-three years, David Frankfurter died of natural causes. For a Jew who had lived through the years of the Third Reich, it was a rare achievement.

Part Three

A Taste of Jews

22

The Eastern Jewish Question

During his brief life, Andrei Yushchinsky achieved nothing that would have given him a place in history. To make his mark, he had to be murdered. Even then, in spite of the cruelty of his death, it was not such an important crime that it would have been recorded in history.

On March 20, 1911, the battered corpse of the twelve-year-old was found in a cave on the outskirts of Kiev. As far as the local police were concerned, the murder was an open and shut case. Andrei Yushchinsky was a youthful member of a group of gangsters. During a feud with a rival gang, the boy was killed. Police sought a warrant for the arrest of the prime suspect, Vera Cheberiak. If everything had followed the routine procedure, the public prosecutor would have issued the arrest warrant, the criminal, a woman, would have been brought to trial, and the matter settled. There would have been nothing of importance to make the murder a footnote to history.

But the case of Andrei Yushchinsky did not follow procedure, because this was the age of the pogrom, which had begun with the assassination of Czar Alexander II. Over the previous thirty years Ochrana (the Russian secret police) and the Black Hundred, a right-wing extremist organization, had encouraged anti-Jewish violence. Pogroms were used as Roman Emperors had once employed the circus and the persecution of Christians, to distract public attention from corruption and oppression. Andrei Yushchinsky was to be one more burning coal in the furnace of violence.

The director of Ochrana in Kiev approached the public prosecutor, I. G. Shcheglovitov. The official was urged to ignore the police evidence and to permit Ochrana to provide another set of facts that would suit the purposes of the secret police and the extremist members of the Black Hundred. For Shcheglovitov, it was not a difficult decision. He was known as an active anti-Semite. Vera Cheberiak was to be allowed to escape prosecution to permit Ochrana to arouse the public with the blood ritual case of Menachem Beilis. The idea was to stir stories of Jewish blood rituals that had long circulated among the general public. According to the tales, Jews murdered Christian children to use their blood in secret religious practices.

Ochrana found a lamplighter who was prepared to testify that he had observed Menachem Beilis, the foreman of the kiln in a brick yard, kidnap the youngster while the innocent child was playing in the yard. Then, the Ochrana circulated the story of the blood ritual to ignite smoldering anti-Semitism.

Underlying the discontent was the conversion of the vast agricultural estates to the production of cash crops. The change was filling the cities with hundreds of thousands of dislocated, disgruntled peasants. For the Black Hundred and Ochrana, the growing unrest in the Ukraine had to have an outlet. Menahem Beilis fitted their purposes.

The Beilis case sent shock waves across the Russian Empire as far as the town of Radomsk in the Polish provinces, where Sendel and Rifka Grynszpan were caught up by the fear of another pogrom. In April 1911, along with many of their family members, they took to the road and headed westward, away from the immediate danger. The couple had nothing to hold them. They had been married for just one year and did not have children to slow their flight or property to lose.

Two years later, to the surprise of everyone, the court acquitted

Menachem Beilis of the obviously false charges, but that no longer mattered. By the time the court had rendered its decision, thousands of lives had been disrupted. The Grynszpan family, which had already reached its destination, would not return willingly to Poland.

Before Sendel and Rifka Grynszpan had been born, the road westward had been well trodden. A mass migration of Eastern European Jews had begun in 1881, driven by the violence of the pogroms throughout imperial Russia. As their numbers swelled into a swarm, they aroused among Western Europeans the fear that they were going to be drowned beneath the hordes of Jewish foreigners.

On their way across Europe many passed through Germany. The Germans, especially, were concerned with the "Eastern Jewish Question." These strangers, these *Schnorrers* (peddlars), were seen to carry in their genes the virulent cultural virus that enabled them in a generation to adopt their new culture in order to subvert it from within. In a generation they were expected to undergo the transformation from beggars and trouser peddlers to masters of the culture, economy, and politics of their new land. Newspaper cartoons played upon the popular anxiety with vivid portrayals of the transformation from impoverished peddler to sophisticated wealthy financier.

In spite of the imagined danger from their presence, Germans were pleased to see the Eastern Jews, just as long as they passed through Germany and did not attempt to remain. They were good business. They bought food and other necessities, they stayed in hotels, and they booked rail and ship passage. The German American Line, which operated ships between Hamburg and the United States, carried by 1910 seven hundred thousand refugees away from Europe to America. When the Austrian Empire closed its frontiers to the fleeing Jews, Germany held hers open, urged to do so by businessmen eager to reap the benefits of the persecution in the East.

To assure themselves that these foreigners did keep moving out of Europe, or at least out of Germany, the Germans issued

them very few residency permits, a mere seventy thousand by
1910. These few recipients of the permits were condemned from
the outset. The existing German Jews, who had sought safety
from the general hostility by assimilating to the point of disappearance, feared the arrival of their coreligionists, who looked
and behaved differently and brought with them the means to
stir the disease of prejudice.

Although Jews in Germany had achieved positions of prom-
inence in many areas of the society, there remained an awareness
of an earlier time, when the mobs looted and murdered. At any
time it could happen again, and the Eastern Jews made the lurking
danger a clear and present threat. Jewish groups gave financial
aid to their coreligionists, but that was the extent of their brotherly
embrace. Keeping a good distance from the strangers seemed to
many to be the prudent course to follow.

Sendel and Rifka Grynszpan were among the few to receive
the scarce residency permits. They settled in Hanover, where
Sendel opened a tailor business. Other family members scattered
across Europe to establish themselves in other parts of Germany,
in Belgium, and in France. Sendel Grynszpan was the stereotype
of the *Schnorrer,* the trouser peddler who had the powers to
seize control of the country, except that Sendel was scarcely able
to feed his growing family. For a time, he had escaped the violence
that had been ignited by the bombs of Narodnaya Volya, but
the greatest pogrom of all time was coming. From it there would
be no escape.

23

Perpetual Strangers

By the time of the birth of Herschel Feibel on March 28, 1921, childbirth had become for Rifka Grynszpan a painful, seemingly unavoidable routine. Herschel was her sixth child in ten years, and he would be followed by two others. But the Grynszpan family would never experience the happy event when Sendel and Rifka would preside over a gathering of their eight children and numerous grandchildren to celebrate their family bonds and to salute the parade of the generations. Of their eight children, Berta, the fourth, Marcus, the fifth, and Herschel were the only ones to survive to adulthood. The other five died at birth or during their early years.

Powerless and impoverished, the Grynszpan family was forced to ride the waves of the time as though they were flotsam on a turbulent sea. On the day of Herschel's birth at Burgstrasse 36, in the Jewish quarter of Hanover, chaos was the way of the world around them. Four years of bloody warfare had given way to turmoil and uncertainty. The currency was collapsing, erasing the wealth of millions of Germans; the newly born Weimar Republic was stumbling from crisis to disaster.

Across Germany, fear of a Communist revolution aroused the extreme right. Communist-led uprisings in the Ruhr in April 1920 and in Hamburg in October 1923 strengthened the extreme right in the *Freikorps,* a forerunner of the Brown Shirts that would eventually carry Hitler into power.

Although Sendel Grynszpan took no interest in politics, he could not escape the consequences of his Jewishness. The assassination in June 1922 of Foreign Minister Walther Rathenau was an important signpost on the road to the coming pogrom that would overshadow anything that had ever occurred previously in Jewish history.

In April 1922, Foreign Minister Rathenau concluded the Rapallo Treaty with the struggling Soviet Union. Both Germany and the Soviet Union were seeking trade outlets for their goods and diplomatic legitimacy. Already the extreme nationalists accepted the view that the Communist menace was directed by Jews. Rathenau was a Jew, and he had concluded an agreement with the only Communist government. The linkage between Judaism and Communism was as clear as anyone needed.

In the midst of the turmoil, the only thing that Sendel and Rifka Grynszpan could bequeath to their children was the burden of their heritage. They were Jews. Far worse than that, they were Eastern European Jews, branded by German society as greedy, grasping *Schnorrers* (peddlers), and shunned by the assimilated Jews as a potential source of trouble. Although the Grynszpan children had been born in Germany, they were from the moment of birth de facto and de jure foreigners with Polish citizenship and without the possibility of becoming naturalized Germans. If the boys, when they grew to adulthood, married Germans— Jews or Gentiles—their wives, too, would be branded undesirables and stripped of their citizenship and rights. Like the other Eastern Jews, they were damned for being different and denied the opportunity to become the same.

By the time of Herschel's birth, the Grynszpan family had lived for ten years in the Jewish quarter of Hanover in northern Germany. In spite of their efforts, they had not made much economic progress. During his childhood, Herschel's parents were able to shelter him from the brutal realities of their situation, until he entered school, where Herschel learned from students and teachers the unforgiving way of his world. Among the crucial lessons was the fact that he was a despised minority within a persecuted minority. Equally degrading, he was among the poorest in society and without the prospects of rising above his low place. Without money or the likelihood of acquiring it, Herschel could buy neither respect nor the means to escape persecution.

From the beginning Herschel was a troublesome child and a difficult student. His teachers believed that he had the potential to achieve much more than he did. Always standing in the way of the vital self-discipline of the successful student was Herschel's hair-trigger temper, which made the undersized youth into a dangerous time bomb. His Jewish friends—he had only Jewish friends—were cautious around him, aware of his violent temper and the quickness of his hands to strike, which prompted them to give him the nickname "Judas Maccabaeus," in memory of the Jewish rebel who revolted against the Roman masters.

At the time, when Herschel entered the municipal school, his father was still managing to keep the family clothed and fed. Somehow, Sendel Grynszpan had survived the shortages of the war years and he continued to maintain his family through the galloping inflation of the early 1920s. The Wall Street crash in October 1929 and the subsequent worldwide depression finally proved to be too severe for him to survive, and he closed his business. The family sank to an even deeper level of hardship. Sendel became a used clothing peddler who depended upon welfare supplements to keep his family alive. Their new misery lingered into 1934, when Adolf Hitler rescued the Grynszpan family from their economic hardships.

Soon after Hitler came to power, his new regime imposed a harsh stability upon the nation. For a brief time, there was a flurry of economic revival that permitted Sendel Grynszpan to reopen his business. In spite of anti-Semitism, Sendel's resurrected shop prospered, giving to the Grynszpan family an unfamiliar taste of the good life. It had taken Sendel a quarter of a century to rise above stark poverty, and his success ironically came at a time when Jews were facing a new pogrom.

It was during these years of unfamiliar prosperity that Herschel reached his thirteenth birthday and had his bar mitzvah. One of his first acts as he approached manhood was to join the youth arm of the Mizrahi movement. The organization had been founded in 1902 in response to the upsurge of pogroms in Eastern Europe. As a result of the violence, Eastern Jewish refugees in Western Europe saw more clearly than ever the need to reestablish a Jewish state, and Mizrahi envisaged a state that blended orthodox Judaism with nationalism. The movement spread quickly, especially among the alienated Eastern European Jews who tended to be conservative in their politics and orthodox in their religion.

Alienated from the mainstream of Germanic and Germanized Jewish culture, Herschel had concluded that his future lay in Palestine, where Mizrahi maintained a training center. At the center teenage pioneers were given instruction and assistance until they were able to manage for themselves. Herschel's hope for a new life in Israel was a vision that was capturing a growing number of Jews in Germany. After the violence in Eastern Europe and the underlying anti-Semitism of Western Europe, they had begun to abandon all hope that Europe would ever accept them for what they were.

A steady flow of Jews was leaving the continent for other parts of the world. Forty percent of the emigrants from Germany turned toward the harsh land of their ancestors. Between the census of 1925 and the violence of *Kristallnacht* on November 10, 1938, emigration accounted for a large portion of the decline in Germany's Jewish population, from 535,000 to 400,000. Because of the low birth rate and assimilation—27 percent of Jews were marrying Gentiles—the departing people were not replaced. If Hitler had had a little patience, his policy of a Germany free of Jews would have come to pass through a natural process and the "Jewish Question" would have been answered to everybody's satisfaction.

Establishing a Jewish population in Palestine was viewed by Zionists as a crucial step toward the creation of the resurrected Israel, despite the fact that the British had reneged upon the

Balfour Declaration of 1917, in which it had promised the formation of a Jewish state in exchange for Jewish support against the Ottoman Empire. In spite of the broken promise, Zionists were confident that their time would come, and they proceeded on that premise.

For an adult with $4,000 in capital or an essential skill, the road to Palestine was open. The British administration did not close the door until 1939, when Arab pressure threatened unrest in the territory. Before the Arabs forced the British to end immigration into Palestine, the British administration gave credit to the immigrants for the stimulation of the otherwise stagnant economy. There was a real estate boom in Tel Aviv and a surplus of physicians and other professionals. The foundation of a highly educated, culturally sophisticated, Western-type society was being constructed.

For youths going without their parents and without money, there were several organizations that provided sponsorship. Youth Aliyah, Mizrahi, Hechaluz, and others kept a steady flow of young men and women moving to the ancient homeland. Usually, the move required the young pioneers to undergo a preliminary training period in Europe. Jewish organizations funded the preparation.

By May 1935, Herschel, the youthful pioneer, was ready to begin his journey to Palestine to begin building the new Israel. Set upon the course of his life, Herschel left the public school in which he had learned little. His first necessary step was to go for a year of language and religious instructions at Yashiva Breuer in Frankfurt-am-Main. The school had been founded in 1890 to teach the principles of religious orthodoxy in an effort to counter the secularism of the assimilated German Jews. Frankfurt had become a center for the cultural renaissance of German Jews and the heart of the Zionist movement in Germany.

Herschel's year of training ended in April 1936. Fifteen years old, the age at which many of the young pioneers were making the trip to Palestine, Herschel returned to his prospering family in Hanover, where his older brother, Marcus, had just begun his apprenticeship with a plumber. To an observer of events, Herschel's preparation to go to Palestine had come just in time. Less than a year earlier Germany had passed the Nuremberg Laws, which stripped Jews of their rights. At the Committee for Refugees at the League of Nations the Jewish Agency for Palestine stated that there was no longer any reason for a Jew to remain in Germany. Nobody could have agreed more than Herschel.

As far as Sendel Grynszpan could see, nothing had changed. He had never had any rights to lose. Whether oppressed by the May Laws, the Nuremberg Laws, "the Jewish Question," or some other instrument of persecution, he still had to deal with the more important question of how to put a roof over his family's heads and food in their mouths.

Before Adolf Hitler had come to power and for the months shortly afterward, there seemed to be a return of the pogroms, from which Sendel had fled more than two decades earlier. Once again, he saw a rush of terrified refugees who sought safety elsewhere. It was all very familiar, but then the terror ebbed and the panic eased. Many of the frightened even returned to resume their disrupted lives. By the time Herschel returned from Frankfurt, the situation had stabilized.

A Jew with a sense of history could reach into his collective cultural memory to find that periods of public outbursts against the Jewish people were usually followed by a time when the madness subsided into a familiar, endurable contempt. If history repeated itself, and there was no reason to imagine that it would not, then Hitler, too, would have his moment and pass. As far as Sendel could see, Palestine was too severe a cure for what was surely a temporary ailment. Instead of escaping to far-off Palestine, Sendel expected Herschel to follow his brother into an apprenticeship, which would eventually bring money into the house. For Sendel, time and the first taste of a better life blurred the distant memory of Menachem Beilis and the ritual murders that had forced him to flee from his home in Poland.

Whatever his father thought, Herschel found no reason to remain in Germany, and he expected his parent to release him to seek his future. As a minor, though, Herschel could not act without the parental signature, but Sendel, as stubborn as his volatile son, refused to agree. Unable to persuade his father, explosive Herschel and his immovable parent were like a match and a stone. Every contact between the two in their apartment ignited another outburst of temper.

The youthful rebel had acquired one means to escape the clutches of his father, however. Shortly after he began his course at Yashiva Breuer, he had obtained his Polish passport as the first step to the move to Palestine. Once Herschel realized that he would never be able to move his father to sign the papers for his emigration, he used his passport to leave home. First, Herschel obtained from the Hanover police a reentry permit, which was necessary before he could acquire a tourist visa to Belgium. Next he began visits to his relatives to find an alternative to life with his parents.

Uncle Isaak in Essen gave his nephew a few weeks of family hospitality, but no permanent home. Uncle Wolf in Brussels was less agreeable. He did not want to be burdened with a penniless nephew with family problems. Next door to Uncle Wolf was Zaslawsky, a cousin. He was more hospitable than Uncle Wolf, but the hospitality had a time limit. In short order, the unhappy teenager would have to make arrangements to live elsewhere. Herschel's last hope was in Paris, where he had several paternal and maternal relatives. When a desperate appeal was made to Uncle Abraham and Aunt Clara, the reply was an enthusiastic welcome. The childless couple owned a confectionery shop in the French capital and were enjoying a modest success that they were willing to share. If Sendel and Herschel accepted the arrangement, then they were prepared to adopt their unhappy nephew. Sendel agreed to allow his rebellious son to live in Paris for as long as Abraham would keep him. If Herschel followed his usual pattern, that would not be for too long. An eruption of the famous temper was almost guaranteed. For Herschel, the gods of good fortune were smiling. Even the currents of history were flowing in his direction.

24

The Paper Prison

While Herschel prepared for his adventure in a new land, across the nearby frontier in France the Third Republic had just experienced another change in government. At the head of the Popular Front government was Leon Blum. He was a contradiction of the times—a Jewish prime minister when anti-Semitism was flourishing and a social democrat when totalitarian solutions were in favor.

After the Wall Street crash in 1929, most of Europe collapsed rapidly into an economic depression with social unrest and political instability. France, however, sank steadily, like a leaking rotting ship, into the economic muck. It was a gradual decline that seemed to have no end and left no hope that the future would be better. Blum put into effect a package of measures to revive the economy and to put back to work the four hundred thousand unemployed. As a part of his program he instituted the forty-hour work week and paid vacations in order to improve the conditions of life and create new jobs. He raised production costs at a time when prices were falling. That contributed to a decline in exports and a rise in imports. Blum's policy antagonized the industrialists. Next, Blum nationalized the defense industry in an effort to take the profits out of war. His defense production policy came into effect just as France had begun to rearm in order to counter the threat from Germany. Under the new system of nationalized industry, arms production fell. That added the nationalists to the growing number of groups hostile to his administration.

Blum had a nation with three million foreign refugees. Seven hundred thousand were Italians who had escaped from Mussolini. Forty thousand were Jews who had fled from Hitler. Still, "foreign refugee" became a buzz word for Jew. Anti-Semitism became xenophobia. Blum introduced measures to help the unwanted aliens. This last act antagonized most of the people of France.

It was during this brief flirtation with liberalism, a throwback to the unusual 1920s, when Herschel arrived at the French frontier. In mid-September, Madame Rosenthal, the cousin of Zaslawsky's sister, traveled to Brussels from Paris for a brief visit and to collect her special baggage, Herschel Feibel Grynszpan. The boy did not have the necessary documents to enter France. A lack of documents, though, was a minor problem that could be easily overcome. If Herschel had applied at the French embassy for a visa, it might have taken months of waiting, especially if the visa office had concluded that Herschel intended to remain illegally in France. In spite of the liberal policies of the short-lived Blum administration, the bureaucrats, accustomed to the transitory nature of their political leaders, were able to ignore the brief flirtation with liberalism and to function inside their maze of rules and regulations. To counter the inertia of the bureaucrats, other methods were developed by refugees to slip through the paper barriers.

Madame Rosenthal was Herschel's guide through the political maze. She took the teenager on the train to the Belgian frontier town of Quievrain. There he left the train and was aided by railway workers to cross unnoticed through the porous border into France as thousands of others had done before him. Once inside France, Herschel went into hiding, until Uncle Abraham was certain that authorities were not searching for him as a border jumper. At the end of September, the teenager emerged from his seclusion to begin the process of converting his illegal status into a legal residency.

Herschel had advantages which gave him better prospects than most border jumpers in search of a legal status. Despite the instability of the revolving door French government and the economy with four hundred thousand unemployed, the French Republic was a land of tranquillity on a continent of turmoil. The exaggerated French reputation as a haven for the persecuted drew three million refugees. They fled the oppression of Mussolini in Italy, the dictatorship of Salazar in Portugal, the civil war between the Republicans and Fascists in Spain, the purges in the Soviet Union, the pogroms in Poland, and the violent persecutions in Germany. Not all of them bothered with the legal niceties necessary to enter France. Regardless, the French government did not consider illegal entry to be a serious crime. After a few formalities, anyone without too stained a record could manage to get at least a temporary residency.

Uncle Abraham took his illegal nephew to the Central Committee for the Assistance of Jewish Emigres to begin the conversion from border jumper to resident. The Central Committee had performed the process numerous times. As compared to many of their clients, Herschel was one of the easier cases. He did not have a criminal or political history to mar his record, and he had a qualified sponsor. Next, Uncle Abraham took him to the police, to obtain an identity card. To appease the law, a 100-franc fine for illegal entry had to be paid. The formalities completed, Uncle Abraham signed a guarantee to support Herschel, and the teenager was free. It was all very routine and simple.

Abraham and Clara showered upon their nephew the attention they would have shown their own child, if they had been blessed with one. Pleased to have him, they demanded very little from him and were not disappointed when he gave little in return. Occasionally, he ran a few errands for his uncle, but usually he was too busy enjoying his new adventure in the excitement of Paris, where there was a bright, strange world to be explored. The shackles of years of poverty in Hanover and religious orthodoxy dissolved in the Paris lights. In very short order, Herschel underwent a complete transformation from Zionist pioneer in search of his ancient identity to teenage Paris bon vivant with money in his pocket and plenty of time to spend it. Each day, there were tours to the wine country of the Loire Valley or boat trips along the Seine. After excursions with groups of other Jewish youths, he went to dances at Aurore Sportsman's Club and for snacks and drinks at Tout Va Bien Restaurant.

Herschel soon forgot his family in Hanover. Their lives were occupied with drudgery and self-denial. In Paris, self-indulgence was the way of the world, a world into which he found he fitted comfortably. While he immersed himself in his new pleasures, the paperwork at the Central Committee was moving slowly through the usual bureaucratic channels. At the end of January 1937, nearly four months after he had filed for his residency, the Central Committee submitted the application to the Ministry of the Interior, which responded two weeks later. Herschel received a residency permit for eighteen months. That gave to him enough time to explore ways to convert a temporary residency into a permanent status.

Everything seemed to be going in his direction. Herschel had papers that made him legal in four countries. He had a legal status that many desperate refugees would have envied: a valid passport that entitled him to travel, a residency permit that allowed him to remain in France, a reentry permit and residency permit that made it possible for him to return to his family in Germany, and a tourist visa that permitted him to return to Belgium. Not until the end of May 1937, was there any reason for Herschel to begin to worry.

Herschel's Polish passport was due to expire on June 3, 1937. Shortly before the expiration date, he reported to the Polish Embassy that he had lost the document and requested a replacement. A new passport was issued in August, but the replacement was valid for only six months. With the loss of his original passport, his tourist visa to Belgium was gone. One country had been struck from his lands of possible refuge.

Herschel's next critical change occurred in October, when his German reentry and residence permits expired. That struck Germany from the list of countries he could go to. Herschel was now legal in France, and in Poland, which did not want him and where he had never been.

Then Herschel's Polish passport expired at the end of February 1938. Without a valid passport, Herschel was stateless. One year after Herschel had received his eighteen-month residency permit, it was his only valid document. That put him at the mercy of the French bureaucracy, which had little mercy to give. Blum's Popular Front government was gone, taking with it any sympathy for Jewish refugees. The leader of the new administration described the condition of the country as "saturated." France would not absorb any more of the fleeing. While Herschel was dancing to the rhythm of the tango, he was sinking into a legal quagmire.

If Herschel had been able to turn back the calendar to the days of Samuel Schwartzbard, then it would have been a different world. During the years after World War I, when Samuel Schwartzbard touched the conscience of the nation, France experienced a flirtation with an unfamiliar liberalism. She invited foreigners to replace the one and a half million Frenchmen who had died on the battlefields. French women alone could not accomplish the task of rebuilding the nation. In 1927, the foreigners were seen to be the salvation of the republic. Just ten brief years later, they were thought to be its doom.

France had changed. The prosperity of the exciting 1920s had been supplanted by the despair of the decaying 1930s. Foreigners were accused of taking French jobs, dominating the economy, polluting the culture. Foreigners were told to go back home, and many did. The guest workers of the time, Arabs from Algeria, blacks from Senegal, and Asians from Indochina, took the hint and left, but the Jews from Germany did not have the option to go. They were forced to stay and to face the growing hatred of the French public.

Hitler read correctly the mood of the time in France and elsewhere. The Führer declared that the tears shed for the plight of the Jews were tears of hypocrisy. In March 1938, he implemented a program that proved his claim.

Anschluss (the unification of Germany and Austria) had just been completed. Adolf Hitler sent German soldiers into Austria to incorporate his old homeland into his new *Vaterland*. Soon afterwards, he sent his fellow Austrian Adolf Eichmann to rid Austria of some of her 180,000 Jews. Eichmann was the Nazi whip who would drive an unwanted horde at the nations of Europe, to give to them just a small taste of what was to come. If anything were certain to ignite the anti-Semitism, which Hitler believed permeated every European nation, then this wave of homeless, impoverished Jews would.

Across Europe and beyond in North America, the receiving countries slammed shut their frontiers and appealed to Germany to expel the Jews in a more orderly fashion. President Roosevelt called for the Evian Conference, to be held in June 1938, to establish an orderly system of migration. North America and Europe wanted to solve the problem without dealing with it. Among the ideas discussed, a favored view was to create a new Jewish homeland on the French-controlled African island of Madagascar.

Hitler had proved his point. If just 50,000 Jews from Austria could evoke such panic, he held in reserve the 500,000 Jews of Germany and Austria.

In France, there was little doubt who would receive the brunt of the tidal wave of the desperate. Under those conditions, French xenophobia was an easy well to tap. *L'Action Française, La Croix de Feu*, and numerous other right-wing extremist groups clamored to keep out the newcomers and to drive out those already in the country. The old anti-Semitism, which had sent Dreyfus to Devil's Island, was alive and flourishing. As far back as the late 1920s, the National Socialist Party, before it had seized control of Germany, had already an active movement in France. Hitler's ideas grew well in the rich fields of French bigotry. Oblivious to all of the changes around him, Herschel Grynszpan was still dancing to the rhythm of the tango.

The significance of the German strategy of threatening Europe with waves of desperate Jews had a special impact in Poland, where anti-Jewish pogroms were worse than those in Germany.

Forty thousand of the Jews who were being driven out of Austria were Polish citizens. Seventy thousand of Germany's Jews carried Polish passports. If Germany followed through with her threat to give the world a second taste of Jews, then Poland would be forced to accept the return of her own unwanted people. On March 31, 1938, the Polish government announced that any Polish citizen who had lived outside of Poland for five years or longer would lose his citizenship, unless he returned by October 29, 1938, which the Poles knew would be impossible for the great majority of expatriate Polish Jews. Cunningly, the Poles imagined that they had turned back upon the Germans their own practice of denying German citizenship to Eastern European Jews. The Polish action alerted the Germans to a potential problem. After October 29, 1938, about 110,000 people (many did not actually have Polish passports yet), including Herschel's family, would be rendered stateless. As a stateless people, there would not be any country with the obligation to receive them. As a result of the loss of citizenship, Germany would be stuck with the unwanted Jews of Poland.

While Poland and Germany engaged in their diplomatic fencing match over the lives of 110,000 expatriate Jewish Poles, Herschel's own legal status continued to deteriorate. But none of these diplomatic or personal events altered Herschel's carefree life, until the last legal blow fell upon him. In August, his eighteen-month residency permit expired. A ministerial order instructed him to leave French soil by August 15, 1938. Instead, he went into hiding in the servants' quarter on the fifth floor at 8 Rue Martel.

Upon the expiration of the residency permit, Herschel's last legal claim to live anywhere on earth had gone. He was a teenager without a country or any rights. For whatever it was worth, his one compensation was that France could not deport him, because no other country was obligated to admit him. France, therefore, was stuck with her unwanted visitor.

Under Blum that might not have been a serious problem, but history had changed. The sympathetic government had been replaced by an administration hostile toward Jewish refugees. Under the new Daladier administration that could mean detention in one of the new internment camps, which the Third Republic was building to solve the refugee problem.

Having issued the order for Herschel to leave France, the authorities showed no more interest in the teenage refugee. Once that became clear, Herschel left his place of hiding and returned to his amusements in the thick of Paris life. Once again he ignored the current of history that was sweeping him toward unknown perils. As the Polish deadline approached, the government in Warsaw took a further step to assure that the maximum number of expatriate Jewish Poles would lose their citizenship. On October 6, the government announced that by October 29, 1938, Polish passports had to be validated in Poland.

In Berlin the real objective of the Polish strategy was understood. The German government decided to act. Among the victims of the German response to the Poles was the Grynszpan family in Hanover. In 1911, at the time of Sendel and Rifka's departure from Radomsk, a town between Krakow and Warsaw, their home territory was ethnically Polish but politically Russian. The collapse of the Russian, Austrian, and German empires led to the creation of several new nations. Poland was one of those new states cut out of the pieces of the old empires. Radomsk became Polish. Sendel Grynszpan could have retained his old Russian citizenship or adopted the new Polish flag. He chose Poland. It was the wrong flag; the time now arrived to pay for the error of twenty years earlier. On the evening of October 27, 1938, the Polish Jews were taken from their homes to be deported.

At the Adolf Eichmann trial in Israel in 1961, Sendel Grynszpan was called as a surprise witness.

> We didn't know anything. That day, it was Thursday evening, a policeman came and told us to go to Police Zone 11 with our passports. He said, "You'll be right back."
> When I reached Zone 11, I saw all sorts of people sitting, standing, weeping. A police officer was shouting: "Sign! Sign!"

and forcing deportation papers on them. I had to sign, like all of them. One of us did not, and his name, I believe, was Gershon Silber—he had to stand in the corner for twenty-four hours.

They took us to a concert hall. There we found people from all over—about six hundred of them. They took us in police vehicles, prison vans. They brought us to a railway station. The streets were black with people shouting: "Send them to Palestine!"

At the border they searched us for money. If anyone had more than ten marks, the rest of the money was taken away. They told us: "Ten marks. You did not bring more to Germany, so you cannot take more out." The SS men used whips to hurry us across fields to the frontier line. Those who faltered were struck, blood spurted, bundles were grabbed from people's hands. It was the first time I had seen the barbaric behavior of Germans. They told us to run. I was struck and fell into a ditch. My son helped me up and cried: "Run, Papa! Otherwise we shall die."[96]

The Jewish deportees came from many German cities. They were forced into freight cars and shipped eastward to the Polish frontier, where twelve thousand deportees were assembled. In the midst of a heavy rainstorm these people were driven out of Germany. Women and children led the "invasion" of Poland. The uprooted Jews hoped that the sight of desperate women and children waving their Polish passports over their heads would stop the stunned frontier guards from shooting.

Newspapers around the world carried the story of the mass deportation. In Paris *Pariser Haint,* a Yiddish language daily, informed the Jewish population what horrors were occurring to their coreligionists. As tragic as the plight of those Jews was, it was an abstract horror, occurring to people without names or faces, without personalities or importance, until on November 3, a postcard arrived from Zbonszyn, a town on the Polish-German border. Berta, Herschel's sister, wrote for the family.

Dear Herschel,

You must have heard about the disaster. I will tell you what
happened. Thursday evening, rumors were going around that
Polish Jews in our town were being deported. None of us believed
it. At nine o'clock that night, a policeman came to the house
to order us to report to the police station with our passports.
We went as we were to the police station. Just about the whole
neighborhood was there. Almost immediately, we were taken
to the town hall in a police car. So was everyone else. No one
told us what was happening, but we knew it was the end. They
pushed deportation orders into our hand and told us we must
leave Germany by October 29. We were not allowed to return
home. I begged to be allowed to collect a few things, and a
policeman accompanied me. I packed a bag with a few essential
clothes, but that was all we could save.
    We haven't a penny. Could you send some money to Lodz?
    Love from all of us.
    Berta[97]

The letter jarred Herschel from his preoccupation with the
amusements. Daily reports in the newspapers added to the scene
of desperation which included his family. By Sunday, November
6, his frustration led to outbursts of temper. Herschel demanded
of his Uncle Abraham that he rescue the family in Poland.

"You don't give a damn about them!" Herschel charged his
uncle. For a time, their tempers flared. Then, Uncle Abraham
gave his volatile nephew two hundred francs, and the dispute
passed until four o'clock in the afternoon, when it erupted anew
and rose to a fury.

"If you don't like it here, then go somewhere else!" Uncle
Abraham shouted back.

Herschel stormed out of the house, slammed the door behind
him, and went away with his closest friend, Nathan Kaufmann,
a neighbor. The two teenagers went to the Aurore Sportsman's
Club, where Herschel could dance away his despair.

On their way across the city, they passed through the San

Martin District. There was nothing new to be seen, but when Herschel passed the Sharp Blade, a gun shop, at 61 Rue de Faubourg Saint Martin, he saw revenge for the twelve thousand Jews who were suffering and dying in the Polish mud, where he would have been if he had not abandoned his family to indulge himself with the liberties of Paris. By striking at the Nazis, he could make a political statement against brutality and raise the guilt over his pleasures from his sagging shoulders.

25

The Voice of the Gun

Herschel Grynszpan was seventeen years old and barely five feet tall, a teenager without a country, a human being without rights. At any time the authorities could arrest him and do whatever they wished with him. They had the power to deport him or to intern him, and he was helpless to stop them, as helpless as the twelve thousand Jews in the muck of a Polish internment camp, where the desperate were killing themselves to escape the horrors of a world no longer endurable. Was he next?

A gun, a small steel instrument, could in the hands of someone weak and insignificant equalize the imbalance of power. A gun speaks with the eloquence of death. Who better than the corpse of a German could argue before the court of the public opinion the case of the persecuted?

In a moment, Herschel Grynszpan, who had undergone the transformation from Zionist pioneer to Paris bon vivant, underwent a new transformation, from carefree, powerless teenager to history-shaping assassin. Although Nathan Kaufmann was with Herschel Grynszpan, he did not see the transformation. If he had noticed the gun shop, the significance of its wares had not registered in his mind.

Nothing more was said by the newborn assassin of the plight of the Jews in the muck and misery of Poland. At the Sportsman

Club, Grynszpan carried on as though he had not heard of the mass deportation. Once again, he seemed to be concerned solely with his private amusements. Around seven o'clock the two friends parted at the Strasbourg–St. Denis Metro Station. They arranged to meet in two hours for supper at Tout Va Bien.

After deceiving Nathan Kaufmann as to his real intentions, Grynszpan walked the short distance from the station to the Hotel Suez, where the desk clerk was his first real obstacle. If Grynszpan was going to carry out his hastily contrived scheme, he would need a room for the night. Under French police regulations, all foreign hotel guests were required to present valid identification and to fill out a registration form. Grynszpan did carry his expired Polish passport, but if the clerk were observant, and the law-abiding type, he would be compelled to report the irregularity to the police.

Grynszpan informed the desk clerk that he was Heinrich Halter, a salesman from Hanover. He asked to postpone the legal formalities until he brought from the station his luggage, which included his identification papers. The clerk agreed. Having overcome his first obstacle, Grynszpan went to his room, to avoid further questions and to write a brief letter to his suffering parents. He wrote on the back of a personal photo.

> My dear parents,
>
> I could not do otherwise. May God forgive me. My heart bleeds at the news of twelve thousand Jews' suffering. I must protest in such a way that the world will hear me. I must do it. Forgive me.
>   Herschel[98]

At nine o'clock, when Grynszpan was locked in his hotel room, Nathan Kaufmann arrived at Tout Va Bien for their prearranged meeting. He waited until he was certain that his friend would not keep the appointment. Alarmed that Grynszpan had not appeared, Kaufmann returned home to learn that his friend was not there either.

Uncle Abraham began a futile search for his hot-tempered nephew. To the worried uncle, the disappearance was connected with the violent quarrel, but he could never have imagined what his nephew was planning. Over the previous two years, the teenager had never thought of anything beyond his next pleasure.

Not until the next morning did Grynszpan emerge from his room, when he ate breakfast, paid for his meal, and left the Hotel Suez to begin his mission. Soon after, he entered the Sharp Blade gun shop, where the proprietor, Monsieur Carpe, served him. In little time, the proprietor realized that his customer had no knowledge or experience with firearms.

"Why do you want a gun?" he inquired.

"My father owns a business. I must carry large amounts of cash," Herschel explained.

"Then, you will need a weapon that is easy to conceal," Monsieur Carpe advised. He recommended a 6.35 mm, short-barrel, five-shot revolver.

He gave Grynszpan a few moments of instruction in the use of the gun, checked his identity, and wrapped the gun and ammunition.

Grynszpan was now an armed assassin with a mission fixed in his mind. Amazingly, the transaction had taken little time and had cost a meager 240 francs. Since the previous night, Grynszpan's progress from powerless teenager to deadly assassin had gone smoothly. Armed with his revolver, Grynszpan's next stop was the washroom at Tout Va Bien, where he loaded five bullets into the gun. Ready now for his mission, he stopped at the bar for a drink. It was just around nine o'clock, Monday morning, November 7, 1938. The assassin was prepared to kill.

Grynszpan took the Metro to Solferino Station, the closest stop to 78 Rue to Lille, the location of the German Embassy. Outside, Constable François Autret was walking his beat near the main entrance of the embassy. Grynszpan stopped the policeman. "Where is the entrance?" he asked. Constable Autret directed him and saw the young man enter. Nothing prompted the policeman to give Grynszpan a second thought.

Inside, door porter Nagorka greeted Grynszpan in the lobby. Despite German fears of attacks upon their officials, there was no security to check visitors.

"I have a special document for the ambassador," Grynszpan informed him.

"I will deliver it for you," Nagorka offered.

"I must deliver this in person," Grynszpan informed the porter, who was not surprised by the response. There were many matters too important for him to handle.

Nagorka left Grynszpan in the lobby while he went to find someone with the authority to receive a confidential document. Before leaving Grynszpan alone in the unguarded lobby, the porter had not asked for identification or proof that a document existed. People simply accepted the word of a stranger. After deceiving the desk clerk at the hotel and the owner of the gun shop, Grynszpan was still surprised to see how easy everything was.

A moment later, Nagorka returned to inform Grynszpan that he had located someone with the authority to accept the document. Unfortunately, it was not the ambassador, Count Johannes von Welczeck; he was not available. It was just 9:30 in the morning. At that early hour, many officials had not yet started the day or were busy elsewhere. Third Secretary Ernst vom Rath was the best Nagorka could manage. The twenty-nine-year-old low-level diplomat was at his desk awaiting the confidential document from the messenger.

Vom Rath had not planned on a diplomatic career. He had studied law at the universities in Bonn, Königsberg, and Munich. In 1932, he began his law career as chief court clerk. For a young man from an influential Prussian family, the diplomatic service seemed to offer more opportunity than did a life in the field of law. In 1934, vom Rath left his position as chief court clerk and went to the foreign ministry. After one year, he took and passed a civil service examination, was assigned to duty in the foreign ministry in Berlin for a year, then was sent to Paris in 1936 to serve for one year as the personal secretary to Ambassador Koester, his uncle.

From Paris, vom Rath was assigned to Calcutta, where he contracted a serious intestinal infection that required four months of recuperation in a Black Forest sanatorium. Paris was his first post-recovery assignment. He had arrived in July and was on duty to receive his killer, Herschel Grynszpan.

Vom Rath directed the unidentified messenger to take a seat in front of his desk. "Do you have an important document to deliver?" the third secretary asked.

Grynszpan, who was wearing an overcoat over his suit, rose from the padded leather chair. As he faced vom Rath Grynszpan reached into the left inside pocket of his jacket. When his hand emerged, it was holding the loaded, five-shot revolver.

"You are a filthy Boche, and here, in the name of twelve thousand persecuted Jews, is your document!" The words exploded from Grynszpan's mouth.[99]

As he shouted at the diplomat, Grynszpan fired all five rounds in the gun. Once the time had arrived to commit the fatal deed, the assassin, who had behaved with such cunning, lost control of his volatile temper. While the weapon fired, the teenager underwent a transformation from cold-blooded assassin to frenzied child. One bullet lodged in the ceiling. Two were buried in the wooden panelling behind vom Rath. One hit vom Rath in his left shoulder. The fifth bullet struck him in the groin.

Once the gun was empty, the injured diplomat attempted to flee from the office. He managed to reach the open door before he collapsed. From elsewhere in the embassy, the sound of gunfire and Grynszpan's shouts brought Nagorka and another employee, Kruger. They found the still-conscious vom Rath lying wounded in a spreading pool of blood in the open doorway and Grynszpan frozen to the place from where he had shot the diplomat. Grynszpan had stunned himself into immobility. It was a simple matter for the Germans to disarm him and take him prisoner. Grynszpan had fulfilled his mission to strike at a German, to avenge the suffering Polish Jews. Yes, the gun had spoken, but it was still unclear what it had said and who had heard.

Shortly after they captured Grynszpan, Nagorka and Kruger

gave their prisoner to Constable Autret, who a few minutes earlier had directed Grynszpan to the main entrance of the embassy. An embassy official offered to accompany the constable and the assassin to the police headquarters on rue Bourgogne, but Constable Autret declined the offer. Grynszpan had become a police matter with which outsiders were not permitted to interfere.

Once placed under arrest, the teenager gave Autret no problems. On his way to the police station, Grynszpan was eager to tell everything. He confessed to the policeman that he had gone to the embassy to shoot the ambassador but was unable to reach him. So, he shot the first German official available. Vom Rath was simply an unfortunate target of opportunity.

At the station, Constable Autret gave his report to Inspector Monneret. The police inspector conducted a preliminary questioning of the suspect and was preparing to take a written statement when an irregular order came from the Foreign Ministry to admit a German observer, Herr Lorz, who soon took charge of the interrogation. The embassy official's one concession to French authority was to conduct the interrogation in French. Afterward, a police board of inquiry condemned the violation of the police procedure, which had succumbed to external political forces.

Grynszpan made no effort to conceal his guilt. Proudly, he described to his interrogators how he had planned the assassination and why he had done it. By afternoon, Berlin knew as much as there was to know about the shooting of the third secretary. Berlin knew that behind the attempted assassination was the persecution of the Jews. That information had a number of critical ramifications.

Inspector Monneret, once he had reclaimed command of the case, retraced with Grynszpan the path that had taken him from the apartment of Uncle Abraham and Aunt Clara, to the Hotel Suez, to the Sharp Blade gun shop, and finally to the embassy. Every detail of Grynszpan's story was confirmed. Monneret was satisfied that the case was just what it appeared to be, the irrational act of an irrational teenager.

Later that night, Grynszpan was transferred to Chief Inspector

Badin, who reviewed the evidence and reexamined the young assassin. At the end of the questioning, Grynszpan signed a statement in which he admitted guilt and the police investigation was over, a simple, open and closed case. In the morning, Grynszpan was taken to the office of the public prosecutor, where the police gave him over to the Republican Guard.

The next phase of the procedure had begun, as the judicial machinery slowly began to turn. About eleven o'clock, for the first time since his arrest on the previous day, the accused teenager met his legal advisors, Maitres Szwarc and Vesinne-Larue. The two Yiddish speaking lawyers had been retained by another of Herschel's uncles, Salomon Grynszpan, who was one of his more prosperous relatives in Paris. During the brief period before he was to be taken to the court of the investigating magistrate, Judge Tesniere, Grynszpan described to the lawyers what had occurred while in police custody.

Under the direction of his legal counsel, Grynszpan's first act in court was to renounce his signed confession. In the preliminary court hearing the teenager claimed that the statements to the police had been obtained after hours of severe questioning and after he had been denied sleep. Once that legal step was completed and the charges were read, the hearing ended. Grynszpan was charged with the attempted murder of the third secretary of the German Embassy, Ernst vom Rath, and was remanded for trial. The first step of the legal process completed, Judge Tesniere issued warrants for the arrest of Abraham and Clara Grynszpan as accessories to the crime.

26

Men of Honor

Despite the severity of his injuries, Third Secretary vom Rath remained conscious and able to explain what had occurred in the embassy. While he was being taken to the Alma Clinic at 166 rue Universite, he described to First Secretary Achenbach how his unidentified attacker had entered the office, drawn his revolver, shouted about "persecuted Jews," and fired. More than this vom Rath could not explain.

Just to learn that a Jew or Jews had been involved revived memories of Wilhelm Gustloff in Switzerland. Such an event in an embassy was feared by German officials to be the first sign of massive Jewish resistance. Officials of the Gestapo had been warning the government of a potential uprising. All that was lacking from their certainty was the time, the place, and the precise nature of the Jewish revolt.

Ambassador Count von Welczeck went immediately to the French Foreign Ministry. He needed to learn who was behind the shooting. The sudden arrival of the German ambassador at the ministry did not alarm Foreign Minister Georges Bonnet, who was awaiting a reply to the question of a Franco-German peace declaration. Obtaining the agreement had become for the French minister an important goal to crown his career, because at a time when Europe seemed to be sliding toward another bloody war, Bonnet had chosen for himself the mantle of the "Peace Maker."

French Prime Minister Edouard Daladier and Foreign Minister Bonnet had gone to Munich in September to join British Prime Minister Chamberlain and Foreign Minister Lord Halifax in the serving of a portion of Czechoslovakia to appease the imperialistic appetite of Chancellor Hitler. That deed having been accomplished, the delegations returned home to assure their voters that peace had been secured for the price of only a small portion of an unimportant Central European state. To silence his critics, Chamberlain had an Anglo-German declaration to prove that appeasement had its reward. Bonnet, however, had not received similar treatment. France was being given less than was Britain for doing as much to meet Hitler's wishes. Correcting that failure became a crucial part of Georges Bonnet's policies.

"Peace Maker" was for Bonnet an unfamiliar role. Just one year earlier, during 1937, while ambassador to Washington, he had advocated a U.S.-British-French alliance. According to his plan, the three powers were to coordinate economic policies to combat the persisting depression and to synchronize military strategies to counter the growing military threat from Germany. No one took his proposal seriously. As Germany rearmed, it seemed to Bonnet certain that a war was coming. To the foreign minister it became clear that France, possessing a common border with the growing power, would have to face the danger of the coming war alone. He was certain that France could not survive.

Bonnet's appointment as ambassador to the United States had been his first taste of diplomacy. Previously, his career had been limited to areas of finance. Through a series of administrations he had served as minister of the budget, minister of commerce, and minister of finance. As a result of his concern with economic and financial policies, Bonnet's supporters were the conservative business interests that opposed the anti-fascist Socialists and Radicals.

While Georges Bonnet had the support of the conservative elements for his economic policies, they opposed his program to form an anti-German alliance. Support for that policy came from the Socialists, who rejected his economic philosophy. Bonnet's divided support proved fatal to his ambition to become prime minister. During January 1938, the fall of the Chautemps administration caused President Lebrun to invite Bonnet to form a government. He tried and failed, opposed by the Socialists. Bonnet's conservative followers were only lukewarm in their support and too weak to carry the day. But now he always referred to himself as a former prime minister.

Bonnet took the Foreign Ministry portfolio in the Daladier government in April 1938 and stepped into the forefront of the peace movement. Agreeing with the Socialists in foreign policy and the Conservatives in domestic policies had not won him the prime ministership. Therefore, he became completely the man of the right, a man of appeasement and peace.

Aware of his obsession to be known as a peacemaker, the Germans delayed, employing Bonnet's own ambition to extract more concessions from him. Foreign Minister von Ribbentrop postponed visits to Paris to sign an agreement. When Count von Welczeck arrived at Quai d'Orsay on the morning of November 7, the minister was expecting to receive his long overdue reward, until he learned about the shooting in the embassy.

Third Secretary Ernst vom Rath was an accredited diplomat under the protection of the French Republic. The French Republic had failed to protect him. Ambassador Count von Welczeck was within his rights to lodge a formal protest. If Berlin wished, the ambassador could turn the matter into a diplomatic incident that would cloud Franco-German relations and delay once again the peace agreement that was so important to Bonnet's image. In his own mind, Georges Bonnet faced a time limit in which to acquire the agreement. The British prime minister and foreign minister were scheduled to visit Paris on November 24. Bonnet wanted to have in his hand a similar declaration to demonstrate to his British colleagues and rivals that France had equal standing in Berlin.

In his communication of that morning sent at 11:38 to Berlin, Ambassador Count von Welczeck said, "He said spontaneously and with some emotion that a Franco-German rapprochement would mean the fulfillment of his life's dream."[100] No mention was made of the discussions about the shooting of Ernst vom Rath, who had been moved out of the realm of diplomatic channels into a special category.

Getting the German ambassador to reduce the shooting from an international incident to a mere unfortunate event had been bought by a simple order to the police to allow a representative from the embassy to participate in the interrogation of the assassin. For Bonnet it was a relief to find how by a minor violation of police regulations he could dispose of the diplomatic problem.

Earlier, the foreign minister had violated agreements with Czechoslovakia, in order to please Chancellor Hitler. Going even further than the British to win the approval of the German chancellor, after Munich, he had attempted to create a joint French-German press office, to censor the French press to assure the Germans that they would not be offended by newspaper articles. When that failed, Bonnet sought to obtain the power to silence the press by legal actions. Again, he failed, but he had demonstrated his willingness to try. In comparison, ordering the police to admit an official of the German embassy to question Grynszpan was a very insignificant concession.

While the diplomats made their demands and gave their concessions, the subject of the discussion, Ernst vom Rath, was still struggling for his life. Upon his arrival at the clinic, he had undergone emergency surgery, which had taken two hours. Grynszpan had used a small caliber weapon. When one bullet penetrated vom Rath in the groin, the slug wandered throughout his body and inflicted a trail of damage. Vom Rath's spleen had been ruptured. The hemorrhaging organ was removed, and bleeding was controlled. The wall of vom Rath's stomach had been perforated at two points. Dr. Baumgartner, who was the chief attending physician, treated the wounds. Finally, the wandering bullet had ended its course in vom Rath's left lung. The slug was removed, the bleeding was stopped, and the lung revived. During the surgical procedure one transfusion was administered.

Hitler himself took a direct interest in the case from the outset. He sent his personal physician, Dr. Karl Brandt, and the director of the Munich University Hospital, Dr. Georg Magnus, to Paris to assist in the care of the minor diplomat and to provide the Führer with frequent, detailed reports. A military aircraft carried Magnus from Munich to Berlin, where he was joined by Brandt. Then the aircraft flew to Cologne, to pick up Ernst vom Rath's father, Gustav vom Rath, and fly him to Paris, but the old Prussian junker, who was the chief of police of Cologne, refused the offer. Instead, he and his wife took the slower means of train to the French capital. Shortly afterward, the event and subsequent episodes gave life to rumors of a deep hostility by the old Prussian toward the Nazi leader of Germany.

The two physicians arrived in Paris early in the morning. From their first examination they gave little hope for the survival of the diplomat. They declared in a medical report: "The condition of Consul vom Rath* is grave as a result of the injuries to the stomach. A major loss of blood from the rupture of the spleen has been treated with transfusions. The excellent treatment given by Dr. Baumgartner permits us to look forward to an improvement."[101]

Prior to the shooting, Third Secretary Ernst vom Rath had been an insignificant bureaucrat. When Consul Vom Rath died, as was expected, it would be a more serious offense against German dignity than would have been the assassination of Third Secretary Vom Rath. Already the propaganda machine was in full swing to make the event into a battle for the preservation of German national dignity. Frequent medical bulletins kept the public aware of a German warrior's struggle for his life in a hostile world.

Sir Michael Bruce, a retired British diplomat, received an appeal from Chaim Weizmann of the Jewish Agency in London to apply his influence through British diplomatic channels to

---

*As soon as Berlin learned of the grave condition of the diplomat, Adolf Hitler elevated him to the far more important rank of consul.

persuade the German government to control anti-Jewish violence. In response, Michael Bruce traveled to Berlin to speak to British Ambassador Neville Henderson who was not available; he was in London. The trip was fruitless. As far as the British Foreign Office was concerned, "peace in our time" was the operative policy of the moment, and the diplomats had been instructed not to antagonize Herr Hitler. Michael Bruce found himself speaking to a collection of unresponsive embassy officials.

Hitler's increasing strength at home and abroad made the German government indifferent to international views about the rising level of anti-Semitism. Immediate revenge for the shooting of Consul vom Rath was the theme sounded in the newspapers. The official news agency, Dienst Aus Deutschland, declared on the afternoon of the shooting that it was a proof of the "international Jewish conspiracy." At the bottom of the conspiracy, the newspapers claimed, was an effort by International Jewry with the assistance of Winston Churchill to create a rift between France and Germany. *Völkischer Beobachter,* the newspaper used by Hitler as his personal platform, gave the direction of official German thinking. The newspaper spoke about revenge for the crime and recalled how *Landesgruppenleiter* Gustloff had been assassinated in Switzerland. Two years after the case of Wilhelm Gustloff had been buried, Hitler was enraged anew that the Jewish conspirators behind the convicted assassin, David Frankfurter, had escaped their just punishment. In the case of vom Rath, the same would not be permitted to occur. This time, Germany intended to act.

Over those two years conditions had changed a great deal. When Wilhelm Gustloff was shot, Hitler was not in a position to protest too loudly. Gustloff had been an official of the National Socialist Party, without any diplomatic standing in Switzerland. In fact, his conduct had been skirting illegality. Diplomatically, Germany had little claim on Switzerland, and it was better to let the question fade. In the meantime, Hitler had other matters more important than the death of Wilhelm Gustloff and a dispute with Switzerland to deal with.

On November 7, 1938, the Führer was free to make vom Rath Germany's entire agenda, the cause of the moment. *Völkischer Beobachter* noted, "It is an impossible situation that hundreds of thousands of Jews in Germany should still be prominent in business, own houses, and populate public resorts."[102] *Der Angriff,* the paper under Dr. Josef Goebbels, spoke on November 8 as if the diplomat were already dead and it knew where to place the blame.

It is no coincidence. While in London the Churchill clique, unmasked by the Führer, was busy with sanctimonious deception, in Paris the murder weapon spat in the hands of a Jewish lout and destroyed the last measurable remnants of credibility in the assertion that agitation for war and murder against the Third Reich had never been carried on or contemplated. The Jewish murder-urchin Grynszpan also assumed the pose of a world improver and avenger. Thereby, he took the same line as is pursued by Messrs. Churchill, Eden, Duff, Cooper, and their associates, indefatigably and in the most varied fashion, in association with the international conspiracy of Jews and Freemasons.[103]

The newspaper continued the theme that the Jews in Germany were enjoying too good a life. Then *Der Angriff* published a list of streets where Jewish businesses could be found and the addresses of Jewish homes. Following the lead, other newspapers across the country copied the pattern set by Goebbels' paper.

Clear to everyone, the stage was being set for a major event that was to cover the length and the breadth of Germany. Throughout the country, the people were waiting for the news of Consul vom Rath's death. In Kassel and Hesse the mobs could not wait. They attacked Jewish homes and businesses. By the middle of the day on November 9, the doctors at the clinic abandoned hope. Bleeding had resumed, and an infection had started. Ernst vom Rath sank into a deepening coma. At 4:30 in the afternoon, he died. Herschel Grynszpan was a murderer.

That evening, several hundred members of the German community in Paris gathered at the Alma Clinic to escort away the body of vom Rath. A minor diplomat had died; an important martyr for the cause of National Socialism had been born.

27

A German Hero

Three days after the death of Consul Ernst vom Rath, memorial services were held at the German Church on rue Blanche in Paris. French Prime Minister Daladier and French President Lebrun sent representatives. Foreign Minister Georges Bonnet attended in person. Adolf Hitler was represented by State Secretary Baron Ernst von Weizsacker.

Nothing was said in the eulogies of how or why Ernst vom Rath had died. Soon after the shooting, it had been decided in Berlin not to lay the blame upon France, in order to assign all of the guilt to the international Jewish conspiracy. Affixing that guilt was being withheld until Ernst vom Rath was back on German soil. Once home, the propaganda machine with Hitler himself at the lead was to give the waiting public the full impact of the deed. The ceremony in Paris was preserved as a solemn, nonpolitical affair. In the presence of the parents of the diplomat, State Secretary von Weizsacker, addressing the body, said, "Ernst vom Rath, your country greets you. Germany awaits you."[104]

The dead diplomat, accompanied by his parents, was taken by special train from the French frontier to Düsseldorf. On the way across the country vom Rath was saluted at each station by contingents of SA, SS, and Hitler Youth.

In Düsseldorf, Rheinhalle was draped in the colors of the

National Socialist Party. The flag-decorated casket, with four men as the guard of honor, was on public display to give vom Rath's countrymen an opportunity to see their newest national hero. On November 17, 1938, vom Rath was given a state funeral and proclaimed a martyr for National Socialism.

The Führer himself sat in the front row. While party and state officials watched, the chancellor approached the casket, saluted the fallen martyr, and resumed his seat. Throughout the ceremony, Hitler sat silently, while Foreign Minister von Ribbentrop made a speech placing the death into the midst of the conflict between Germany and the world. More than two and a half years earlier, the theme had been set at the funeral of Wilhelm Gustloff, when Hitler said, "We recognize the challenge, and we accept it."

That statement was to echo at vom Rath's funeral and elsewhere. Vom Rath's murder was declared an attack against the whole of Germany and a clear challenge to the nation. Foreign Minister von Ribbentrop told Germany and the world outside:

A hostile world, paralyzed by outmoded usages, thinks to stop the march of fate by rejecting everything that is young and strong, and by blind hatred of the creators and standard-bearers of a new age. Lies and calumny, persecution, terror, and murder, are the weapons of international Jewry and of other destructive powers which seek to deny to National-Socialist Germany her path into the future.

Their last victim is our Party member, vom Rath. While he was doing his duty abroad for the Führer and the Reich, he was struck by the bullets of the cowardly hired assassin. . . .

Slowly but inevitably the old world is declining. No agitation, no calumny, no terror, can reduce the German people again to vassalage or stay Germany's progress. What new thing may arise from the collapse of the old order of society in other countries, from the ruins of the old, declining civilization, we do not know. One thing, however, is our sacred belief and our deepest conviction: after this world change eternal Germany will still stand, united, strong, and as great as never before. . . .

Wilhelm Gustloff and Ernst vom Rath are blood-witnesses who died abroad for the resurrection of Germany. From the sacrifice of all these German men, true, unto death, coming generations will draw strength to maintain, defend, and increase the Reich. The death of Ernst vom Rath was not in vain. . . .

While now in the rest of the world new hatred has broken out against us, while an attempt is made to desecrate the sacrifice of our dead Party member by fresh lies and insults, a storm of rage sweeps through our people, and their intention to give themselves at any time for Führer and Reich becomes only harder and more determined. I repeat the words which the Führer spoke at the grave of Wilhelm Gustloff: "We recognize the challenge and we accept it!"[105]

Everyone had expected Hitler to address the mourners and to honor the fallen diplomat, but the chancellor remained silent and left quietly at the conclusion of the ceremony. After the propaganda buildup to the funeral, Hitler's silence aroused questions.

Genevieve Tabouis, the Paris columnist for *L'Oeuvre,* in an article titled "Argument Around the Casket" gave a theory for the Führer's silence. According to Tabouis, Gustav vom Rath, an old Prussian aristocrat, had blamed the low-born Austrian corporal for the murder of his son. As the men stood over the body, the aristocrat condemned the chancellor. The Führer, offended by the Prussian, refused to speak. Afterward, Hitler had the old Prussian arrested and held in prison until the baron retracted his charges. The elder vom Rath's earlier refusal of the airplane ride to Paris gave indirect support to such speculation. Elsewhere, the story circulated that Third Secretary vom Rath had not been a party member and had opposed the policies of the Hitler regime, which considered him a threat. Vom Rath's questionable loyalty, therefore, had placed him under the watch of the Gestapo. In the end, the story said, the diplomat was murdered by the government. By killing vom Rath, the Gestapo could eliminate a diplomat of doubtful loyalty and fix the blame upon the Jews. That made Herschel Grynszpan a German agent or an unwitting dupe.

Gustav vom Rath denied Tabouis's statements. In January 1939 he traveled to Paris to file a libel action against Tabouis' newspaper and to state publicly that his son had been a loyal supporter of the Nazi movement. Whether true or not, the charges in Tabouis' column struck home. Hitler himself gave credence to her charges when he named the journalist specifically in one of his speeches. She was to be the only journalist given the singular honor of being condemned personally by Adolf Hitler.

Soon after *L'Epoque* and other Paris journals released the story that the Gestapo had sent an agent to France to silence the newspapers. The articles said that the agent had been given $7 million to buy anyone with a price and he had orders to silence anyone not for sale. Silencing the press was made a crucial step in the program of softening France for its eventual conquest.

Another important step for German propaganda was to establish a cause for the coming war. Herschel Grynszpan provided just what the propagandists needed. Here was a Jew who had entered a German embassy and shot to death an innocent diplomat. Herschel Grynszpan was to be raised by German propaganda to the plateau of symbol of the international Jewish conspiracy.

28

A Festival for Wolves

At the end of October 1938, two German tourists were assaulted in Antwerp, Belgium. The German government immediately attributed the attack to international Jewry and punished the Third Reich's 500,000 Jews by forbidding for one month all public meetings of Jewish organizations. Hitler was declaring to the world that he had hostages who would suffer for any and all offenses against Germany. The half million Jews of the Reich were a weapon to keep other nations under Hitler's control. Either he would inflict suffering upon the Jews, or the waves of Jewish refugees would inflict disorder upon Europe and North America.

Adolf Eichmann had given the world just a small taste of the Jews already that year. The rush of penniless, dispossessed refugees had caused other governments to plead with the Germans for a more orderly emigration and to permit the dispossessed to take with them a portion of their assets. No other country was willing to absorb the refugees. American immigration quotas were fixed in cement. "The Lady with the Lamp" had cancelled her invitation, although it had been written by a Jew, Emma Lazarus.

During the early days of the Third Reich Jews were encouraged to leave, free to carry away their wealth. The first objective of National Socialism was to make Germany *Judenrein*, cleansed of Jews. Gradually, as foreign exchange was drained from the central bank and the Nazis realized that there was money to be made by expelling Jews, restrictions were imposed to limit what could be taken, until the limit was reduced to nearly nothing.

Not only were the Jews forced to leave empty-handed, they also had to find someone willing to accept them. An industry of selling visas developed to fill the pockets of German and foreign government officials who could issue the right stamp or document to open a border, until Switzerland's Chief of Police Rothmund branded every German Jew with the mark of the beast.

German tourists did not require visas to visit Switzerland. Jews with German citizenship could use their passports to enter Switzerland and hide, or seek clearance for another destination. Rothmund wanted to have an easy means to separate the Jews from the tourists. He persuaded the Germans to stamp the letter "J" onto Jewish passports. After October 5, 1938, when the law went into effect, Jews could no longer escape detection. Officials who had been able to sell travel documents, had a more difficult time covering their illegal activities once the buyers could no longer disguise their Jewish identities.

Five days later, Julius Streicher, nicknamed the *Judenfresser* (Jew eater), added a new urgency to answer the "Jewish Question." The former publisher of *Der Sturmer* personally directed the destruction of the main synagogue in Nuremberg. When Hitler forced him to sell his hate sheet, he lost his public voice, but he had not been silenced or discouraged from seeking control of the Nazi movement. His unsanctioned action inspired local Nazi leaders throughout Germany to imitate him, to begin their private pogroms against Jewish centers. By following his lead, the freelance terrorists were taking anti-Semitism out of governmental and party control and putting it into the unpredictable hands of the mob. If he hoped to continue to rule, Hitler had to reclaim control of the Brown Shirt mobs that had carried him into office. The news from Paris on November 7, 1938, was what was needed to focus the public hatred. Hitler himself could not have planned it any better.

On the evening of November 9, der Führer was in Munich to attend the celebration of the fifteenth anniversary of the Beer Hall Putsch. The putsch had been a failure, a moment of personal disgrace for Hitler. Whatever the truth, he and the party had managed to rewrite history and to convert shame into a glorious episode that began on the evening of November 8, 1923, at 8:45, when Bavarian State Commissioner Kahr was addressing a gathering of three thousand burghers in Munich's *Burgerbraukeller,* a large beer hall.

The nationalists of the time were disturbed about French occupation of the Ruhr and the Versailles Treaty's ongoing requirement for reparation payments. The federal government was submitting to humiliating demands. The Bavarians wanted the national government to expel the French and forgo the payments. As Kahr spoke, a group of armed, uniformed men invaded the beer hall. Adolf Hitler, a revolver in his hand, jumped onto a table and fired a shot into the ceiling. While eyes were fixed upon Hitler, the remainder of the band of SA, under the command of Hermann Göring, positioned a machine gun at the door to cover the unarmed audience.

With that one action, Hitler had captured many of Bavaria's officials. Then, by bluff and threats, he extracted from them pledges of support and their recognition that he was the rightful head of the national government. Over the next hours, however, one by one, Hitler's prisoners slipped away, taking with them their pledges of support. In the fresh light of morning the Führer found himself a leader without followers.

Hitler had one ploy left. Later in the morning, he formed his men into ranks, and they marched through Munich toward the center of government. At some point the authorities would be forced to take a stand to stop him or to surrender. Hitler expected the authorities to throw their support to his movement. A few months earlier he had created civil disturbances, and the authorities had done nothing. Hitler read their inaction as approval.

No one knows who fired the first shot, but it was fired. The police stood their ground, and a number of National Socialists were killed. In the face of police fire, Hitler fled the field of battle. Hitler's arrest could have consigned his movement to a historical footnote, except that he had landed in the midst of a conflict between the indecisive Weimar government and the harder-willed Bavarians. As an Austrian citizen, Hitler could have been deported, or he could have been imprisoned for years for rebellion and insurrection. Instead, he was given a mild sentence intended to demonstrate the defiance of Bavarian politicians toward the central government. During his time in the Bavarian prison, Hitler wrote the bible of the Nazi movement, *Mein Kampf* (My Battle). Hitler was given a second chance, and his movement was resurrected.

Each year the party celebrated the putsch. On the evening of November 9, 1938, thousands of SA officers and party officials were in Munich to hear the Führer speak and to salute their resurrection from the disgrace of Versailles to the triumph of international power. Prime Ministers Chamberlain of Great Britain and Daladier of France, a few weeks before, had both presented Czechoslovakia to Germany. More would come. About eight o'clock, the expected news, that Consul Ernst vom Rath had died, arrived. Everyone in the audience knew the story. Goebbels's paper, *Der Angriff*, and Hitler's paper, *Völkischer Beobachter*, had both explained in their November 8 issues the Jewish conspiracy behind the shooting, and there were hints that some form of retaliation was coming. Why else would *Der Angriff* publish the addresses of Jewish homes and businesses?

Hitler and Goebbels discussed the killing of the diplomat privately. Then the leader of the National Socialist Party, who had been expected to speak, left, leaving to his minister of propaganda the honor of inspiring the faithful by feeding them a long overdue feast of Jewish blood. Being given such an assignment was for Goebbels an opportunity to redeem himself. Goebbels was universally hated within the upper circles of the government and among the party members. He had the nickname of the "shrunken German," a reflection of his shortness and club foot, which he claimed was the result of a childhood accident.

Goebbels also bore the even less complimentary name of the "he goat," because of his practice of demanding sexual favors from the actresses who performed in the propaganda films. Such unscrupulous tricks were said to be the usual method used by Jewish film producers and directors to gain control over Aryan women. That branded Goebbels as the "Jew Producer."*

One of Goebbels's many affairs was with Czech actress Lida Baarova. After the secret of their relationship became widely known, the scandal brought catcalls whenever he spoke in public. His conduct was a violation of the Nazi credo of the strong family and a reverence for motherhood and gave his numerous enemies in government the ammunition to remove him from the circle of power. In spite of their efforts, Hitler kept the scandal-ridden minister. The Führer said that, "Only Goebbels can deliver the right kind of propaganda."

News that Magda, Goebbels's wife, planned to divorce him was more than even the Führer could accept. He gave Goebbels the option of repairing his marriage or leaving office. Goebbels chose power; his mistress was promptly deported. Soon afterward, the minister of propaganda could declare that Magda was pregnant again, to the glory of the Aryan family. Although the episode had passed, Josef Goebbels was not certain whether or not it was over. Then, Hitler asked him to address the waiting officers of the SA. The opportunity seemed to be the Führer's vote of confidence.

Moments after the speech began, the audience realized that they were hearing more than the usual anti-Semitic harangue. Goebbels told them that the National Socialist Party could not organize violence against the Jews, but "spontaneous actions" would be understood, and the Führer would not be displeased. The long-delayed license to act had been issued.

Since the National Socialist Party had come to power, the SA had been awaiting the order to punish the Jews for their many crimes against Germany. The Nazis charged that the Jews

---

*Victor Reimann, *Goebbels*, p. 225.

had caused the German defeat in 1918 by aligning all of the other nations against her.

Shortly after the party had come to power on January 30, 1933, there had been a brief flurry of violence against Jewish shops. These, though, were just appetizers that entirely failed to satisfy the taste for Jewish blood that the SA troopers had developed. When Wilhelm Gustloff was assassinated, he was the first German official to have been killed by a Jew. Across Germany, the Brown Shirts were ready to show the Jews that the assassination would be avenged. Instead, Berlin instructed them to stay calm.

The SA had to wait until it suited Adolf Hitler to unleash them. On November 9, 1938, their waiting was over. Hitler was master of Germany, and Germany was master of Europe. No longer did the Führer need to worry about the opinions of other nations.

Lina Heydrich wrote in her memoirs that she and her husband, the director of the Gestapo, were asleep in their room at the Four Seasons Hotel in Munich on the night of November 9, 1938. They were awakened at 11:15 when the regional Gestapo office informed him that urgent instructions had been received from the Ministry of Propaganda. The urgent news was that *Kristallnacht* (the Night of Broken Glass) had begun. He was to inform the security forces. Through the hotel window, Heydrich saw the flames from a burning synagogue.[106]

At 11:55, Heinrich Mueller, the deputy director of the Gestapo, sent preliminary instructions over the teletype.

Attention, office leaders and their deputies. These instructions must be forwarded to all SS quarters immediately:

1) Within the shortest time possible action against the Jews will start all over Germany, especially against their synagogues. Interference of any kind will not be tolerated.

2) Important material in the archives of the synagogues must be confiscated and removed to a safe place.

3) Between 20,000 and 30,000 Jews within the Reich must be arrested. They are to be chosen from among wealthy Jews. Special instructions pertaining to this phase of the actions will be issued during the night.
(Signed) Gestapo 2 Mueller[107]

This was a night for the Brown Shirts. The Gestapo and the SS were not to participate. They were to assure the SA, rampaging in civilian clothes, that the public would neither join the violence nor interfere with it.

After Goebbels's speech, SA officers left the beer hall to telephone their posts across Germany. Their instructions were to begin cleansing Germany of the Jews. By mid-morning, attacks were under way in seventy-six cities and regions of the Third Reich, including Austria and the Sudetenland.

Somewhere in the inner circles of the government, plans for these events had been under way for weeks. Under normal circumstances, the arrest of twenty thousand Jews would have strained the capacity of the concentration camps. But these were not normal times. For several weeks, in anticipation of a large influx of new prisoners, barracks in the camps underwent rapid expansion. Other preparations had been under way. Chief of Police for Berlin, Count Wolf Heinrich von Helidorf, disarmed the Jewish population. He collected guns and ammunition, swords, and other possible weapons. When the SA gangs struck, there was little danger that their victims could resist.

Planning the night of violence was limited to a select few. Heydrich appears to have been excluded from the inner circle. Once the rampage began, he had to confirm with his superior, Heinrich Himmler, the instructions that had come from the Ministry of Propaganda. By 1:20 on the morning of November 10, the instructions had been confirmed. Heydrich sent his order by teletype.

Confidential, Blitz. Munich. To all State Police offices, to all Security Units, and all Special Shock Detachments.

Concerning actions against the Jews tonight.

Because of the assassination of a member of the German legation in Paris, vom Rath, demonstrations against the Jews in the Reich, Austria and the Sudeten area are to be expected in the night from November 9 to 10, 1938. To deal with these events the following orders are to be obeyed:

Leaders of the State Police . . . must at once call for a meeting to secure coordinated action of demonstrations.

For such actions only orders are to be issued which do not endanger the life or property of German citizens. Synagogues are to be set on fire only if buildings of German citizens are not endangered by the flames. As many Jews as possible must be arrested. Arrest first only healthy Jews of not too advanced age.

After arrests have been completed, communications are to be established with the nearest concentration camp, and the arrested Jews are to be shipped to those camps at once.

(Signed) Heydrich SS Gruppenführer[108]

Once released to rampage among the Jews, the SA wolf packs could not be held on a short tether. Kristallnacht was for the long waiting soldiers of hate their festival for wolves. They had been instructed to select their targets so as not to damage Aryan property. But as buildings were fired, the flames quickly jumped the ethnic barriers to reach the homes and shops of Aryans. Under the Nuremberg Laws of 1935, to preserve the purity of the German race, there was not to be any sexual contact across ethnic lines. Yet, rapes were numerous. The police even arrested some of the German attackers, but the courts dismissed them all on the grounds that they were under orders. Looting was strictly forbidden. The morning of November 10, 1938, was to be a time of public outrage, a "spontaneous expression of anger" for the murder of vom Rath and a history of other Jewish crimes. It was not to be a time for personal gain. Despite the proscription, fur shops were cleared of pelts and coats. On *Unter Den Linden,* in the fashionable district of Berlin, the fashionable Margraf store suffered the loss of one billion seven hundred million marks worth of fine jewellery, gold, and precious stones. Little of the loot was ever recovered.

By late morning, most of the damage had been done. Goebbels instructed the SA that afternoon that they had tasted enough Jewish blood, destroyed enough Jewish property. The night of "spontaneous vengeance" was over. He had given the SA fresh infusion of the revolutionary spirit that had sent them into the streets to battle the police and political opponents until der Führer became chancellor.

When the night of violence ended, the destruction extended across Germany. Two hundred synagogues had been pulled down or torched, 7,500 homes and businesses had been wrecked, 20,000 people had been imprisoned, and about 100 Jews had been murdered.

29

Reaping the Harvest

During the early hours of rioting, Air Marshal Hermann Göring was travelling by train from Munich to Berlin. From his train window he saw the fires, but he had not been included within the circle of the *Kristallnacht* planners, and he did not know that the night of violence had begun. Göring's role in government was centered on the development of the military industrial complex. He was the economic czar, the commissioner for the Four Year Plan for industrial development. If Germany intended to be the military giant of Europe, then it would have to have the newest weapons and the most modern industrial facilities to produce the requisite tanks and aircraft. To fulfill his objectives, Göring required Jewish capital and skills. Under his supervision, Jewish-owned enterprises were left to operate freely, although the official policy had been for the Aryanization of the economy.

On a local level small shops and businesses were forced to close or sell out to Aryans. The program was supposedly voluntary, but Jews had nowhere to complain when threats were made and violence was applied. Larger industries were less vulnerable to local pressure. With Göring's consent, they continued to function, until the SA gangs set them afire. As the smoke cleared, Göring saw his Four Year Plan endangered by the very pleased Goebbels.

Göring held a special conference on November 12, 1938. At eleven in the morning, one hundred government and party officials were at the Air Ministry. Heydrich brought his reports of the destruction. In attendance were the ministers of interior and of finance. Although the conference was concerned with the economic consequences of the rampage, Goebbels was there to take credit for the destruction.

The corpulent air marshal began with a message.

I have received a letter from Bormann, the Führer's deputy, written by order of the Führer, stating that from now on the Jewish question must be treated in accordance with an overall plan, with a view to a final resolution. Yesterday, the Führer again confirmed by telephone, that I must centralize decisive measures.[109]

A policy change had been declared. The freelance terrorism of Julius Streicher was over. Henceforth, the violence toward the Jews was to be managed through the economic czar. Such matters had to be directed centrally and coordinated to match established policy.

The primary reason for the conference was to discuss money. Before *Kristallnacht*, Germany had serious financial problems. Because of the massive rearmament and the numerous programs to establish the totalitarian regime, National Socialism had become a costly form of government. The Reich treasury was empty. *Kristallnacht* had converted a serious economic problem into a critical one. At the conference, Göring raged at his audience:

The result has been an outbreak of anarchy and chaotic demonstrations. We must act immediately, because, gentlemen, I have had enough of demonstrations. They don't damage the Jews. They damage me. I am responsible for the economy. Whenever a Jewish shop is wrecked and merchandise is scattered in the street, the insurance companies have to pay damages to the Jews while the public is deprived of the consumer goods which belong to them. If demonstrations are deemed necessary in future, I would ask you to be certain that they do not harm us. It is folly to plunder or burn large Jewish shops for which German insurance companies will have to pay damages. It is folly to burn up entire racks of clothing and other goods which are urgently needed when I shall be made to feel the pinch later on. We might go straight ahead and burn up raw materials.[110]

At the conclusion of the long discussion Herr Hilgard, a representative of the insurance industry, was permitted to address the conference. The insurance industry faced a grave situation. Göring offered to relieve the companies of their obligations to pay, but that was not a real solution. Most of the damage had been suffered by Aryans. Whatever the public view of Jewish wealth, the reality was that most of the Jews had been lessees. The buildings were Aryan owned. Jewish shopkeepers or families lost the contents of the businesses or homes, while the burned and wrecked property was a loss to Germans. If the insurance carriers refused to pay the just claims, then no one would bother to buy policies, and the insurance industry would collapse.

At the conclusion of the conference a four-point plan was announced. Göring turned *Kristallnacht* into a good business deal for Germany.

1. Earlier in the year, a survey had determined that Jews in the Third Reich owned collectively seven billion marks. That gave the Jewish population a per capita wealth four times greater than that of other Germans. A one billion mark fine—about $500 per Jew—was imposed on Jews for the murder of vom Rath, on the principle that all Jews were guilty for the act of one. The money was to go into the empty treasury.

2. The voluntary Aryanization of the economy was to be replaced immediately by a mandatory program. The government would purchase at bargain prices Jewish businesses and property and resell them to Aryans for the true market value. The profit was to be kept by the government. The Jewish seller was to be paid in bonds from which he would have to live.

3. The Jewish victims of the violence were to repair the property at their own expense. The insurance companies would be permitted to pay Jewish claims at a reduced rate, and the government would confiscate the insurance payment. Foreign carriers were to be required to pay, and the government was to claim the foreign currency.

4. Jews were to be denied access to most public places. The final provision of the four-point plan had nothing to do with economics and was Dr. Goebbels's contribution to the conference. The "shrunken German" was determined to add humiliation to the extortion and violence.

Göring's introduction of punitive taxes was not an original idea. In 1936, the Ministry of Finance had proposed the tax to punish Jews for the assassination of Wilhelm Gustloff. Due to the pressure from the Ministry of Justice, the proposal was abandoned, although not forgotten. Early in 1938, the German government had the confidence to impose punitive taxes upon the Jewish population. On April 25, blinded Jewish war veterans had their tax exception for their guide dogs canceled. Such changes went unnoticed by the outside world.

There was little international response to the violence of *Kristallnacht*. When Eichmann expelled fifty thousand Jews from Austria in March 1938, Hitler claimed that the cries of protest were empty hypocrisy. The rest of the world talked about settling the problem of refugees by sending them to colonies in Madagascar. *Kristallnacht* stirred a similar response. Foreign Minister Bonnet of France told German Foreign Minister von Ribbentrop in December 1938 that he was trying to deport ten thousand Jews to Africa. Prime Minister Chamberlain told the British Parliament that a Jewish colony should be created somewhere within the vast British Empire or in Brazil. President Roosevelt recalled Ambassador Wilson and extended for six months the tourist visas of twelve thousand refugees who were in the United States, but there was not to be more, except financial aid for the development of a Jewish colony somewhere else.

In 1923, Hitler had interpreted the silence of the Bavarian

government and its mild treatment of him as secret support of his movement. As the democracies sought to avoid the subject of the persecution of the Jews, Hitler saw a quiet support for his policies. Once again he had proven his point about the rest of the world.

The Gestapo was not so certain about the German reaction, however. *Kristallnacht* frightened the secret police as was revealed in the study.

DOCUMENT CDXXXIII

Gestapo

Berlin, 8 December, 1938

B-#2114/38g-IIA4

Secret!

Report on the Situation of November, 1938

A) Illegal movement of the communists—illegal activities
Overview of the organization and tactics

In their declarations [on the subject of the pogrom] the communists proclaim their solidarity with the Jews. To them *Judenaktion* is the political arm of the "Fascist war," whose purpose is to hide the difficulties both inside and outside the Reich. . . . The sympathy which the communists show toward the Jews can be seen also among the middle class, especially among the clerics. It has been determined, therefore, that the communists, together with the above mentioned groups which oppose the State, influence the public opinion and find support in the population which, while disapproving of Judaism themselves, nevertheless disapprove of the events of 9 to 10 November. The destruction of properties, the resulting contradictions, as well as the Four Year Plan, have been used by the communists for their own purposes to attack the worldview of the Nazi Party.

That there is no doubt about the revival of Leftist agitation is not only seen in connection with anti-Semitic measures. We must give credence to the information supplied by our sources that this agitation has reached the zenith unknown in many years. Since November functionaries and members of the party do not seem to do well while those who plead the Jewish cause (from communists to Catholics) command a much larger audience. Numerous rumors arise with the party. . . . The similarity between the Reichstag fire and the fires of the synagogues seem to give rise to these rumors.

B) Illegal Marxist movements
Social Democratic Party

The propaganda from the German Social Democratic Party for both internal and external consumption seems to revolve around the Jews. . . . Marxist newspapers claim that the *Judenaktion* was not an expression of the will of the people but was Nazi expropriation and pillage.[111]

Kristallnacht was the dividing line. After a brief flurry of violence in early 1933, conditions in Germany eased to an endurable general hostility. Some of the refugees who had fled for safer countries returned. Immigration quotas to the United States went unfilled. At the time of *Anschluss* in March 1938, Jews from Austria sought safety in Germany.

Kristallnacht shattered the last hope. Every remnant of rights was lost; the community had to pay out two billion marks in repairs, for damaged property, punitive taxes to the national government, and fees to be released from concentration camps. Lines formed at embassies. But the German government, eager to cleanse the world of the hated minority, canceled the issuance of exit permits. The age of destruction had begun; the Nazi machine was beginning its drive toward "the final solution."

On November 24, two weeks after the rampage of *Kristallnacht*, the newspaper of the S.S., *Das Schwarze Korps* (the Black Corps), announced what was to become official policy thirty-eight months later at the Wannsee Conference.* "The fate of such Jews as the outbreak of war should still find in Germany would be their final end, their annihilation [*Vernichtung*]."[112]

Before the outrages of *Kristallnacht,* a large percentage of the Jewish population of Germany and of the world had not yet realized the intensity of Nazi hatred and the thinking underlying it. The Jews, the people of the Testament, had not yet learned the truth, as preached by National Socialists, that their era was over. The Führer proclaimed it. "The Jews, the ancient 'Chosen People of Israel,' are the mortal enemy of the 'New Elect,' the Chosen People of Germany."[113] According to Nazi mythology, a war of the gods was being fought out as though the world were a Wagnerian opera stage. In such a war there could be no mercy and only one victor.

---

*The Wannsee conference was the occasion at which the proposal for "the Final Solution" (exterminating all the Jews) was made.

30

The Price and the Cost of Justice

Anti-Nazis could not ignore the outrages of *Kristallnacht* or Hitler's challenge to the world to do something about his actions. Thus, the time to fight had come; the place to fight was in a French courtroom. Like it or not, the battlefield was to be the case of Herschel Feibel Grynszpan.

Here was the opportunity to place Adolf Hitler in the court room dock and to try him for crimes against humanity. For the prosecution of the Führer only two attorneys in France were qualified, Maitre Henri Torres and a Corsican, Maitre Vincent de Moro-Giafferi. Both famous, high-priced lawyers had been involved in other human rights cases.

The World Jewish Congress approached Torres, who had successfully defended Samuel Schwartzbard for the 1926 murder of General Petliura, to handle the Grynszpan case. Unconnected with the World Jewish Congress, a committee of liberal journalists and publishers approached Moro-Giafferi to take the case. In 1933, he had joined the anti-Nazi struggle when he volunteered to defend a mentally retarded Dutchman, Marius van der Lubbe, who had been charged by the Nazi regime with the burning of the Reichstag. Moro-Giafferi was denied the opportunity to challenge the Nazi government. Van der Lubbe was hanged, and Moro-Giafferi publicly accused Hermann Göring for the fire and condemned Hitler for the injustice. Later, serving as a consultant, Moro-Giafferi had been associated with the unsuccessful trial of David Frankfurter.

As it had been with his predecessors, there was no doubt of Herschel Grynszpan's guilt. If he had been an ordinary murderer, his defense counsel might plead temporary insanity or claim a crime of passion, but Grynszpan could not be presented as an ordinary criminal. In the case of Schwartzbard, putting the victim on trial had led to the acquittal of the defendant. When the Swiss had prevented Frankfurter from presenting evidence against Wilhelm Gustloff, it resulted in his conviction. There could be just one defense. Ernst vom Rath would have to be presented as the substitute Hitler. *Kristallnacht* and all of the other crimes of the Third Reich had to be fixed upon the third secretary.

Grynszpan's prospects were not bright. The brief flirtation with liberalism that had saved Schwartzbard from the blade of guillotine had succumbed to a return to traditional French anti-Semitism. Despite the poor chance for a victory, Torres accepted the case. Moro-Giafferi vacillated.

Pertinax, one of the prominent liberal journalists of the time, took the corpulent, flamboyant, reluctant lawyer to meet Edgar Mowrer, the Paris-based American correspondent for the *Chicago Daily Tribune*. Mowrer was associated with the American Committee, which was composed of American journalists and publishers. Behind the movement was Dorothy Thompson Lewis, the wife of the Nobel Prize–winning author Sinclair Lewis and Mowrer's sister-in-law. She had the popular daily column, "Let the Record Speak," in the *New York Herald Tribune*.

Members of the committee had been seeking a chance to confront the evils of Nazism on the public stage. If handled properly, Herschel Grynszpan could be just their means to humble Hitler. Mowrer was reluctant to employ Moro-Giafferi and he did not want Torres.

> I saw Moro-Giafferi this morning. I am not altogether pleased with the choice, because Moro is considered here as being

extreme left. But he is one of the big shots and will do a good job and manage to put Hitler in the prisoners' dock. . . .

Moro told me he had already been asked to defend young G., whom he calls "the child." He, therefore, gladly accepts to represent your Committee at the same time.[114]

Rumors about vom Rath and Grynszpan added to Edgar Mowrer's uneasiness about the case. Anyone could hear the stories being whispered in the night clubs—The pair were not strangers. They were homosexual lovers, and proof could be found at the German Embassy. Why was door porter Nagorka returned post haste to Berlin from where he could not be called to testify in a French court? Why was it so simple for a Jew to enter the embassy? For some the answer was obvious. Grynszpan had been a frequent caller who was known to the security staff.

A secret homosexual love affair was not the only rumored explanation of the assassination. It was said that Ernst vom Rath had not been a dedicated Nazi and had been under surveillance by the Gestapo. Beyond that the confirmed devotees of the rumor mill claimed that the Gestapo was behind the murder. The purpose: to rid Germany of a security risk and create an anti-Jewish incident at the same time, which was why *Kristallnacht* was so well-organized. Most rumor mongers, though, were satisfied to blame the killing on a lovers' quarrel.

Mowrer did not intend to become involved in a sex scandal. Not until Moro-Giafferi assured him that none of the stories was true and that he had the police reports to support the denial, was the journalist convinced. Urged by Pertinax to finance the flamboyant Corsican, Mowrer pledged the support of the American Committee. Grynszpan acquired one of the most famous lawyers in France. Altogether, five defense counsels had been retained for Herschel Grynszpan. Still, it was unclear who would defend him.

The World Jewish Congress had retained Torres and pressured Salomon Grynszpan to accept him. In the beginning Salomon had employed Maitres Szwarc and Vessine-Larue, who did not intend to withdraw. Separately, Abraham Grynszpan had retained Maitre Gillet. Once Grynszpan became a cause for the anti-Nazi groups, Moro-Giafferi was recruited. The famous lawyer would never play fifth or even second fiddle to anyone else.

Before Grynszpan could be saved from the guillotine, the puzzle of the lawyers had to be sorted out. Moro-Giafferi had the winning arguments. He was the senior counsel with over a thousand cases to his credit. Far better than that, he had a deep American pocket into which to dip. With him as a chief counsel and the others as assistants, everyone could share the riches. Torres, Moro-Giafferi's former student, had graduated to become his chief rival in the theater of justice. When Torres agreed to serve as cocounsel, the others readily accepted their secondary roles.

Moro-Giafferi had a good reason to be generous. As he approached the climax of his prestigious career, the famous lawyer wanted to crown his long professional life with a term as the president of the French Bar Association. His only real rival for that office was Torres. Now, the younger Torres was content as his cocounsel on the defense committee.

With American money to secure Torres and the other attorneys in his corner, the prominent human rights lawyer was able to wage his campaign to gain the jewel for his private crown. Moro-Giafferi's strategy, however, brought him into conflict with the American Committee, which had not wanted to support the World Jewish Congress's selection, because Henri Torres was a Jew. In spite of their protests, however, now they had Torres coming in through the back-door. According to Mowrer,

> At my first meeting with Moro he candidly told me that he was sharing the defense of Grynszpan with Maitre Torres, his only rival in French criminal law of a sensational kind. Torres is moreover, a Jew, and precisely the sort of person who should have had nothing to do with the trial. Moro's verbal explanation was that in a matter of the importance of the Grynszpan trial he dared not refuse an offer by Torres to share the responsibility with him. In point of fact, other lawyers told me that Moro

hopes ultimately to be elected Batonnier, or President, of the French Bar, and needs Torres' support for it. Torres, having scented money and a chance for fame, insisted on coming into the Grynszpan affair as part of his price for ultimately supporting Moro. This is the atmosphere in which the whole affair started.[115]

While the French lawyers engaged in their personal squabbles, the German propaganda machine was in full operation. No sooner had Maitre Moro-Giafferi joined the case than *Der Angriff* in Berlin on November 19, had a headline, "Moro-Giafferi Defends World Jewry." The newspaper tried to find some Jewish ancestor perched on Moro-Giafferi's family tree. Search as the Nazis might, not one Jewish gene was found in his ample body.

The first courtroom battle did not involve Herschel Grynszpan. His Uncle Abraham and Aunt Clara were to stand trial for violation of article 4 of the government decree on immigration. If they were found guilty of aiding an illegal immigrant, they could receive one year of imprisonment. Moro-Giafferi had agreed to accept Herschel's case, but nothing had been said of the uncle or the aunt. Suddenly, he found himself with two other clients he did not want to defend. At first, Moro-Giafferi resisted. Then he changed his mind, persuaded by the possibility of his dismissal.

On November 21, supported by a squad of assisting counsels, Moro-Giafferi stood before the court. He had attempted to postpone the trial, but examining magistrate Judge Tesniere was under pressure from the minister of foreign affairs to conclude the case quickly and quietly.

On November 14, a week after the assassination, Foreign Minister Georges Bonnet had tabled in cabinet a decree to close to the press and the public any court proceedings that might have a harmful impact upon French foreign policy. Bonnet had already violated police procedures to accommodate the Germans. One more concession to protect German sensitivities was nothing. So the trial was encased in secrecy. Bonnet was still in search of his mantle of peacemaker and German Foreign Minister

Joachim von Ribbentrop was the only man who could drape it around him by signing a Franco-German agreement. Alert to his advantage, the German foreign minister was hesitating, playing cat and mouse with the dreams of the Frenchman.

Critics of the foreign minister attributed his eagerness to accommodate the Germans to a more mundane cause. They noted that the minister's standard of living had improved substantially since he had acquired the portfolio of foreign minister. Their conclusion was that Bonnet had been bought. It was certianly something Hitler would have tried:

> I am opening dossiers on all the influential people in their countries. These dossiers will contain only the information that counts. Can he be bribed? Can he be bought in any other way? Is he vain? Does he have erotic interests? What kind of women does he like? Is he homosexual?. . . . It is with these things that I shape politics, that I win people to my cause, that I force them to work for me, that I guarantee my advance and influence into all countries.[116]

Despite Bonnet's efforts, as soon as it was known among his colleagues that Moor-Giafferi was to perform on the legal stage, a crowded courtroom was assured. An army of lawyers, who could not be excluded, attended the trial of Abraham and Clara Grynszpan. Through them, the public would learn everything that occurred behind the closed doors.

Maitre Moro-Giafferi argued that the aunt and uncle were not in violation of article 4. Under article 11, if an illegal immigrant could not be deported, then to shelter that person was not an illegal act. As of August 15, when Grynszpan lost his residency, he had been stateless. France could not deport him. Without an interpreter, Abraham and Clara Grynszpan were forced to explain in inadequate French why they had sheltered an illegal immigrant. They told the court that their nephew had become a substitute for the son never born to them. In spite of their personal situation and of the legal arguments, the quality of French judicial mercy was limited. The couple was sentenced to four months each and fined a total of one hundred francs.

That part of the case resolved, the couple was remanded for trial in January 1939 for the more serious charge of complicity in the murder of Ernst vom Rath. Their trial would come immediately after Herschel's trial had begun. Already, a sign of the lack of sympathy of the court and the fortunes of justice had been revealed, and it did not augur well for Herschel.

Moro-Giafferi faced powerful enemies inside the court and outside in the political circles. The Paris newspaper *Le Petit Parisien* reported that twenty French newspapers were controlled by German interests. From the beginning of the Grynszpan affair, the matter had been under Goebbels's direction. He appointed Friedrich Grimm to supervise the legal interests of Germany and named Wolfgang Diewerge director of propaganda; both men had participated in the trial of David Frankfurter.

To represent Germany, Grimm retained French lawyers, Maitres Loncle and Garcon. Diewerge made anti-Semitic material available to them and to sympathetic journalists.

31

In the Vise

The battle for the life of Herschel Grynszpan began on November 30, 1938. Moro-Giafferi had everything going against him. His best strategy, his only possible strategy, was to delay the trial while he waited for the political currents and public opinion to shift.

From the outset the public prosecutor used Grynszpan's photograph with the message to his parents to demonstrate premeditation. The defense claimed the ambiguous phrases to be a sign of his intent to commit suicide.

My dear parents,

I could not do otherwise. May God forgive me. My heart bleeds at the news of twelve thousand Jews' suffering. I must protest in such a way that the world will hear me. I must do it. Forgive me.
Herschel[117]

Three court-appointed psychiatrists, who had examined Herschel, Drs. Genil-Perrin, Ceillier, and Heuer testified about his state of mind. They found him to be of normal intelligence and fully responsible for his actions. When they asked why he had not killed himself, Grynszpan replied that "In our day and age the death of a Jew would not have attracted attention and that his [Grynszpan's] protest would have failed."[118]

Grynszpan told the court that he had been disturbed by the news about the deportation of twelve thousand Polish Jews, among whom were his family members. He stated that his initial intent was to kill himself, to protest the brutality. Then, he decided to appeal to Ambassador von Welczeck. At the embassy he was directed to vom Rath. According to Grynszpan's version of events, he said to this low-ranking diplomat, "They are interning Jews in concentration camps—but that was not enough, they are now pursuing them like dogs," to which Grynszpan said the diplomat replied, "Jewish filth!"[119] That statement triggered a moment of uncontrollable rage. Unable to control himself, Grynszpan said he drew the revolver to inflict injury on the German. Instead, his inexperience with the weapon and his rage caused him to shoot wildly and to inflict a fatal wound. Vom Rath's death, therefore, was accidental.

The deportation of Polish Jews was to be a keystone in the defense strategy. By parading the massive suffering through the pages of the newspapers and across the stage of the court, Moro-Giafferi hoped to win sympathy for the Jews and mercy for the assassin. The conduct of the Polish government aided the strategy of the defense. A month after the Jews had been driven out of Germany and dumped into the muck, the Grynszpans and five thousand others remained in a camp, deliberately kept in misery by the Polish government, which was using them to get aid from other countries and to have the world pressure the Germans to keep the remaining Polish Jews in Germany.

Upon learning that a Catholic priest had been dispatched to Poland to bring Grynszpan's family to Paris to exhibit their misery before the courts and the press, Friedrich Grimm sent a message to Berlin to pressure the Polish government to keep the Grynszpan family where they were. Since it had been made public that a Jew had shot vom Rath, the Germans had attempted to deny a link between the deportation of Polish Jews and the killing of the diplomat. The German press made no references to it. German diplomats were to deny any connection. Now Grimm had to limit exposure in the French papers and prevent it from being discussed in the courts.

German diplomats had a lot of influence over the Poles. Shortly after the expulsion of the twelve thousand Jews, German and Polish negotiators had been discussing the disposition of Jewish property in Germany. Those who had been deported were limited to one suitcase and ten nonconvertible marks. They arrived paupers and imposed a financial burden upon the Polish state. Poland wanted Germany to release their assets. The shooting of vom Rath had disrupted the talks. For the Poles to have the talks continue, they had to agree to keep Grynszpan's family in Poland. Moro-Giafferi lost another battle.

On January 11, 1939, Abraham and Clara Grynszpan were back in court. They won one important victory, when the court dismissed the charge of complicity in the murder of vom Rath. Instead, Abraham had his sentence raised to six months, Clara had hers reduced to three months, and their combined fine was increased to two hundred francs. Despite the victory, the defense had little reason to celebrate. Grimm had every reason to be confident that Grynszpan was going directly to the guillotine. To hurry the teenager on his way, Grimm wanted a speedy trial. In a report to Goebbels, Grimm wrote: "Judge Tesniere does not conceal his irritation at the barrage of messages from Grynszpan and his family. He reckons that [the] further north one goes, the more truthful the people, and the further south—towards the Mediterranean, Italy, Spain—the less people adhere to what is true, particularly the Jews in the East."[120]

Failure in Paris was countered by success in America. Before the trial Dorothy Thompson had dedicated a column to Grynszpan.

A week ago today an anemic-looking boy with brooding black eyes walked quietly into the German embassy in the rue de Lille in Paris, asked to see the ambassador, was shown into the office of the third secretary, Herr vom Rath, and shot him. Herr vom Rath died on Wednesday.

I want to talk about that boy. I feel as though I knew him, for in the past five years I have met so many whose story is the same—the same except for this unique desperate act. Herschel Grynszpan was one of the hundreds of thousands of refugees whom the terror east of the Rhine has turned loose in the world. His permit to stay in Paris had expired. He could not leave France, for no country would take him in. He could not work because no country would give him a work permit. So he moved about, hoping he would not be picked up and deported, only to be deported again, and yet again. Sometimes he found a bed with another refugee. Sometimes he huddled away from the wind under the bridges of the Seine.[121]

For those who did not read her column, Thompson spoke on national radio to explain the battle between totalitarianism and democracy. Grynszpan was presented as the symbol of the struggle, which people could support with cash contributions. In response to her appeal, $10,000 flowed into the war chest of the American Committee. French newspapers covered the American campaign for Grynszpan's defense. Reports of the swelling funds in America ended the fundraising in Europe. Once control of the case was claimed by the Americans, the World Jewish Congress in Paris withdrew its support.

Grynszpan became completely dependent upon his distant American benefactors. At the moment Herschel fired two bullets into vom Rath, the teenager lost control over his life. He became an object, tossed upon the colliding currents. He was a freedom fighter and an international Jewish conspirator. He was a political hot potato and a fat cow to milk. Locked in a cell in Fresnes Prison, he had become a cause and ceased to be a human being.

The first hopeful sign for the acquittal of Herschel came on March 15, 1939, and was spread across the front pages of the newspapers. Throughout France readers learned how Adolf Hitler had violated his agreement to leave the rest of Czechoslovakia untouched. Overnight the Führer turned public opinion against treacherous Germany.

Journalists rushed to the scene to report the action. On March 16, when Dr. Nahun Goldmann of the World Jewish Congress called at the office of Edgar Mowrer, he, too, was gone. Goldmann had come with a request for $5,000 (two hundred thousand francs).

> It is impossible to collect monies in Europe for the continuation of the necessary work, since your generous action in the United States has been widely advertised and the fact that you have collected large sums of money precludes us from any possibility of raising money in Europe, if only pending further remittances from America.[122]

From the outset, money had been a point of conflict between Mowrer and Moro-Giafferi. Finally, they agreed upon two hundred thousand francs. The first one hundred thousand francs arrived in February. That was supposed to have been enough to finance the defense.

The second instalment was to be made at the conclusion of the trial, which Moro-Giafferi had told Mowrer in November 1938 would be in four or so months. Then the time frame was being pushed further back, and the legal defense committee had asked for more cash. The World Jewish Congress did not have it. Such greed was exactly what Mowrer had feared would dominate the minds of the lawyers.

> In many ways the announcement of the formation of the American Committee and the money collected for the trial was a misfortune. It apparently gave Moro-Giafferi and his associated lawyers the impression that they had struck oil. Therefore, they hesitated to name any kind of sum as what they could use for expenses and fee, for fear that it be less than the Committee had in mind to give them.[123]

Under French law the attorney who is to plead a case cannot accept payment in advance. To evade the law, a special defense committee was formed to collect the money. Maitre Ellie Soffer, the director of the League to Oppose Hitlerian Oppression, was made administrator of the fund. No sooner had the one hundred thousand francs arrived in Paris than it was gone. Forty thousand was paid to Maitres Szwarc and Vesinne-Larue, to withdraw from the case. Ten thousand francs went to Maitre Gillet for unspecified services. Fifty thousand francs covered the investigations in Poland. Despite the agreement to accept the total of two hundred thousand francs, Moro-Giafferi attempted to double his fees by seeking additional funds from the World Jewish Congress, which had retained Torres before he joined Moro-Giafferi's defense team.

Beyond the power of the lawyers, changing international conditions promised to bring the entire matter to an end. As public opinion shifted against the Nazis, and as the general public viewed war with Germany to be likely, Moro-Giafferi demanded an immediate court date. Reversing his position, Grimm sought a delay.

Unmoved by the arguments of the defense or of the Germans, Judge Tesniere continued the laborious efforts of gathering evidence. In his court, French justice would not be hurried. More court hearings were held to question Monsieur Carpe, the owner of the gun shop. At the same time, the Germans were permitted to read into the record their description of the deportation of the Polish Jews. By summer of 1939, Edgar Mowrer had tired of the case. He urged Thompson to withdraw her support.

Dear Dorothy:
Acting in full concert with Pertinax, I am writing to suggest that you authorize me to close up the connection between your Committee for Grynszpan and Maitre Moro-Giafferi in Paris, and return to you the 100,000.—francs still in my hands. The situation here developed badly from the beginning:
The press clamor about the immense funds collected by you

for the Grynszpan defense excited the appetite of every lawyer in Paris. . . .

I received the impression that except for Moro himself we are dealing with people whom we cannot trust. Moro himself is probably sincere and honest, but he is surrounded by parasites and deals with them in a lofty manner at other people's expense. . . .[124]

Far from the legal arena, Thompson remained committed to the cause. She wrote to the flamboyant lawyer, Moro-Giafferi, to assure him of her support. "I am putting myself in your hands completely. If you believe you need it, then so be it. We will give you the 300,000 francs still in our possession."[125]

Meanwhile a great deal of time had passed. It was late summer 1939. Before Moro-Giafferi could make arrangements to get the balance of the money in the coffers of the American Committee, events in Europe exploded. On September 3, 1939, France and Great Britain declared war on Germany. For Grynszpan the news was the best sign of hope. No French court would convict a Jew for the killing of a German diplomat when all Germans were the enemy. Again, Moro-Giafferi requested a court date. Again, he was denied, and Grynszpan's appeals to have himself released to join the French Army were ignored.

On September 14, 1939, a minor change with critical importance to the teenage assassin occurred within the French government. Georges Bonnet, who had opposed the declaration of war, was removed from the foreign ministry and given the portfolio of justice minister. Because of that cabinet shuffle, he gained direct control over Grynszpan's case.

Grynszpan demanded his release. In a series of letters, he accused Moro-Giafferi of indifference. On February 17, 1940, Moro-Giafferi responded to his unhappy client. He informed Grynszpan that there was no hope of a trial in the foreseeable future. The public prosecutor told Moro-Giafferi that "further progress, either by beginning the trial or by granting provisional release, would arouse formidable opposition of which it was not his responsibility to uncover the source."[126]

The famous lawyer had recognized his defeat, but he had one last legal ploy. It was a claim that Grynszpan would have to make at the right time. The idea was a time bomb in the hands of the teenager, who would be forced at some time to defend himself in a hostile environment.

Once he had determined to pursue Herschel Grynszpan, Minister of Enlightenment and Propaganda Goebbels was tenacious. At the outbreak of the war, he retained Swiss attorney Marcel Guinand to stop the case from going to trial. Somehow the strategy was successful. Grynszpan was left suspended in time in his prison cell. On behalf of the teenager, Victor Bosch, the president of the League of Human Rights, demanded that the public prosecutor release Grynszpan or bring his case to trial. Neither was to happen.

By the summer of 1940, the American Committee had forgotten about the symbol of the struggle between totalitarianism and democracy. The remainder of the funds was sent to the foster children's program in Britain, to aid in the evacuation of children from the cities to the safety of the rural regions. Only Goebbels remembered Herschel Grynszpan. The minister of propaganda intended to place on "the little Jew from Hanover" responsibility for the outbreak of World War II.

32

Wolves and Sheep

After Britain and France had presented him a large portion of Czechoslovakia for an empty promise, after the rest of the world had done little more than weep over the outrages of *Kristallnacht,* after no government acted to stop the invasion of the remainder of Czechoslovakia, Chancellor Hitler had every reason to believe in the rightness of his tactics. When Hitler presented to Poland the same offer once made to Czechoslovakia, there was little doubt in his mind that the eastern neighbor would capitulate, because the Poles had no reliable allies to come to their defense.

Within the democracies, the public attitude was to avoid any conflict with Germany, especially over Poland. "Who wants to die for Danzig?" the peace factions in France and in Britain asked. Their unwillingness to confront the reality of the time had been anticipated by the Nazi leader. "All democracies, all the propertied classes would be too happy to be free of responsibilities and have the peace which I will guarantee. . . . They don't ask for anything else except to grow flowers, go fishing, or spend their evenings by the fire, Bible in their hands."[127]

The Führer did not have to worry about his position with the German population. At home Hitler had the public's approval. Many Germans were willing to die for Danzig. From the advent of National Socialism, German policy had been to recover all

271

lost territories and to incorporate into one Greater Germany all
ethnic Germans. The imposed humiliating settlement of World
War I gave to Poland the eastern regions of Germany and sep-
arated from the fatherland thousands of ethnic Germans, who,
Hitler claimed, desired to return to the Reich. An invasion of
Poland was said to be simply the reunification of one people.

As seen from Berlin, Poland could scarcely resist the power
of the *Wehrmacht* (the German Army). The Third Reich had the
most powerful modern military force on the European Continent,
while Poland was disorganized, backward, and ill-prepared.
Poland's one weapon was a stubborn determination to defend
its two decades of independence after centuries of dreaming of
it and sacrificing for it.

On August 23, 1939, the Ribbentrop-Malenkov Agreement
cleared the invasion road. Germany would attack from the West.
The Soviet Union would attack from the East. With these two
powerful states united in their determination to dismember
Poland, who would dare come to the aid of the hopeless nation?

On September 1, 1939, Germany attacked. Trapped between
the German army in the West and the Soviet army in the East,
the nation was doomed from the outset. Despite her disadvan-
tages, Poland gave the German army a better fight than the
generals in Berlin had anticipated. Nonetheless, Poland was
quickly conquered and occupied. The Gestapo arrived with its
execution teams to clear the new lands of enemies. Before the
war, the Gestapo had established among the local ethnic Germans
a network of informants. The local spies led the Gestapo killing
squads to Jews and potential Polish resistance leaders. In little
time, their zeal and their methods brought the Gestapo into
conflict with the army. The generals who held the ultimate power
over the conquered territories did not intend to have within their
midst an independent force that took its orders from a different
authority and had a different agenda.

Back home, the secret police flourished in a self-made atmosphere of terror. In the public mind the Gestapo was watching
everywhere, knew everything, and could do as it wished to punish

enemies of the government. Reinhard Heydrich was a methodical technocrat who had made the midnight knock into an instrument of terror. Through use of random searches and questioning, by unexpected visits in the middle of the night, he planted in the public mind an exaggerated fear of his powers. To avoid an examination at Gestapo headquarters, friends betrayed each other, children renounced parents. Janitors and generals alike quivered at the name of the secret police.

After their experience with the Gestapo in Poland, the generals told the authorities in Berlin to keep the secret police out of France when the time came for them to subdue their western neighbor. Inside Germany, the generals may have trembled at the name of the Gestapo, but outside the Reich they could control and enforce their will. Heinrich Himmler, director of national security, was ordered to keep the Gestapo home. Outwardly, he complied with the command. In reality, he instructed Heydrich to find a method to circumvent the policy that kept his forces out of France. While a secret war was being waged within the massive German bureaucracy, the shooting war was proceeding. Norway and Denmark were conquered in the spring of 1940. In their trenches the British and French waited.

On May 10, the Western Allies, who had sought for nine months some means to avoid a bloody conflict with Germany, no longer needed to consider the question. German forces struck the Dutch frontier. Four days later, they breached the French border. By June 14, they were marching victorious through the streets of Paris. After a brief and not too costly battle, the City of Lights had fallen untouched into their hands. Hitler had conquered the jewel in the crown of his instant empire.

War created a swarm of refugees who sought safety in flight. Far ahead of the advancing German troops, ten million refugees had taken to the road. Included were the officials of the crumbling Third Republic. Even prisoners from Fresnes Prison, where Herschel Grynszpan had been kept, were moved to safer cells in Orleans Prison. Among the units to enter Paris were troops of the *Geheime Feld Polizei* (Security Territorial Police), the occupation police. They were under the command of the military, but there was one special force of twenty men under the command of SS *Obersturmführer* (First Lieutenant) Helmut Knochen. Of his unit, the army had no knowledge.

Knochen had joined the Gestapo in 1937. He had lived in France, spoke the language, and was familiar with the culture. All of this made him a natural candidate to lead the Gestapo in the French capital, except that the secret police were not permitted to operate in France. As the arm of national security, the Gestapo had a mission. To fulfill that mission, the elimination of enemies of the regime, agents had to be on French soil. Heydrich selected Knochen, who was instructed to devise a plan to thwart the demands of the generals.

Knochen needed just a small, well-trained force to accomplish his objectives. SS *Sturmbannführer* Karl Bomelburg was chosen to lead the hunters. Before the war, Bomelburg had been the police representative at the German Embassy. As part of his duties he had maintained contact with the International Police Office in Paris and the French police. In reality, his function had been to penetrate the French police and maintain surveillance over enemies of Germany.

German authorities worried about the thousands of refugees living in France. Some were considered dangerous to the Hitler regime. Unknown to the military authorities, Colonel Knochen dressed his men in occupation police uniforms and had them travel in occupation police vehicles. In the confusion of the occupation no one noticed three vehicles and twenty men who moved into rooms at the Louvre Hotel, from where they went to work immediately.

First they conducted a series of raids at the offices of Jewish and anti-Nazi organizations, such as the World Jewish Congress. They rifled the files of Vincent de Moro-Giafferi and other political opponents.

Next they began the search for the enemies of the Third Reich, an operation in which the prewar policies of the Daladier administration were a great help. Since 1938, the French Republic had maintained concentration camps for the thousands of unwanted refugees who had sought asylum in France. Eighty thousand men and women had been confined, including survivors of the International Brigades, people from various countries who had fought for the defeated Spanish Republic. The survivors were imprisoned in camps in Gurs, near the Spanish border, from where the Germans shipped them to die in labor camps.

Herschel Grynszpan, of course, was among the wanted enemies of Hitler. He had been one of the easier cases, until the evacuation in June. Up until then, the Gestapo could find him in a cell in Fresnes Prison. After that he was on the move.

A special search party reached Orleans Prison on June 19, to arrest Grynszpan, but they were two days too late. Herschel and ninety-six other prisoners had just been sent in a convoy to Bourges, to escape the rapidly advancing *Wehrmacht*. The convoy never arrived at Bourges. Along the road the vehicles were attacked by German fighter aircraft. During the strafing, the guards abandoned the prisoners, who fled into the countryside, except for a handful who stayed with the convoy. Among these was Grynszpan, who refused to seize an opportunity to escape. Instead, he demanded of a French army officer who found the abandoned convoy that he be taken to the prison at Bourges. Uncertain what else to do with the prisoners, the officer escorted Grynszpan and the others to Bourges. The town had become a refugee center. To house the thousands of homeless, the prison had been converted into a hostel. When the handful of prisoners was brought to the warden, he had no idea what to do with them, especially with the famous teenage assassin.

The warden, the chief of police Taviani, and Paul Ribeyre, the public prosecutor, considered their problem. Together, the officials decided that Herschel Grynszpan should be sent unescorted further south to Chateauroux. The warden was advised not to record the arrival of the prisoners. If somehow they disappeared into the hordes of refugees, then no one could hold the authorities in Bourges responsible.

A couple of days later, the Gestapo followed the route of the convoy. At Bourges the trail ended. There were no records of the arrival of the prisoners. As far as the evidence revealed, a chance encounter with German aircraft had freed Grynszpan or killed him. He could be anywhere, fleeing for his life or lying dead in a ditch.

Gestapo agents could not imagine the drama that was occurring just ahead of them. At Chateauroux, Grynszpan collided with the immovable mountain of French bureaucracy, which refused, in spite of his protests, to give him his rightful place in a French prison cell. When Grynszpan reached Chateauroux the police had no orders to arrest him. Not until a central authority had been reestablished and orders had been issued would the police consider his case. If he insisted upon his own arrest, and Grynszpan did, then he must continue southward to Toulouse, where someone else might be more agreeable.

Toulouse was the end of the line for thousands of refugees. The city was crowded with the frightened and the desperate from across France. Included were Uncle Abraham, Aunt Clara, and one of Grynszpan's many lawyers, Isidore Frankel. None of them knew that Grynszpan was nearby. They thought he was still in prison.

Just when the Gestapo was ready to give up the chase, their luck changed. Grynszpan was mentioned during the interrogation of a captured French army officer, the same officer who had escorted the abandoned prisoners to Brouges. The hunt was resumed. Grynszpan was still missing, but now the secret police knew why. Public Prosecutor Paul Ribeyre had assisted the escape of an enemy of Germany, a crime for which he was arrested and sent to Cherche-Midi Prison in Paris to await execution. On July 15, guards came to his cell. Ribeyre saw the few moments of his future fly away, but the prison gate was opened and he was freed with a warning.

During Ribeyre's imprisonment events were leading the Gestapo to Grynszpan and to the release of the public prosecutor. For two weeks Grynszpan had survived amidst the chaos. Finally, he stood before the gates of Toulouse Prison to demand his rightful place in a cell where he would have food and shelter. In a disorderly world, the teenage assassin wanted a secure place, where he did not have to provide for himself. During his confinement in Fresnes Prison, life had not been unpleasant. Although he had been confined, and his routine had been fixed by the prison authorities, a steady flow of visitors with an interest in his case kept him occupied and at the center of attention. When not a celebrity for the lawyers and the journalists, the guards amused him with checker or card games and provided him with chocolates. All of that had been taken from him by the war.

From the time that he had jumped the border in 1936 to his involuntary escape in 1940, the teenager had not learned to speak more than elementary French. According to Grynszpan's view of the situation, his lack of skill with the French language and his thick German accent would betray him. He would be viewed as either a German spy or as a German fugitive. It was just a matter of time, Grynszpan believed, before someone shot him for one reason or another.

Other fugitives from the advancing Nazi machine attempted to escape over the mountains into Spain. Before the Germans were able to secure the frontier, a regular route had developed. As he had refused to escape from the convoy, Grynszpan did not consider the still open road to Spain or participation in the underground units organizing to resist the German occupation. His determination not to escape was matched by a German obsession with blocking his flight, but the teenage assassin was only one of a long list of enemies of the state. The Gestapo could not expend all of its limited resources upon him. In order to capture Grynszpan and the other eight hundred or so priority targets, the Germans had to establish an orderly system that could be used as a broad net.

On June 22, 1940, Germany signed an armistice agreement with France. The Third Reich had foreseen the eventuality. Article 19 required the French to surrender all enemies of the regime.

All German prisoners of war and civilian prisoners in French custody, including detained or convicted persons who have been arrested and sentenced for acts committed in the interests of the German Reich are to be handed over immediately to the German troops.

The French Government is obligated to hand over on demand all Germans in France, in the French possessions, colonies, protectorates, and mandated territories who are named by the German Government.

The French Government undertakes to prevent German prisoners of war or civilian prisoners from being removed from France to French possessions or abroad. Correct lists are to be supplied of prisoners already removed from France as well as of sick and wounded German prisoners of war unfit for travel, with particulars of their whereabouts. The German High Command will take over the care of the German sick and wounded prisoners of war.[128]

The German Foreign Ministry established the Kundt Commission for the purpose of locating the wanted enemies who were living in the zone under the rule of Vichy France. Previously, Dr. Ernst Kundt had made his reputation facilitating the absorption of the Sudetenland into the Third Reich. The commission was to be one of the lesser episodes in his career. During the few months of the commission, Kundt had the authority to search the prisons, refugee centers, and concentration camps as well as police records. Agents of the Gestapo sat on his commission.

Not long after the disguised Gestapo unit had gone into operation, the occupation police, the Geheime Feld Polizei, learned of its existence. In Berlin the enraged generals demanded the removal of the unit. Finally, a compromise was reached. Colonel Knochen was to report to the military governor and to clear Gestapo operations with army authorities. The colonel, who was to earn the title "the hangman of Paris," promised everything, but he had no intention of keeping his pledges. To the constant irritation of the generals, the Gestapo continued to follow its own policies. Once the squabbling was over, the secret police benefited from their unmasking. They moved into more comfortable headquarters in a wealthy district of the city. No longer forced to hide, they operated openly along with agents on the Kundt Commission.

The Vichy government was eager to assist the search and urged the Germans to take away as many prisoners as possible. Each one occupied scarce space in a concentration camp or prison. Each ate food that was in short supply. Kundt's report about his efforts noted, "The French government is grateful for every one taken out of their charge."[129]

To the distress of the French authorities, Kundt had a limited objective. He was interested only in enemies of the Third Reich who were considered to be threats to the Nazi power. When his search was completed, eight hundred of the known enemies were found and deported.

Waiting in his cell to be discovered was Grynszpan. Once Goebbels' obsession was found, the Nazis demanded that he be surrendered. Here, though, the French asserted their imaginary independence. In this case only, the Vichy government demanded a formal request for extradition. Grynszpan may have committed a crime against Germany, but he had committed that crime within French jurisdiction; and the French guarded jealously the facade of their national sovereignty, however flimsy it might be. All of the other enemies of the German state had not committed any crimes in which the French had an interest.

On July 18, 1940, Herschel Grynszpan was brought from Toulouse Prison to the demarcation line between the German Occupied Zone and the Free Zone, where he was placed into German hands, to be held in Sante Prison in Paris. The *New York Times* reported the event on September 8, 1940.

> Herschel Grynszpan, the young Polish Jew who assassinated a Nazi diplomat and touched off Germany's unprecedented November 1938 persecutions of Jews, has been delivered into the hands of the Gestapo (secret police) by the government of Marshal Henri Philippe Petain and Pierre Laval.
>
> Nothing has been heard of Grynszpan since.[130]

Dr. Otto Abetz, plenipotentiary to France, notified Berlin of Grynszpan's transfer: "Upon German request Grynszpan was brought to the German representatives at the line of demarcation today, July 18, 1940, to be transferred to Berlin."[131]

During the prewar years, Abetz had directed the German-French Friendship Society, which functioned under *Ausland Organisation*. The objective of the society had been to disseminate German propaganda and to undermine France for eventual conquest.

The process of softening France had been so successful that the Third Republic fell with little resistance. In part, credit for the victory went to Abetz, who was rewarded for his achievement with the office of ambassador to the Vichy government.

On September 9, 1940, a day after the United Press International release revealed the transfer of Grynszpan from Vichy to German jurisdiction, German propaganda provided the false information that Grynszpan had been convicted of murder by a French court and sentenced to twenty years imprisonment. According to the *New York Times*,

Herschel Grynszpan, the Polish Jew who killed Ernst vom Rath, a member of the German Embassy staff in Paris, was disclosed today to be serving a twenty-year penitentiary term to which he was sentenced by a French court "under German supervision."

Nazi sources suggested that this meant that Grynszpan probably had been transferred to a jail in Nazi-occupied Paris or Germany. He was found, they said, in the Sante Prison in Paris after German occupation of the French capital.[132]

Under orders from Goebbels, the Gestapo had been hunting "the little Jew from Hanover." Once news reached Berlin that the quarry had been found, Grimm was sent to Paris to complete the transfer from French to German hands. He submitted the request under Article 19 of the armistice agreement. There was no argument from the French, and Grynszpan was transferred to Germany. The shrunken German at last had his boy.

Once the French had failed to convict and execute him, Goebbels made his own plans for Grynszpan. Here was the Devil incarnate, the flesh-and-blood proof of an international Jewish conspiracy. Herschel Grynszpan, the diminutive teenager, was to be presented as the spark who had set the globe afire to fulfill a secret Jewish plan to dominate the world. Everyone was to have the entire horror revealed in a public trial, which was to be Goebbels' ultimate triumph.

33

The Problem Child

Chancellor Adolf Hitler had read correctly the lack of will of the European democracies. Even after war had been declared, France and Britain attempted to avoid taking responsibility for their own survival. During the nine months of the "phony war," when the British and the French armies sat inert in their trenches, the politicians and the generals refused to take the initiative.

The last prime minister of the Third Republic, Paul Reynaud, had not been able to wage war or to make peace. At the end, he summoned from Fascist Spain the retired ancient hero of World War I, Marshal Henri Philippe Petain. The old soldier despised the liberal democratic Third Republic, which he considered to be a decaying regime. Nearby in Germany and Italy he saw examples of strong men in command of vigorous, motivated states. No better man could have been chosen to administer the coup de grace to the Third Republic. On June 22, 1940, Petain signed the Franco-German armistice. Less than a month later, on July 10, 1940, to ratify the agreement, he reconvened in Vichy the remnants of the National Assembly. With Nazi approval, he appointed himself the strongman president of the new state, named Pierre Laval prime minister, and introduced the French echo of German Nazism, the National Revolution.

Such a humiliating death for the Third Republic required an

equally shameful burial of the abandoned institutions. Two weeks after the new state was declared, Laval informed the U.S. representative in Paris of a trial to prosecute many of the leaders of the dead Republic.

> I do not want their lives but the country demands that those responsible for the errors committed in persuading France to enter the war for which she was not prepared and the aims of which she did not clearly understand be fixed and those responsible be punished. If this is not done voluntarily by the Government in an orderly fashion the country will rise up and accomplish it by revolutionary force and violence.[133]

In preparation for the trial, on September 7, former Prime Ministers Edouard Daladier, Leon Blum, and Paul Reynaud and General Maurice Gamlin were arrested. The *New York Times* announced the arrests with the headline, "French War Chiefs Put Under Arrest."[134] Georges Mandel, a former minister of interior and minister of colonies, had been arrested earlier in Morocco to where he had escaped in order to organize resistance to France's conquerors and deny them her overseas territories.

Following such an easy victory over the French and their eager capitulation, Hitler could have asked for nothing better than to have the conquered French condemn themselves in a spectacular trial. To aid the French in their self-humiliation, Grimm was sent to Vichy to consult with the officials about the nature and scheduling of the trial. Marshal Petain planned to establish a court at Riom, in the fashion of the Nazi People's Court in Germany. During the show trial, numerous important witnesses were to be called to heap upon the defendants blame for the war. Among the chief witnesses was to be Georges Bonnet, who made available vast quantities of Foreign Ministry documents.

Under the Vichy administration, the courts moved at the same laborious pace as they had under the defunct Third Republic. Nothing was able to hurry the examining magistrates as they gathered the evidence. By October 17, 1941, Marshal Petain, tired of the legal process, decided that he was as much justice as anyone needed or would get. He pronounced all the defendants guilty as charged. Justice Minister Joseph Barthelemy protested the arbitrary decision. The minister had been a university lecturer in law and a famous jurist. In the name of justice and the rule of law, he insisted that the defendants must have their day before the bar. Marshal Petain agreed to permit a court to condemn the already condemned. The trial began on February 17, 1942.

Le Temps, the government controlled newspaper, vilified the accused and lionized Bonnet. He was presented as the lone fighter for peace in an assembly of warmongers. Lurking in the background was the international Jewish conspiracy. Leon Blum and Georges Mandel were Jews. Grimm supported the trial with a book, *Attentat Contre la France* (The Assault on France), that he wrote under the pseudonym Pierre Dumoulin. The book described how France and Germany were both victims of the same Jewish conspiracy, which led them into an unwanted and unnecessary war. Although he was a German diplomat, Ernst vom Rath's murder by Herschel Grynszpan was presented as an attack against France.

Grynszpan himself arrived in Berlin on October 25, 1940, where preparations for his trial were under way. Of all his propaganda triumphs, the trial and the inevitable execution of Herschel Grynszpan was to be Goebbels's most magnificent. Such a spectacular trial required the proper theatrical setting. Appropriately, Goebbels planned to have the show in the Bellevue Theater, where a select number of members of the German public and journalists from friendly countries could share the drama. Here Goebbels would expose the depth of the global Jewish conspiracy. Then, just as everything was ready for the legal stage, the grand moment of the shrunken German's career had to be postponed, until the Riom trial was completed.

Hitler had taken a personal interest in the Riom trial. After being defeated by the Germans, he enjoyed the irony of having the French condemn each other. Each of the prosecution witnesses testified against the accused. In reply to the condemnation from his defeated former generals, Daladier called them "those who were my subordinates yesterday and will be my subordinates in the future."[135] He charged them with incompetence and cowardice. Leon Blum, who had learned to speak in the upper-class salons, spoke in his high, feminine voice. He explained how he had nationalized the munitions industry to produce better and more arms to benefit the nation and not to enrich the industrialists. All of the defendants identified the persons responsible for the defeat, the appeaser, Georges Bonnet; the admirer of totalitarianism, Henri Philippe Petain; and the supporter of the rightists, Pierre Laval. Through their scheming and because of the incompetence of the military leaders, France had been betrayed and doomed to a disgraceful defeat.

Two months after the trial had begun, it took a direction the prosecution had never anticipated. The accusers became the accused, charged with failing to kill more Germans and to drive them out of French territory. In spite of the altered course of the trial, the public prosecutor did not prevent the defendants from making their damning statements.

News from the trial had been censored. Still, the events became known to the general public, who heard it from the BBC in London. What had seemed in the beginning to have been a wonderful propaganda event had turned sour. Riom had become a circus, and the leaders of the Vichy government were the star clowns. To end the humiliation, Adolf Hitler sent Ambassador Abetz to the French town. On April 14, 1942, the trial was recessed indefinitely.

Although they had not been convicted by the kangaroo court, the defendants remained in French custody. Paul Reynaud and Georges Mandel were confined in the primitive ancient fortress of Portalet near the Spanish border, where they remained until November 20, 1942, when the political structure of France underwent a critical change. The Allied invasion of North Africa caused the Germans to abolish the army of the Vichy government and to occupy the former Free Zone. Even the fiction of independence was erased. Reynaud and Mandel were taken to Oranienburg

Concentration Camp near Berlin, where they were held incommunicado in isolation cells until April of 1943. During July 1944, Mandel was returned to Paris and placed in French hands. On July 7, men from the German-directed French paramilitary police, *Milice,* took Mandel to the Fontainebleau Road, where he was murdered by Milicien Jean Mansuy. At the Nuremberg Trials Ambassador Abetz was sentenced to twenty years of imprisonment for his involvement in the murder of Mandel. For the same murder the court sentenced to death German commandant Knipping of the French Milice. Of all the accused, Georges Mandel was the only one to be murdered by the Nazis. Among them all, he was the only one to have actively opposed the German conquest. To compound the offense of opposing Hitler, Mandel was guilty of a worse crime. His real name was Louis Rothschild; no other name was more symbolic of the international Jewish conspiracy than that of the hated Rothschild family.

While the failed Riom trial was being played out, events in Germany were under way for Goebbels's grand performance. Nothing was to be left to chance in order to assure the Führer a first-class propaganda achievement.

First, there was the legal formality to begin the process of condemning Grynszpan and the secret army of conspirators. During the summer of 1941, Public Prosecutor Ernst Lautz indicted Grynszpan. About the same time, Justice Minister Dr. Franz Guertner died. State Secretary of Justice Franz Schlegelberger was named acting minister of justice. Goebbels formed a joint committee with representatives from the ministries of justice, foreign affairs, and propaganda, to oversee the direction of the case and to "stage manage" the trial. Unlike the drawn-out French affair in Riom, the German performance was to last a mere seven days. For the first six days, expert witnesses describing the international Jewish conspiracy would be paraded on stage. On the seventh day Grynszpan would be permitted to read a statement and be subject to questioning. Grynszpan was to answer for the murders of both Ernst vom Rath and of Wilhelm Gustloff. "Goebbels asserted that the Grynszpan case would demonstrate yet another evidence of the power of the World Jewry which goes beyond international borders. As in the case of Frankfurter-Gustloff, the Jewry had its 'filthy finger in the game.' In the death of Ernst vom Rath, naturally, the preparations were made by a longer hand."[136]

While preparing the case, Goebbels encountered a serious problem with the Ministry of Justice. Officials considered the extradition of Grynszpan to Germany to be a violation of international law, because Germany had no legal claim upon him. At the same time, Josef Goebbels wanted to try Grynszpan for treason, but the Ministry of Justice limited the charge to murder. Under the German legal code, treason could not be committed by a stateless person. Although Grynszpan had been born in Hanover, he had been refused German citizenship. As a result of the German policy, he had been a Polish citizen until October 29, 1938, when the Polish government stripped all of their expatriates of their citizenship.

The decision spoiled Goebbels's drama. A charge of murder made a difference in the type of evidence permitted in the court. The Ministry of Justice intended to permit Grynszpan to discuss why he had killed Ernst vom Rath.

For the purpose of gathering evidence for the trial, legal counsel Jagusch had been sent to question Grynszpan in his cell in Saxenhausen Concentration Camp near Berlin. The defendant was among the privileged residents who were not subjected to hard labor and minimal rations. Grynszpan made no effort to deny his guilt. Instead, he revealed the real reason, the reason that the audience in the Bellevue Theater would hear.

Here was the secret defense strategy, the time bomb, that had been imparted to Grynszpan by Vincent de Moro-Giafferi, when the flamboyant lawyer knew that he had been defeated. The lawyer struck at the heart of the Nazi façade, their claim to moral superiority, their obsession with their racial supremacy.

Herschel Grynszpan revealed to his interrogator that he had been a pimp who procured male prostitutes for homosexual clients. A regular customer was the unmarried twenty-nine-year-old diplomat, Third Secretary Ernst vom Rath.

Not only was the dead diplomat to be presented as a moral degenerate, he was to be described as a common cheat, a petty thief. After he had enjoyed his sexual pleasures, he refused to pay. Then, Herschel, who had a record of an uncontrollable, violent temper, lost it and shot the cheating German. Presented with the nature of Grynszpan's defense, Grimm said:

> That is the most evil battle of the international Jewry against Hitler and Germany. It shows that the Jewry does not know the limits of propriety. It insults, reviles, and it soils its victim; it takes delight in rolling him in filth. . . . It proves that Jewry does not shrink away from any deceit or lie.[137]

Goebbels wrote in his diary, "It is an absurd, typically Jewish claim. The Ministry of Justice, however, did not hesitate to incorporate this claim in the indictment and to send the indictment to the defendant."[138]

Because of the conflict between Goebbels and the Ministry of Justice, Grynszpan had acquired an ally in his struggle against the Nazi regime. Still more deadly, the secret weapon he had brought from Paris was fatal to Goebbel's efforts to display the long-claimed Jewish conspiracy. Grynszpan had struck the most sensitive nerve in the Nazi psyche. Under article 175 of the criminal code, homosexuality was despicably illegal. If Grynszpan were allowed to cast the slightest degree of doubt upon the man who had been raised to the standing of a fallen martyr, then it could bring ridicule upon the regime.

The defendant had planted a seed of disgrace in the Nazi field, and he could harvest a bumper crop of scandal. Always lying just beneath the surface were the whispered stories from the night clubs of Paris. Soon after the killing in Paris, rumors had floated everywhere about the homosexual relationship between the teenage killer and his unmarried victim. Grynszpan could draw upon that. In such a trial the taint of scandal would overshadow the testimony of Georges Bonnet, who was to come to Germany to confirm the existence of a Jewish conspiracy.

Josef Goebbels did not dare repeat the disaster of Riom; Adolf
Hitler had no stomach for a sex scandal. On May 11, 1942, plans
for the grand show trial were postponed indefinitely. The trial
was never to occur. At the end, Maitre Vincent de Moro-Giafferi
managed to defeat Adolf Hitler.

Destruction of the Third Reich did not expunge the homosexual
taint from the reputation of Ernst vom Rath. During the early
1950s, Count von Soltikov published reports of the widely believed stories of the sexual practices of the murdered diplomat.
In 1953, Gunther vom Rath, Ernst's brother, sued von Soltikov
for defaming the name of the vom Rath family. Wolfgang
Diewerge, former aide to Goebbels, testified for the vom Rath
family. Under oath Diewerge stated that homosexuality had never
been a question. The false testimony cost von Soltikov the case.

Thirteen years later, Wolfgang Diewerge stood trial for perjury
in an Essen court. Franz Schlegelberger testified for the prosecution. Schlegelberger had been state secretary of justice and
acting minister of justice. He had been involved in the planning
of a program to sterilize Germans with one Jewish parent. He
informed the court that one secret plan was to use Grynszpan's
conviction to justify the implementation of the "Final Solution,"
which had begun on July 31, 1941, and was moved into a priority
status in January 1942.

Goebbels' scheme was to have a spectacular show trial to
set the stage for the organized murder of the Jewish population
of Europe. This had been thwarted by the resistance of the
judiciary, which asserted the remnants of its independence. That
independence ended on August 24, 1942, when Hitler removed
Schlegelberger from the offices of acting minister of justice and
state secretary of justice. The ministry was given to Otto Thierack,
the hard-core Nazi Party member who had been the president
of the People's Court, which had sentenced to death numerous
political opponents of the Führer. Minister of Justice Thierack
was instructed by the Führer to subordinate the law to the needs
of the Nazi Party. Whenever it became necessary for the state
to curtail rebellion by force, Hitler did not want to have

interference from lawyers and judges. In the inner circles of the government there was a growing fear of a public rebellion. As the armies retreated in the face of stronger forces in Africa and in the Soviet Union, fear of a general uprising multiplied.

At last, Goebbels had his friendly court, but his interest in the trial had waned. No longer of interest to the propaganda minister, Grynszpan sank into obscurity within the sea of misery. He emerged during 1943 for a brief visit to the director of the "Final Solution," Adolf Eichmann. On the stand during his 1961 trial in Israel, Eichmann recalled that Grynszpan was "a mere slip of a boy." The chief of Hitler's killers instructed that the prisoner be taken away to an "unspecified future."[139]

Next, near the end of the war, Grynszpan appeared before a tribunal in Hanover. He was sentenced to be executed on May 8, 1945. On May 7, Germany surrendered.

There is no evidence that Grynszpan died in prison camp and no proof that he survived. His family believes that he, with millions of others, went into a mass grave. Torres, on inadequate evidence, draws the same conclusion. "Betrayed by his German accent, Grynszpan was arrested by Nazi police near Toulouse. He was sent to Germany where he was summarily judged and executed."[140] In 1949, Torres' associate on the defense committee, Serge Weil-Goudchaux, informed a French court of the same conclusion.

Others believe that Grynszpan still lives. Supporters of this view claim that through a chain of unbelievable luck the teenage killer slipped through the Nazi death machine. They assert that he has adopted a new identity in Paris, where he lives in fear of assassination. Declares writer Egon Larson, "It is little short of a miracle that among the survivors of the slaughterhouse that was Hitler's Europe there should be the boy who first pulled the trigger against the oppressors of his people."[141]

Perhaps yes. Maybe no.

Epilogue

Samuel Schwartzbard was a haunted man. He saw the battered corpses of thousands of murdered Jews, who had died for the sole reason that they were Jews.

David Frankfurter did not see the heaps of mangled Jewish corpses that were scattered across the pages of history. Instead, he saw future horrors which would soon engulf Switzerland and the rest of Europe.

Herschel Grynszpan peered into the cold mud of Poland. There, he looked into the faces of twelve thousand expelled penniless Jewish refugees among whom he saw the accusing eyes of his brother, sister, and parents.

As Schwartzbard, Frankfurter, and Grynszpan considered their different views of conditions, they realized that the murdered of the past, the murdered of the future, and the suffering of the present were being ignored by the peoples of the world. Each concluded that it remained to him alone to awaken the indifferent non-Jewish communities and the apathetic Jewish people by shouting through the barrels of their guns a protest and a warning. Schwartzbard raged about justice denied, Frankfurter alerted about lurking danger, and Grynszpan wept about misery and suffering.

However each of these men came to the point of decision, they all followed widely different roads to reach the same fatal point. Schwartzbard came from an environment of rebellion and defiance against a hostile authority. Frankfurter came from a family tradition of intellectual development, but had to take a personal stand against the unyielding authoritarianism of his father in order to preserve his private dignity. Grynszpan was raised in a home of oppressive poverty and was harangued because of his physical smallness, to which he responded with outbursts of lashing rage.

Thus, the seeds of violence had been planted in the three assassins by their very different circumstances. Once planted, the seeds were watered and fertilized by the general persecution of the Jewish people and by the failure of the Jewish people to acknowledge that they were the victims of unforgiving hatred. What grew from the cultivated seeds in the rich soil of history was assassination.

All of the assassins understood that words of appeal or protest could not penetrate the barrier of indifference that the world had erected around the brutality of reality. To be heard, the three assassins felt, each in his own way, that violence was the only tool available to break through the barrier. The gun was to be the means of protest, and they killed. Because their deeds had a political element, the killings were separated from the normal crime of the dark street and were called assassination, not murder.

Herschel Grynszpan's act was the least planned of the three and was an outburst of rage. A lifetime of anger was focused upon the misery within Poland and became the killing of an insignificant diplomat, Third Secretary Ernst vom Rath.

Samuel Schwartzbard performed the most calculated killing as he stalked and shot the former leader of the short-lived Ukrainian Republic, Simon Petliura. His rage was tempered by the skill of a professional soldier, who waited for his opportunity and struck when he had the advantage and the certainty of success.

David Frankfurter viewed his role to be that of the surgeon. He had to cut away the cancerous tumor which was threatening the survival of the entire body by removing the menacing growth of Wilhelm Gustloff.

However each of the killers saw himself, he had to abandon his Jewish traditions of debate in order to preserve his people. In doing so, the very same potential victims, whom the assassins sought to preserve, turned upon them for breaching the code of tradition and left them to the mercy of the general non-Jewish society.

Before the three assassins had taken up the gun, they were all alienated men within their private universes, from which they saw a very different world from the one the general Jewish and non-Jewish societies knew. After they stepped upon the world stage to declare through their weapons their outrage at the human condition, their alienation was compounded by their abandonment.

Not until the liberation of the Nazi concentration camps did the whole world witness the enormity of the horrors that were perpetrated in the name of Nazism. What had been one of the most advanced societies in terms of culture and technology had shed its veneer of civilization to turn its genius toward the destruction of an entire people. It had been these horrors of which the assassins had warned, but they had spoken before the world was willing to listen. When the world was finally ready to learn, six million Jews and millions of others had paid with their lives for their own indifference and for the callous apathy of most others.

Since the world was awakened to what extreme lengths civilized human beings could go toward barbarism, millions of others have died in the killing fields of Cambodia and elsewhere, on numerous battlefields, and in the hidden torture chambers of various secret police agencies. In spite of all of the horrors, apathy remains the rule and invites new Schwartzbards, Frankfurters, and Grynszpans to take up the gun and to step upon the stage to make their violent statements.

For these three men, violence was the vehicle that was to carry them and the world toward a destination of justice. Their private rages and the stubborn indifference of others was the energy that fueled the vehicle.

Did they make a difference? Schwartzbard received widespread support from the French public and caused the National Assembly to liberalize citizenship laws to admit more refugees. The French generosity, however, lasted scarcely a decade before the course was reversed and the fleeing Jew became an invading plague.

David Frankfurter killed the leader of the National Socialist Party in Switzerland and received general support from the Swiss public. Politicians within the government, however, had another agenda, which was not concerned with democracy and human rights. Among these political leaders, the preservation of their personal power was far more important than was the advancement of any principle and those leaders remained in office.

Grynszpan was caught in the reversal of the tidal wave of French liberalism. He faced a politically influenced court and a public without sympathy for the sufferings of a handful of Jews when their own standard of living was at threat. In Grynszpan's case, the most important feature was how he caused the rival international political forces to focus upon a point of collision. As each flexed its political and ideological muscles on the global platform of Grynszpan's life, he and his purpose were forgotten.

More than half a century has passed since the third assassination momentarily filled the newspaper headlines. In retrospect, it appears as though the bullets of the assassins changed little. If any lesson was taught, and perhaps learned, then it was how shallow is the commitment of humanity to itself.

Endnotes

1. Raul Hilberg, *The Destruction of the European Jews*, p. 666.
2. Ibid., p. 83.
3. Lucy Davidowicz, ed., *Golden Tradition*, p. 406.
4. Schwartzbard was given the name Shalom but adopted the name Samuel after he moved to France.
5. Taras Shevchenko, *Testament*, trans. John Weir.
6. Petliura's letter to Osyp Nazaruk, in Taras Hunczak, ed., *The Ukraine, 1917-1921: A Study in Revolution*, p. 193.
7. "First Universal," in T. Hunczak, *The Ukraine*, p. 382.
8. "Fourth Universal," in T. Hunczak, *The Ukraine*, pp. 392, 393.
9. Matthew Stachiv and Nicholas Chirovsky, *Ukraine and the European Turmoil, 1917-1919*, vol. 2, p. 373.
10. Lansing Papers, *Papers Relating*, vol. 2, pp. 25-26.
11. Stachiv and Chirovsky, *Ukraine and the European Turmoil*, p. 338.
12. Ibid., p. 330.
13. Matthew Stachiv and Jaroslav Sztendra, *Western Ukraine at the Turning Point of Europe's History, 1918-1923*, vol. 1, pp. 164-65.
14. Ibid., pp. 168-69.
15. Anton Mohr, *The Oil War*, pp. 155, 156.
16. Ludwell Denning, *We Fight for Oil*, p. 16.
17. Stachiv and Chirovsky, *Ukraine and the European Turmoil* (Vynnychenko's diary, November 28, 1918), p. 12.

18. Hunczak, *The Ukraine*, p. 257.

19. Stachiv and Chirovsky, *Ukraine and the European Turmoil*, pp. 24-25.

20. Saul Friedman, *Pogromchik*, pp. 252-53.

21. "Letter from General Petliura," *The Review* 1, no. 29 (November 29, 1919), pp. 621-22.

22. Henry Alsberg, "The Situation in the Ukraine," *Nation* 109, no. 2835 (November 1, 1919), pp. 569, 570.

23. *Jewish Chronicle*, October 21, 1927, p. 26.

24. "Lurid Trial of Petliura's Slayer," *Literary Digest* 95 (November 19, 1927), pp. 36-42.

25. Lucy Davidowicz, ed., *Golden Tradition*, p. 452.

26. Friedman, *Pogromchik*, pp. 215, 216.

27. *New York Times*, June 3, 1921, p. 1.

28. *New York Times*, June 6, 1921, p. 12.

29. The description of the assassination is a composite from a variety of sources.

30. Henri Torres, *Le Proces de Pogroms*, pp. 255-57.

31. This letter to the *Free Workers' Voice* as well as the preceding letter to Schwartzbard's family in Odessa are quoted by Henri Torres, *Le Proces de Pogroms*, pp. 255-57.

32. *Jewish Chronicle*, October 21, 1927, p. 26.

33. Friedman, *Pogromchik*, p. 108.

34. Loc. cit.

35. Torres, *Accuses Hors Serie*, p. 93.

36. Friedman, *Pogromchik*, p. 290.

37. *New York Times*, October 25, 1927, p. 5.

38. *New York Times*, October 26, 1927, p. 7.

39. Torres, *Accuses Hors Serie*, p. 96.

40. Friedman, *Pogromchik*, pp. 312-16. Notes stenographiques fasc. 9, 20.

41. Torres, *Proces de Pogromes*, pp. 52-54.

42. Alice Meyer, *Anpassung oder Widerstand*, p. 45.

43. G. E. W. Johnson, "Switzerland Is Next," *North American Review* 237 (June 1934), p. 526.

44. Ewald Banse, *Germany Prepares for War*, p. 315.

45. *Documents on German Foreign Policy*, A532, Series C., II, p. 772.

46. Meyer, *Anpassung*, p. 34.

47. Adolf Hitler, *Mein Kampf*, p. 3.

48. Johnson, "Switzerland Is Next," p. 523.

49. Hermann Rauschning, *Voice of Destruction*, p. 145.

50. Hitler, *Mein Kampf*, p. 257.

51. Meyer, *Anpassung*, p. 34.

52. Baron Ernst von Weizsacker, *Memoirs of Ernst von Weizsacker*, p. 95.

53. T. R. Fehrenbach, *The Swiss Banks*, p. 64.

54. Jost N. Willi, *Der Fall Jacob-Wesemann*, p. 279.

55. Wolfgang Diewerge, *Ein Jude Hat Geschossen*, p. 13.

56. Meyer, *Anpassung*, pp. 35, 36.

57. Willi, *Der Fall Jacob-Wesemann*, p. 298.

58. Von Weizsacker, *Memoirs*, p. 94.

59. Willi, *Der Fall Jacob-Wesemann*, p. 299.

60. Ibid., p. 386.

61. Diewerge, *Ein Jude Hat Geschossen*, pp. 88, 89.

62. Emil Ludwig, *Davos Murder*, p. 39.

63. Jean Pierre Bloch and Didier Meran, *L'Affaire Frankfurter*, p. 9.

64. David Frankfurter, "I Kill a Nazi Gauleiter," *Commentary* 9 (February 1950), p. 135.

65. Ibid., 136.

66. Ibid., 137.

67. The description of the shooting and the aftermath is based on the *Commentary* article.

68. "Ice Carnival Revenge," *The Literary Digest* 121 (February 15, 1936), p. 15.

69. *Documents on German Foreign Policy*, series C, IV, 540, pp. 1093, 1094.

70. Ibid., 541, pp. 1094, 1905.

71. "Ice Carnival Revenge," *The Literary Digest* 121 (February 15, 1936), p. 15.

72. *New York Times*, February 13, 1936.

73. Raul Hilberg, *The Destruction of the European Jews*, p. 656.

74. *New York Times*, February 19, 1936.

75. "The Murdered Nazi Leader," *Jewish Chronicle*, February 7, 1936, p. 8.

76. Ludwig, *Davos Murder*, p. 121.

77. *New York Times*, February 7, 1936.

78. Ludwig, *Davos Murder*, p. 106.

79. Ibid., p. 126.

80. *New York Times*, February 7, 1936.

81. "Guns Again, an Assassin's Pistol Makes Europe Shiver: Nations Prepare for Next War," *Newsweek* 7, no. 7 (February 15, 1936), p. 7.

82. Bloch and Meran, *L'Affaire Frankfurter*, p. 19.

83. Ibid., p. 32.

84. Diewerge, *Ein Jude Hat Geschossen*, pp. 42, 43.

85. Bloch and Meran, *L'Affaire Frankfurter*, p. 26.

86. Diewerge, *Ein Jude Hat Geschossen*, p. 46.

87. Ibid., pp. 46, 47.

88. "Saint v. Jew," *Time* 28, no. 19 (December 21, 1936), p. 19.

89. *Berner Tageswacht*, December 15, 1936.

90. *Die Front*, no. 292.

91. *Documents on German Foreign Policy*, series C, VI, p. 181.

92. William Dodd, *Ambassador Dodd's Diary, 1933-1938*, p. 431.

93. Meyer, *Anpassung*, p. 9.

94. Alfred A. Hasler, *Lifeboat Is Full*, p. 233.

95. Ibid., pp. 245, 246.

96. *New York Times*, April 26, 1961, p. 15.

97. *Reichsministerium für Volksaufklärung und Propaganda*, file 991, F54-55, Deutsches Zentralarchiv, Potsdam.

98. *Reichsministerium für Volksaufklärung und Propaganda*, file 979, F49, Deutsches Zentralarchiv, Potsdam.

99. Rita Thalmann and Emmanuel Feinermann, *Crystal Night*.

100. *Documents on German Foreign Policy, 1918-1945*, Series D (1937 to 1945), IV, doc. 347.

101. Wolfgang Diewerge, *Anschlag Gegen den Frieden*, p. 50.

102. *New York Times*, November 8, 1938, p. 4.

103. *New York Times*, November 9, 1938, p. 13.

104. Von Weizsacker, *Memoirs of Ernst von Weizsacker*, p. 159.

105. *New York Times*, November 18, 1938, p. 13.

106. Lina Heydrich, *Leben mit einem Kriegesverbrecher*.

107. International Military Tribunal, Nuremberg (IMT), XXV, doc. 374-PS, pp. 376-80.

108. IMT, XXXI, doc. 3051-PS, pp. 515-19.

109. Edouard Calic, *Reinhard Heydrich*, p. 192.

110. Graber, *The Life and Times of Reinhard Heydrich*, p. 130.

111. Lucien Steinberg, "La Nuit de Cristal," *Le Monde Juif* 20 (1965), pp. 10–11.

112. Gerald Reitlinger, *The Final Solution,* p. 8.

113. Herman Rauschning, *Hitler M'a Dit,* p. 263.

114. Letter of Edgar Mowrer to Dorothy Thompson, November 19, 1938, Dorothy Thompson Collection, George Arents Research Library, Syracuse University, New York.

115. Mowrer, ibid., July 25, 1939.

116. Rauschning, *Hitler M'a Dit,* p. 304.

117. *Reichsministerium für Volksaufklärung und Propaganda,* file 979, F49, Deutsches Zentralarchiv, Potsdam.

118. Thalmann and Feinermann, *Crystal Night,* p. 52.

119. *New York Times,* December 1, 1938, p. 13.

120. *Reichsministerium für Volksaufklärung und Propaganda,* file II, 983, F 68, Deutsches Zentralarchiv, Potsdam.

121. Dorothy Thompson, "Herschel Grynszpan," *Let the Record Speak,* p. 256.

122. Letter of Nahun Goldmann to Dorothy Thompson, March 16, 1939, Dorothy Thompson Collection, George Arents Research Library, Syracuse University, New York.

123. Letter of Mowrer to Dorothy Thompson, January 20, 1939. See note 114.

124. Letter of Mowrer to Dorothy Thompson, July 25, 1939. See note 114.

125. Letter of Dorothy Thompson to Moro-Giafferi, August 4, 1939, Dorothy Thompson Collection, George Arents Research Library, Syracuse University, New York.

126. Thalmann and Feinermann, *Crystal Night,* p. 165.

127. Rauschning, *Hitler M'a Dit,* p. 304.

128. *Documents on German Foreign Policy,* 1918 to 1945, IX, p. 205.

129. Aufwärtiges Amt: Inland II, A1B, 80–41 (November 1, 1940).

130. *New York Times,* September 8, 1940, p. 44.

131. *Reichsministerium für Volksaufklärung und Propaganda,* file 988P63, Deutsches Zentralarchiv, Potsdam, and Thalmann and Feinermann, *Crystal Night,* p. 169.

132. *New York Times,* September 10, 1940, p. 6.

133. *Foreign Relations of the United States,* 1940, II, pp. 378–79, and Murphy to Hull, July 29, 1940.

134. *New York Times,* September 8, 1940, p. 44.

135. Milton Dank, *French Against the French,* p. 87.

136. Kurt Grossmann, "Herschel Grünspan Lebt!" *Aufbau,* May 1957, p. 5.

137. Ibid., p. 6.

138. Louis Lochner, *Goebbels' Diary,* p. 161.

139. *New York Times,* April 26, 1961, p. 16.

140. Torres, *Accuses Hors Serie,* p. 299.

141. Egon Larsen, "The Boy Who Pulled the Trigger," *World Jewry* 2, no. 8 (1959), pp. 10–11.

Bibliography

BOOKS

Adamthwaite, Anthony. *France and the Coming of the Second World War*. London: Frank Cass, 1977.

Allen, W. E. D. *The Ukraine*. London: Cambridge University Press, 1940.

——. *The Ukraine: A History*. New York: Russel and Russel, 1963.

Almedingen, Martha. *Emperor Alexander II*. London: The Bodley Head, 1962.

Aster, Howard. *Jewish-Ukrainian Relations: Two Solitudes*. Oakville, Ontario, Canada: Mosaic Press, 1987.

Ball, Max W. *This Fascinating Oil Business*. Indianapolis and New York: Bobbs-Merril, 1940.

Banse, Dr. Ewald. *Germany Prepares for War*. New York: Harcourt, Brace, 1934.

Bauer, Yehuda. *American Jewry and the Holocaust: The American Jewish Joint Committee, 1939–1945*. Detroit: Wayne University Press, 1981.

Bell, J. Bowyer. *Assassin!* New York: St. Martin's Press, 1979.

Black Book. New York: Duel, Sloan, & Pierce, 1946.

Bloch, Jean Pierre, and Didier Meran. *L'Affaire Frankfurter*. Paris: Denoel, 1937.

Boudrel, Philippe. *Histoires des Juifs de France*. Paris: Albin Michel, 1974.

303

Bradley, John. *Allied Intervention in Russia.* London: Widenfeld and Nicolson, 1968.

Brinkley, George. *Volunteer Army and Allied Intervention in Southern Russia, 1917-1921.* South Bend, Indiana: University of Notre Dame Press, 1966.

Browning, Christopher. *The Final Solution and the German Foreign Office.* New York: Holmes and Meier, 1978.

Calic, Edouard. *Reinhard Heydrich.* New York: William Morrow, 1985.

Chamberlain, W. H. *The Ukraine, A Submerged Nation.* New York: Macmillan, 1944.

Cohen, R. *Burden of Conscience.* Bloomington: Indiana University Press, 1987.

Crankshaw, Edward. *Gestapo.* London: Putnam, 1956.

Dank, Milton, *The French Against the French.* New York and Philadelphia: Lippencott & Company, 1974.

Davidowicz, Lucy, ed. *The Golden Tradition.* New York: Holt, Rinehart, and Winston, 1967.

Denning, Ludwell. *We Fight for Oil.* New York: Alfred Knopf, 1928 (Hyperion reprint, Westport, Connecticut, 1976).

Deschner, Gunther. *Heydrich.* London: Orbis Publishing, 1981.

Diewerge, Wolfgang. *Ein Jude Hat Geschossen.* Munich: Verlag Franz Eher, 1937.

———. *Anschlag Gegen den Frieden.* Munich: 1939.

Documents on German Foreign Policy, 1918-1945, Series C, IV, II, VI, Series D. London: His Majesty's Stationary Office, 1962.

Dodd, William. *Ambassador Dodd's Diary, 1933-1938.* New York: Harcourt, Brace, 1941.

Doroshenko, Dmytro. *History of the Ukraine (1917-1923).* Edmonton, Alberta, Canada: The Institute Press, 1939.

Dubnow, S. M. *History of the Jews in Russia and Poland From the Earliest Times Until the Present Day.* Philadelphia: The Jewish Publication Society of America.

Dumoulin, Pierre (aka Friedrich Grimm). *L'Attentat Contre La France.* Paris: Editions Jean-Renard, 1942.

Elcheshen, D. M. *Historical Facts.* Winnipeg, Manitoba, Canada: Historical Research Club, 1975.

Ellis, Albert, and John Gullo. *Murder and Assassination.* New York: Lyle Stuart, 1971.

Fanning, Leonard. *American Oil Operations Abroad.* Ann Arbor, Michigan: Xerox Company, 1971 (McGraw-Hill, 1947).

Fedyshyn, Oleh S. *Germany's Drive to the East and the Ukrainian Revolution, 1917-1918.* New Brunswick, New Jersey: Rutgers University Press, 1971.

Fehrenbach, T. R. *Swiss Banks.* New York: Holt, Rinehart, and Winston, 1985.

Fischer, Louis. *Oil Imperialism, the International Struggle for Petroleum.* London: George Allen and Unwin Ltd., 1926.

Ford, Franklin L. *Political Murder, from Tyrannicide to Terrorism.* Cambridge, Massachusetts: Harvard University Press, 1985.

Friedman, Philip. *Roads to Extinction.* New York: Conference on Jewish Social Studies, 1980.

Friedman, Saul. *Pogromchik.* New York: Hart Publishing, 1976.

Frischauer. *Goering.* London: Odhams Press, 1951.

Gilbert, Martin. *The Holocaust.* New York: Holt, Rinehart and Winston, 1985.

Glaus, Beat. *Die Nationale Front, Eine Schweize Faschistische Bewegung, 1930-1940.* Zurich: Benziger Verlag, 1969.

Godelmann, Solomon. *Jewish National Autonomy in Ukraine, 1917-1920.* Chicago: Ukrainian Research Information Institute, 1968.

Goebbels, Dr. Paul Josef. *Goebbels Diaries, 1939-1941.* Fred Taylor, ed. and trans. London: Hamisch Hamilton, Ltd., 1982.

Gordon, Harold, Jr. *Hitler and the Beer Hall Putsch.* Princeton, New Jersey: Princeton University Press, 1972.

Graber, G. S. *The Life and Times of Reinhard Heydrich.* London: Robert Hale, 1980.

Grew, Joseph. *A Turbulent Era.* Cambridge, Massachusetts: The Riverside Press, 1952.

Gupta, Raj N. *Oil in the Modern World.* Allahabad, India: Kitab Mahal, 1941 (Hyperion Reprint, Westport, Connecticut, 1976).

Hasler, Alfred A. *The Life Boat Is Full.* New York: Funk and Wagnalls, 1969.

Havens, Murray, Carl Leiden, and Karl Schmitt. *The Politics of Assassination.* Englewood Cliffs, New Jersey: Prentice Hall, 1970.

Heydrich, Lina. *Leben mit einem Kriegesverbrecher.* Pfaffenhofen, 1976.

Hilberg, Raul. *The Destruction of the European Jews.* Chicago: Quadrangle Books, 1961.

Hitler, Adolf. *Mein Kampf.* Ralph Manheim, ed. and trans. Boston: Houghton Mifflin, 1943.

Hrushevsky, Mykhailo. *A History of Ukraine.* New Haven, Connecticut: Yale University Press, 1941.

Hunczak, Taras. *The Ukraine, 1917-1921: A Study in Revolution.* Harvard Ukrainian Research Institute, 1977.

Ikle, Max. *Switzerland, an International Banking and Finance Center.* Stroudsburg, Pennsylvania: Hutchinson and Ross, 1972.

Kamenka, Eugene, and Alice Ark-Soon Tay, eds. *Justice.* New York: St. Martin's Press, 1980.

Kennan, George. *Russia Leaves the War.* Vol. 1 of *Soviet-American Relations 1917-1920.* Princeton, New Jersey: Princeton University Press, 1956.

Kirkham, Jim, Sheldon Levy, and William Crotty. *Assassination and Political Violence.* New York: Praeger, 1970.

Lochner, Louis. *Goebbels Diaries (1942 to 1943).* New York: Doubleday, 1948.

Ludwig, Emil. *Davos Murder.* Cedar and Eden Paul, trans. London: Methuen, 1937.

Manning, Clarence A. *The Story of the Ukraine.* New York: Philosophical Library, 1947.

Manning, Clarence A. *Twentieth Century Ukraine.* New York: Bookman Associates, 1951.

Marcus, Jacob. *The Rise and Destiny of the German Jew* (revised edition). New York: KTAV Publishing House, 1973.

Meier, Heinz. *Friendship Under Stress.* Bern, Switzerland: Herbert Lang and Company, 1970.

Mendelsohn, Ezra. *The Jews of East Central Europe Between the World Wars.* Bloomington: Indiana University Press, 1983.

Mendelssohn, John, ed. *The Holocaust.* Vol. 3. London and New York: Garland Publishing, 1982.

Meyer, Alice. *Anpassung oder Widerstand.* Frauenfeld, Switzerland: Verlag Huber, 1965.

Mohr, Anton. *The Oil War.* New York: Harcourt, Brace, 1926. (Hyperion reprint, Westport, Connecticut, 1976).

Paine, Lauran. *Assassin's World.* New York: Taplinger, 1975.

Paxton, Robert, and Michel Marrus. *Vichy France and the Jews.* New York: Basic Books, 1981.

Pereira, N. G. O. *Tsar-Liberator, Alexander II of Russia*. Newtonville, Massachusetts: Oriental Research Partners, 1983.

Pertinax (aka Andre Geraud). *Gravediggers of France*. Garden City, New York: Doubleday, Doran and Company, 1942.

Potichnyj, Peter J., and Howard Aster, eds. *Ukrainian-Jewish Relations in Historical Perspective*. Edmonton: Canadian Institute of Ukrainian Studies, University of Alberta, 1988.

Rauschning, Hermann. *The Voice of Destruction*. New York: G. P. Putnam and Sons, 1940.

——. *Hitler M'a Dit*. Paris: Cooperation, 1939.

Reimann, Victor. *Goebbels*. New York: Doubleday, 1976 (Fritz Molden Verlag, 1971).

Reitlinger, Gerald. *The Final Solution* (2nd edition). London: Vallentine, Mitchell, 1961.

Rudnitsky, Stephen. *Ukraine, the Land and Its People*. New York: Rand McNally, 1918.

Schechtman, Joseph. *The Jabotinsky Story, the Rebel and Statesman*. New York: Thomas Yoseloff, Inc., 1956.

Schleunes, Karl A. *The Twisted Road to Auschwitz*. Urbana, Chicago, and London: University of Illinois Press, 1969.

Senn, Alfred. *Assassination in Switzerland*. Madison, Wisconsin: University of Wisconsin Press, 1981.

Sherwood, John. *Georges Mandel*. Palo Alto, California: Stanford University Press, 1970.

Shevchenko, Taras. *Selected Works*. Moscow: Progress Publishers, 1979.

——. *The Poetical Works of Taras Shevchenko*. C. H. Andrusyshen and Watson Kirkennell, trans. Toronto: Toronto University Press, 1964.

Shirer, William. *Rise and Fall of the Third Reich*. New York: Secker and Warburg, 1960.

Simpson, Sir John Hope. *The Refugee Problem, Report of a Survey*. London: Oxford University Press, 1939.

Stachiv, Matthew, and Jaroslav Sztendra. *Western Ukraine at the Turning Point of Europe's History, 1918-1923*. Vol. 1. Scranton, Pennsylvania: The Ukrainian Scientific Historical Library, 1969.

Stachiv, Matthew, and Nicholas Chirovsky, *Ukraine and the European Turmoil, 1917-1919*. Vols. 1 and 2. New York: Shevchenko Scientific Society, 1973.

Steckel, Rabbi Charles. *Destruction and Survival.* Los Angeles: Delmar Publishing, 1973.

Stucki, Lorenz. *The Secret Empire.* New York: Herder and Herder, 1971.

Swettenham, John. *Allied Intervention in Russia, 1918-1919.* London: George Allen and Unwin Ltd., 1967.

Swiss Credit Bank, 1856-1956. Zurich: Conzett und Huber, 1956.

Tabouis, Genevieve. *They Called Me Cassandra.* New York: Da Capo Press, 1973.

Taylor, J. *The Economic Development of Poland, 1919-1950.* Westport, Connecticut: Greenwood Press, 1970.

Thalmann, Rita, and Emmanuel Feinermann. *Crystal Night.* New York: Coward, McCann, & Geoghegan, Inc., 1974.

Thompson, Dorothy. *Let the Record Speak.* New York: Houghton Mifflin, 1939.

Torres, Henri. *Accuses Hors Serie.* 4th ed. Paris: Gallimard, 1957.

———. *Le Proces des Pogroms.* Paris: Les Editions de France, 1928.

von Weizsacker, Baron Ernst. *Memoirs of Ernst von Weizsacker.* Chicago: Henry Regency Company, 1951.

Willi, Jost Nikolaus. *Der Fall Jacob-Wesemann (1935-1936).* Bern, Switzerland: Herbert Lang, 1972.

Wolf, Walter. *Faschismus in der Schweiz, Die Geschichte der Frontenbewegung in der deutschen Schweiz, 1930-1945.* Zurich: Flamberg Verlag, 1969.

Zimmermann, Horst. *Die Schweiz und Grossdeutschland, Das Verhältnis zwischen der Eidgenossenschaft, Österreich und Deutschland.* Wilhelm Fink Verlag, 1980.

PERIODICALS

Alsberg, Henry. "The Situation in the Ukraine." *Nation* 109:2835 (November 1, 1919), pp. 569, 570.

"American Oil Intervention." *Literary Digest* 69 (April 16, 1921), pp. 17, 18.

"Authentic Record." *New Republic* 81 (November 21, 1934), pp. 31, 32.

Barnes, John K. "The Nations Scrambling for Oil." *World Works* 40 (August 1920), pp. 349-60.

Frankfurter, David. "I Kill a Nazi Gauleiter." *Commentary* 9 (February 1950), pp. 133-41.

Gibson, Hugh. "Switzerland's Position in Europe." *Foreign Affairs* 4 (October 1925), pp. 72–84.

Grabowsky, A. "Crisis of Switzerland." *Contemporary Review* 151 (January 1937), pp. 53–60.

Grossmann, Kurt. "Herschel Grünspan Lebt!" *Aufbau* (May 1957), pp. 4–7.

"Guns Again, an Assassin's Pistol Makes Europe Shiver: Nations Prepare for Next War." *Newsweek* 7:7 (February 15, 1936), pp. 7, 8.

"Gustloff Affair." *The Nation* 142:3685 (February 19, 1936), p. 210.

Hunczak, Taras. "A Reappraisal of Symon Petliura and Ukrainian-Jewish Relations, 1917–1921." *Jewish Social Studies* 31 (July 1969), pp. 163–83.

"Ice Carnival Revenge." *Literary Digest* 121 (February 15, 1936), pp. 15, 16.

Johnson, G. E. W. "Switzerland Is Next." *North American* 237 (June 1934), pp. 521–30.

Larsen, Egon. "The Boy Who Pulled the Trigger." *World Jewry* 2 (August 1959), pp. 10, 11.

"Letter from General Petliura." *Review* 1 (November 29, 1919), pp. 621, 622.

"Lurid Trial of Petliura's Slayer." *Literary Digest* 95 (November 19, 1927), pp. 36–42.

Mowrer, Edgar. "Swiss Rearmament." *Foreign Affairs* 14 (July 1936), pp. 618–26.

"Murders of a Race, Pogroms in the Ukraine and Ruthenia." *Nation* 114 (March 8, 1922), pp. 295–97.

Rappard, William E. "Pluralism, the Swiss Solution." *Survey Graphic* 28 (February 1939), pp. 86–88, 180–81.

"Saint v. Jew." *Time* 28:19 (December 21, 1936), p. 19.

"Schwartzbard's Acquittal—The World's Conscience." *American Hebrew* 121 (1927), p. 891.

"So-Called Little Russia." *Literary Digest* 61 (May 10, 1919), pp. 37–41.

"Swiss-German Crisis Intensified." *Literary Digest* 121 (February 29, 1936), p. 13.

"Switzerland: Anti-Semitic Protocols Get Court Test." *Newsweek* 4 (November 10, 1934), pp. 14, 15.

Steinberg, Lucien. "La Nuit de Cristal." *Le Monde Juif* 20 (1965), pp. 8–10.

"Tiutiuniuk and His Polish Friends." *Nation* 114:2951 (January 25, 1922),
    pp. 106-108.
Wertheim, Jack. "The Unwanted Element." *Leo Baeck Institute Year
    Book* 26 (1981). New York and London: Secker and Warburg, 1981.
"World's Oil Production." *Literary Digest* 64 (February 28, 1920), p. 42.

Index

Abetz, Ambassador Otto, 280, 286, 287
Achenbach, First Secretary, 225
Allied Powers
  accept the Bolshevik victory, 73
  in Odessa, 63, 64
  keeping Russia in the war, 45
  Paris peace conference, 49, 50, 52, 69
  Polish policy, 51, 57, 69
  unwilling to act, 64
  view of Petliura, 60
  view of the Ukraine, 48, 52, 70, 71
Alma Clinic, 225, 231
American Committee, 256, 257, 258, 266–68, 269
Anschel, Axel, 185
Armistice Commission, 50, 70
Ausland Organisation, 121, 122, 124, 136, 169, 178, 186, 281
Autret, P. C. François, 220, 222

Baarova, Lida, 242
Badin, Chief Inspector, 222
Bagge, British Consul John Picton, 45
Banse, Dr. Ewald, 120–22, 124, 136, 169, 178, 280
Barthelemy, General, 49, 50, 52, 55
Barthelemy, Joseph, 285
Baumann, Minister of Justice Johannes, 137, 138, 144, 180, 187, 188
Baumgartner, Dr., 228, 229
Beilis, Menahem, 194, 202
Berenger, Ambassador Henri, 57
Berthelot, General, 44, 47, 62
Black Hundred, 20, 26, 27, 31, 67, 108, 193, 194
Blum, P.M. Leon, 205, 206, 209, 212, 284–86
Bohle, Ernst, 169
Bolsheviks, 20, 24, 43–46, 48, 50, 52–54, 59, 65–67, 69–74, 76, 80, 99–101

Bomelburg, Sturmbannführer Karl, 274
Bonnet, Georges
   accused of appeasement, 286
   divided supporters, 226
   eager for peace treaty, 225, 227, 260
   funeral of vom Rath, 233
   in U.S.A., 226
   named peacemaker, 285
   removed from Foreign Ministry, 269
   silencing press, 260, 261
   supports Nazis, 284, 289
   suspected of corruption, 260
   view of Jews, 251
   violates police regulations, 228
Bosch, Victor, 269
Botha, General, 56
Brandt, Dr. Karl, 228, 229
Bread Peace, 47, 59
Brest-Litovsk Conference, 44, 46
Brest-Litovsk Treaty, 48, 49
Bruce, Sir Michael, 229, 230
Brugger, Attorney-General Friedrich, 178, 182

Campinchi, Maitre Cesar, 90, 101, 102
Canova, Dr. Gaudenz, 137
Carpe, Monsieur, 219, 268
Ceillier, Dr., 263
Central Powers
   agreements with Bolsheviks, 44, 45
   agreements with the Ukraine, 46, 47
   oil requirements, 55
   Ukraine too weak to fight, 45
Central Rada, 37, 40, 41, 43, 45–47, 50
Chamberlain, P.M. Neville, 225, 241, 251
Cheberiak, Vera, 193, 194
Cheka, 66, 76, 99, 100
Churchill, P.M. Winston, 230, 231
Conradi, Maurice, 80, 98, 105, 175, 181, 183
Curti, Dr. Eugen, 174, 181, 182
Curzon, Lord George Nathaniel, 54
Czar Nicholas II, 27, 33, 35

Daladier, P.M. Edouard, 212, 225, 227, 233, 241, 275, 284, 285
De Vries, Dr. J., 175
Dedual, Herr, 163
Denikin, General Anton, 71–73, 90
Der Sturmer, 143, 144, 165, 180, 181, 238
Diewerge, Wolfgang, 136, 140, 180, 229, 261, 262, 290
Divilkovsky, 80
Dmowski, Roman, 51, 52
Dodd, Ambassador William, 186
Dollfuss, P.M. Engelbert, 123
Dreyfus, Capt. Alfred, 211
Dumoulin, Pierre, pseudonym of Friedrich Grimm, 285

Eichmann, Adolf, 210, 213, 237, 250, 291
Evian Conference, 187, 210

Fischer, Theodor, 116
Flory, Judge Georges, 89, 90, 92, 99, 102, 104

Fourteen Points, 51, 52
Frankel, Maitre Isidore, 277
Frankfurter, David
  after the killing, 159–61
  after the trial, 183
  as a student, 125, 128, 129
  assassin, 148–52, 154, 156
  birth of an assassin, 145, 146
  the black sheep, 141
  childhood, 127
  in prison, 184, 189, 190
  in Switzerland, 144
  on trial, 171, 174, 175, 178–80,
    182, 256
  remembered, 230, 288
  revenge for Gustloff, 189
  under arrest, 162
Frankfurter, Rabbi Moritz, 141,
  173, 189
Freikorps, 197
Fremden Polizei, 114, 137, 186, 188
Freydenberg, Col., 65
Frontenfrühling, 117

Gamlin, General Maurice, 284
Ganzoni, Justice Rudolf, 178, 182
Garcon, Maitre, 262
Geheime Feld Polizei, 274, 275, 279
Genil-Perrin, Dr., 263
George, P.M. Lloyd, 54, 73, 257,
  266, 268
Gerhard, Georgine, 187
Gillet, Maitre, 258, 267
Goebbels, Dr. Josef, 120, 148, 170,
  176, 177, 231, 236, 241, 242,
  243, 245–47, 250, 261, 265,
  269, 270, 280, 281, 282, 285,
  287–91

Goebbels, Magda, 242
Goldmann, Dr. Nahun, 266
Göring, Air Marshal Hermann,
  120, 133, 148, 240, 247–50, 255
Grimm, Dr. Friedrich, 176, 261,
  262, 264, 265, 268, 281, 284,
  285, 289
Grynszpan, Abraham, 204, 206,
  207, 215, 219, 223, 224, 258,
  259, 261, 265, 277
Grynszpan, Berta, 197, 214, 215
Grynszpan, Clara, 204, 207, 223,
  224, 259, 261, 265, 277
Grynszpan, Herschel
  assassin, 216–22, 228, 235
  in German hands, 280, 281, 285,
    287, 288, 290
  in Hanover, 197–200, 202, 203
  in Paris, 206-209, 211–13, 215, 216
  out of sight, 291
  preparation, 255
  preparation for trial, 224, 231,
    236, 256, 259, 260, 263, 265,
    266, 269
  runaway, 203-206
  secret defense, 289
  sex scandal, 257
  trapped in a French prison, 269
  under arrest, 222, 223, 260
  wanted, 275–77, 280
Grynszpan, Marcus, 197, 202
Grynszpan, Rifka, 194–98, 213
Grynszpan, Sendel, 194–200, 202-
  204, 213
Guertner, Justice Minister Dr.
  Franz, 287
Guinand, Maitre Marcel, 269
Gurs concentration camp, 275

Gustloff, Hedwig, 121, 122, 124, 136, 155, 156, 159, 162, 169, 177, 178, 186, 281

Gustloff, Wilhelm
  a public view of, 145
  arrives in Davos, 111, 112
  as a young man, 112
  as martyr, 165, 167, 169, 171
  assassinated, 158, 243, 250
  building the party, 115
  the enemy, 147
  forgotten for a time, 185
  funeral, 169
  joins Nazi Party, 113, 114
  Nazi dictator, 121, 131, 132, 136, 138, 139, 152, 156, 157
  Nazi leader, 114, 116, 117, 119
  remembered, 189, 225, 230, 234, 256, 288
  the victim, 152, 155
  the young Nazi, 115

Haller, General Jozef, 49, 50, 52, 57, 69
Halter, Heinrich, alias of Herschel Grynszpan, 218
Hechaluz, 201
Henderson, Ambassador Neville, 229
Hess, Rudolf, 122, 169
Heuer, Dr., 263
Heydrich, Lina, 244
Heydrich, Reinhard, 244–48, 273, 274
Hilgard, Herr, 249
Himmler, Heinrich, 245, 273
Hrushevsky, Dr. Mikchail, 31, 35–37

Hubermann, Dr., 157

International League to Oppose Anti-Semitism, 184
Iron Broom Movement, 116, 142, 143

Jabotinsky, Vladimir, 26
Jacob, pseudonym of Berthold Salomon, 136, 138, 139
Jagusch, legal counsel, 288
Jorger, Dr. J. B., 179, 184

Kahr, State Commissioner, 239
Kaledin, General, 44
Kampfbund, 117
Kaufmann, Nathan, 155, 214, 217–19
Knipping, Commandant of Milice, 287
Knochen, Obersturmführer Helmut, 274, 275, 279
Koester, Ambassador, 220
Kordele, Dr., 178
Kruger, 221
Kundt Commission, 278, 279
Kundt, Dr. Ernst, 278, 279

Lansing, Secretary of State Robert, 51, 52, 63
Lautz, Public Prosecutor Ernst, 287
Laval, P.M. Pierre, 280, 283, 286
League of Human Rights, 99, 269
League of National Socialist Confederates, 116
League to Oppose Hitlerian Oppression, 267
Lebrun, President Albert, 226, 233

Lenin, Vladimir, 24, 32, 43-46, 65, 66
Lewis, Sinclair, 257
Liquidation Commission, 64
Loncle, Maitre, 262
Lord Halifax, British Foreign Minister, 225
Lorz, Herr, 222
Ludwig, Emil, 9, 143, 174, 175, 182, 185
Lvov, Prince, 35

Maey, Erich, 124
Magnus, Dr. Georg, 228, 229
Mandel, Georges, 284-87
Mansuy, Jean, 287
Marx, Karl, 24
May Laws, 21, 202
members of Narodnaya Volya
  Grinevitsky, 18
  Helfmann, Hessia, 19, 20
  Perovskaya, Sofya, 15, 17
  Rysakov, 18, 19
  Yemelyanov, 17
  Zheliabov, The Terrible, 14
Mercier, P.C. Roger, 83, 84
Messinger, Rabbi, 150, 153, 174
Milice, 287
Minger, Rudolph, 119
Mizrahi, 200, 201
Mollard, Police Inspector, 83, 84
Monneret, Police Inspector, 222, 223
Moro-Giafferi, Maitre Vincent, 174, 255-61, 263, 265, 267, 268, 269, 275, 288, 290
Motta, Foreign Minister Giuseppe, 138, 167, 168, 185

Mowrer, Edgar, 256-59, 266-68
Munich Conference, 225, 228
Munier, P. C., 82
Mussolini, Benito, 206, 207
Musy, Finance Minister Jean-Marie, 117, 118

Nagorka, 220, 221, 257
Narodnaya Volya, 13-15, 16, 18, 19, 20, 24, 107, 196
National Front, 115-17, 119, 142, 143, 180, 185
Nationalist Movements
  Ukrainian Revolutionary Party, 32
  Ukrainian Socialist Democratic Labor Party, 32
  Union for the Liberation of the Ukraine, 36
National Revolution, 283
Nazaruk, Osyp, 37
Nightingale Battalion, 107
Nuremberg Laws, 144, 202, 246

occupation of the Rheinland, 171-72
Ochrana, 14-16, 19, 26, 32, 36, 193, 194, 243
Operation Internee, 112
Oranienburg concentration camp, 286

Paul, Coroner, 19, 93, 94, 276, 277, 283, 284, 286
Pelissier, Jean, 71
Pertinax, 256, 258, 268
Petain, Marshal Henri Philippe, 280, 283-86

Petliura, Lessia, 76
Petliura, Olga, 33, 76, 90, 104
Petliura, Oscar, 90, 102, 104, 105
Petliura, Simon
   agreement with Pilsudski, 71
   allied with White Russians, 73
   ally of Poland, 73
   arrested by Skoropadsky, 48
   as a conservative, 33
   as a youth, 31, 32
   as military leader, 40, 44, 46, 49,
      50, 61, 62, 69, 71
   assassinated, 81, 85, 92, 96
   being hunted, 78, 81, 95, 96
   birth of, 31
   blamed for pogroms, 76, 92, 101
   captures Kiev, 73
   chooses silence, 67, 101
   delegate to nationalist confer-
      ence, 36
   facing the Allied Powers, 52, 54
   French view of, 65
   Generalissimo, 60
   imprisoned in Poland, 74
   in desperation, 71, 72
   in exile, 76, 77, 78
   in government, 37
   named as leader, 36
   on trial, 89, 91, 99, 100
   orders from the leader, 61
   publisher, 76
   reformed socialist, 64
   remembered, 181, 255
   rise to power, 66
   summons the peasants to rise, 61
   supports Russia, 36, 37
   treaty with Poles, 73
   victim of Cheka, 100

Petliura, Vassili, 31
Peyre, examining magistrate, 95
Pilsudski, P.M. Jozef
   agreement with Bolsheviks, 73,
      74
   agreement with Petliura, 71
   agreement with White Russians,
      73
   allied with Petliura, 73
   attacks the Ukraine, 69, 70
   secret agreement, 100
   secret plans, 70
Pinsker, Leo, 21
Pogroms
   Balta, 20, 22, 67
   Lemberg, 108
   Odessa, 26
Polish National Committee, 51
Portalet, fortress of, 286
Prader, Salomon, 162
Protocols of the Elders of Zion, 26,
   142, 193, 243

Rapallo Treaty, 198
Rasala Battalion, 43, 57
Rathenau, Foreign Minister Wal-
   ther, 198
red menace, 49, 63, 113–16
Reynaud, P.M. Paul, 90, 283, 284,
   286
Rheinhalle, 233
Ribbentrop-Malenkov Agreement,
   272
Ribeyre, Public Prosecutor Paul,
   276, 277
Riom Trial, 285, 287
Roosevelt, President Franklin D.,
   187, 211, 250

Rosenthal, Madame, 206
Rosenthal, Maitre Gerard, 91
Rothmund, Heinrich, 114, 120, 137, 186–88, 238
Rothschild, Louis, 287
Rothschild oil interests, 55, 56

Salomon, Berthold, 134–39, 162, 222, 259
Saxenhausen concentration camp, 287
Schlegelberger, Acting Justice Minister Franz, 287, 290, 291
Schwartzbard, Anna, 77, 79, 81
Schwartzbard, Chaia, 22
Schwartzbard, Meir, 22
Schwartzbard, Samuel
  after the victory, 105, 106
  as a youth, 22, 24–25
  assassin, 76–82
  death of, 107
  on trial, 89–91, 95–104
  poet, 77
  rebel, 42, 43, 57, 74
  rememvered, 181, 255
  soldier, 38
  the wandering Jew, 28
  under arrest, 83–85
Schwartzbard, Yitzhak, 21, 26
Second International, 43
Sennhof Prison, 184, 189
Shcheglovitov, I. G., 194
Sich Rifles, 46, 47, 60, 62, 66
Skoropadsky, Pavlo
  abandoned by allies, 59
  escape into exile, 62
  loots the Ukraine, 47, 59
  named Hetman, 47

Slovo, 32, 33
Smith, Reginald, 82
Soffer, Maitre Ellie, 267
Spark, 24, 106, 282
Stalin, Joseph, 47
Standard Oil, 54, 55
Steffen, Linnie, 129, 141, 142, 146, 149, 150, 153
Streicher, Julius, 143, 144, 166, 170, 176, 181, 184, 238, 248
Szwarc, Maitre, 223, 257, 268

Tabouis, General, 45
Tabouis, Genevieve, 235, 236
Talaat Pasha, 79
Tarnavskyi, General Myron, 71
Taviani, Chief of Police, 276
Teilirian, Solomon, 79, 80, 105
Tesniere, Examining magistrate, 223, 224, 260, 265, 268
Thalmann, Ernst Alfred, 131, 221, 263, 269, 281
Thierack, Justice Minister Otto, 290
Thomae, Georg, 132–34, 142
Thompson, Dorothy Lewis, 256, 265, 266, 268
Torres, Maitre Henri, 79, 84, 86, 88, 89, 91, 93–104, 181, 255–59, 267, 291, 292
Trident Newspaper, 76, 77
Trotsky, Leon, 45, 46

Ukrainian National Republic
  control of Galicia, 50
  decree of, 61
  leadership of, 62
  threatens French interests, 54

Ukrainian People's Republic
  birth of, 46
  occupied by Germans, 47
  receives recognition, 46
Ukrainian Soviet Socialist Republic
  creation of, 43
Universal Proclamations
  First Proclamation, 37, 40
  Fourth Proclamation, 46
  Third Proclamation, 43
Ursprung, Dr. Werner, 180

van der Lubbe, Marius, 255
Vessine-Larue, Maitre, 257, 268
vom Rath, Gunther, 290
vom Rath, Gustav, 229, 235, 236
vom Rath, Third Secretary Ernst,
    220–22, 224, 225, 227–31, 233–
    35, 241, 245, 246, 249, 256, 257,
    261, 263, 265, 266, 289, 290
von Bibra, charge d'affaires, 178,
    185, 186
von Helidorf, Chief of Police,
    Count Wolf Heinrich, 243
von Ribbentrop, Foreign Minister
    Joachim, 227, 234, 251, 260
von Soltikov, Count, 290
von Steiger, Edouard, 185
von Weizsacker, Secretary of State
    Ernst, 120, 131, 138, 167, 168,
    233
von Welczeck, Ambassador Jo-
    hannes, 220, 225, 227, 263

Vonwyl, Hans, 115, 116
Vynnychenko, Volodymyr
  chairman of UNR, 62
  dedicated Marxist, 65
  French view of, 48, 65
  humiliated, 62
  out of office, 65
  socialist leader, 32
  summons the peasants to rise,
      59
  view of Petliura, 60

Weber Incident, 119
Weil-Goudchaux, Maitre Serge,
    292
Weizmann, Chaim, 229
Wesemann, Hans, 134–36, 144
White Russians, 45, 63, 65, 67, 70,
    71, 73, 74, 101
Willm, Maitre Albert, 89, 102
Wilson, President Woodrow, 51,
    52, 64, 251
Winter Olympic Games, 165, 169
World Jewish Congress, 174, 255,
    258, 259, 266, 267, 275

Yashiva Breuer, 202, 204
Youth Aliyah, 201
Yushchinsky, Andrei, 193
Yussel, 24, 25

Zaslawsky, 204, 206